PHILOSOPHICAL FOUNDATIONS OF ADULT EDUCATION

Third Edition

PHILOSOPHICAL FOUNDATIONS OF ADULT EDUCATION

Third Edition

John L. Elias
and
Sharan B. Meriam

KRIEGER PUBLISHING COMPANY
Malabar, Florida
2005

Original Edition 1980
Second Edition 1995
Third Edition 2005

Printed and Published by
KRIEGER PUBLISHING COMPANY
KRIEGER DRIVE
MALABAR, FLORIDA 32950

Library of Congress Cataloging-in-Publication Data

Elias, John L., 1933-
    Philosophical foundations of adult education / John L. Elias &
    Sharan Merriam.—3rd ed.
        p. cm.
    Includes bibliographical references and index.
    ISBN 1-57524-254-0 (alk. paper)
        1. Adult education—Philosophy.   I. Merriam, Sharan B. II. Title

    LC5219.E46   2005
    374'001—dc22

                                            2004048721

10   9   8   7   6   5   4   3   2

CONTENTS

(Please say "page" with each page number in the Table of Contents)

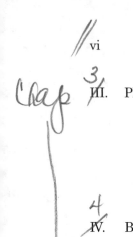

Contents

(Please say "page" with each page number in the Table of Contents)

Chap 8

Chap 9

The Name Index, pp. 275 – 280, will not be read.
The Subject Index, pp. 281 – 286, will not be read

// p. viii is blank

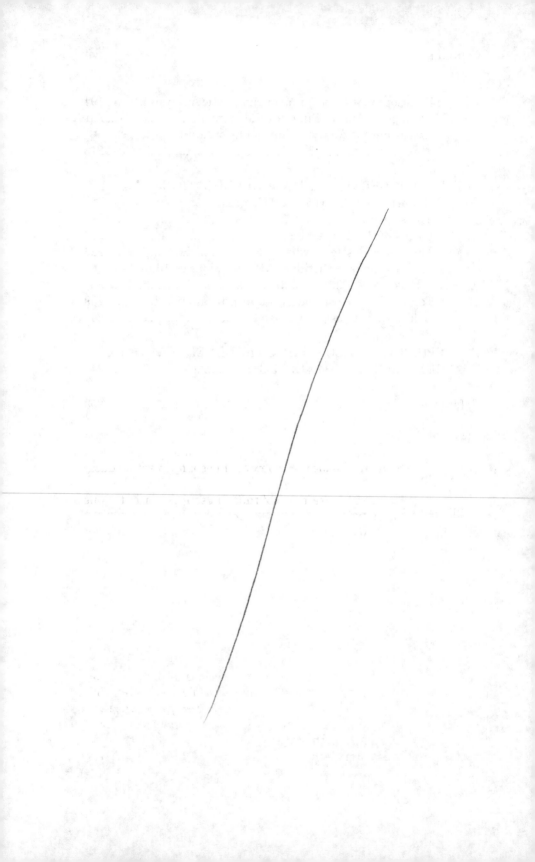

PREFACE TO THE THIRD EDITION

Little did we know that when the first edition of *Philosophical Foundations of Adult Education* was published in 1980, that we would be inspired to write a third, substantially revised edition published twenty-five years later in 2005. In between the original 1980 edition and this third edition, is a second edition published in 1995. In the second edition we attempted to update the book with a self-contained bibliographic essay in which we "revisited" each of the six schools of educational thought in the original edition. This second edition proved somewhat cumbersome to both students and practitioners desiring an up-to-date overview of philosophy in adult education.

Not only had certain examples of the philosophical orientations in adult education practice changed over the years, newer writers had much to add to our understanding of the field. For example, encounter and sensitivity groups of the 1970s have been eclipsed in humanistic adult education by twelve-step programs, and popular self-help/self-development seminars and best-selling books. At the same time, behaviorist outcomes-based evaluation of educational programs has recycled into popularity with federal initiatives such as No Child Left Behind, and evidence-based research.

In addition to programmatic manifestations of various philosophical orientations, there have been additions in philosophical thinking since both the 1980 and 1995 editions. What we labeled "radical" adult education in 1980 was indeed known as radical; however, with the infusion of critical social theory, feminist theory, anti-race and postcolonial theory, we have renamed this chapter "radical and critical" adult education. Further, we have added a new chapter on postmodernism. Postmodernism offers a rigorous critique of all academic disciplines, including education, and most recently, adult education. For this new chapter, we have applied a postmodern critique to each of the philosophies covered in previous chapters.

While we have made these major changes in this third edition, we have maintained the original organization of each chapter in that we review the historical roots, and basic principles of each philosophy, then examine its manifestation in adult education practice. Finally, we end each chapter with an assessment of the philosophy's utility to adult education practice today.

This revision has been an interesting journey for both of us. By going back to our original manuscript and then updating to the present, we have confirmed the fact that although some things change, others remain the same. Behaviorism, humanism, progressivism, radical and critical philosophy are very much in evidence in adult education today as they were twenty-five years ago. Liberal and analytic philosophy of adult education have few adherents today, although the Great Books program still survives. Liberal adult education values are also being called into question by the growing diversity and multiculturalism of our society. Finally, postmodernism challenges us to examine everything about our philosophy and practice.

We hope that you as readers of this third edition of *Philosophical Foundations of Adult Education* will find it useful in providing insights into the practice of adult education, and most importantly, in examining and constructing your own personal philosophy of adult education.

//FOREWORD

During the entire time I have been in the field of adult education, which is almost a half a century, I have heard it being criticized
for not having a philosophical foundation. I can remember reading
many articles in the *Journal of Adult Education* published by the
American Association for Adult Education between 1929 and 1948,
and in its successors, *Adult Education and Adult Leadership,* published by the Adult Education Association of the U.S.A., flailing the
adult education movement in this country for not having a unified
sense of purpose, a cohesive set of aims, a coherent framework of
beliefs and, therefore, a significant impact on society. I remember
attending numerous conferences sponsored by the two national organizations and by the Center for the Study of Liberal Education
(between 1951 and 1961) in which eloquent speakers left me with an
even stronger sense of guilt for not doing something about bringing
some intellectual order into our field.

I remember feeling uneasy about this kind of pressure being
exerted on me, and for several reasons. For one thing, I thought
that the pressurizers were not perceiving the nature and function of
philosophy in the same way, and so they were not helping me think
through how I might get help from it or contribute to it. For another
thing, I resisted the idea of uniformity-of our having (or even aspir-
ing) to agree on a single set of aims, purposes, and beliefs. I attributed much of my own personal growth to having been exposed to a
variety of systems of thought, often conflicting systems of thought,
which forced me to think more critically and deeply about the issues
they were examining. Finally, I didn't see how I could do much about
the situation, since philosophy was not my discipline.

Our field has attracted a few professional philosophers into its fold, and I read their writings avidly and talked with several of them eagerly to try to get help in clarifying the meaning of philosophy for our field. Eduard Lindeman, John Walker Powel, Kenneth Benne, Paul Bergevin, and Jerrold Apps were my philosophical consultants. I got many useful ideas from them, and can see a good deal of influence from them on my way of thinking about adult education. But I didn't get the one thing I wanted most, a broad overview of the philosophical foundations of our field, since each of them was a proponent for a particular philosophical position.

So when Robert Krieger called me to inform me that John Elias and Sharan Merriam had written a book on the philosophical foundations of adult education, and would like me to write a foreword, my hopes soared. I waited for the manuscript to arrive with a mixture of anticipation and wariness. Would it be the usual punishing flailing of our field's philosophical backwardness? Would it exude ideological passion for one position? Would it be written in dull, strange (to me) philosophical 'argon?

I started reading the page proofs the minute they arrived, and had a hard time putting them down to tend to other things that had to be done. It is clear, exciting reading. It presents the nature and function of philosophy as a discipline-but also as a tool for the practitioner to use-in a way that I found completely understandable. It describes the various philosophical approaches appreciatively and respectfully, but with a careful analysis of their strengths and weaknesses as applied to our field. It makes it legitimate for me to take ideas from each approach that make sense to me and to incorporate them into a personal philosophical position. It made me feel more comfortable with philosophy and more secure about philosophizing.

I hope it will do the same for you.

Malcolm S. Knowles
Professor Emeritus
North Carolina State University
1980

CHAPTER 1

INTRODUCTION: PHILOSOPHY OF ADULT EDUCATION

While the roots of philosophical inquiry can be traced back to ancient Greek philosophy, it has only been in the past two centuries that education has received rigorous treatment by philosophers. In the nineteenth century, Immanuel Kant and Georg Hegel directed attention to philosophic issues involved in education. Philosophy of education as a separate discipline of study developed, however, in the twentieth century largely as a result of the writings of John Dewey. His philosophical approach to education provided a critique of traditional education and gave rise to the development of various approaches to philosophy of education.

It has been traditional to discuss educational philosophy in terms of various schools or systems such as realism, idealism, and pragmatism. More recent approaches include reconstructionism, existentialism, behaviorism, analytic philosophy, critical social theory and postmodernism. The problems of classifying different philosophers into schools have long been recognized. Nevertheless, the systematization of the discipline continues and schools of thought develop because similarities and affinities do exist among theorists. Also, the practical necessity of introducing new students to the field warrants some shorthand method of presenting the educational thought and philosophy of numerous theorists.

Although education in general has been systematically analyzed from philosophical perspectives, there has been no extended attempt to explore the various philosophical approaches to adult education. Articles and monographs have appeared in which adult educators have taken positions on questions of a philosophical nature or have espoused personal philosophies of adult education. What this book does is to systematically present a number of philosophical positions and their spokespersons that shape adult education practice today. This effort will add clarity to the enterprise of adult education and enable adult educators to become more consciously purposeful in their educational efforts.

Philosophy

For many people the connotation of the word philosophy is negative. It is thought to be a vague and abstruse subject. It implies a body of abstractions that has little bearing on real life. It deals with theories that are considered abstract, vague, general, and perhaps useless. Most cultures tend to place greater value on the practical and the useful. What is philosophical or theoretical is viewed by many as irrelevant to human life and its problems.

Some of these objections to philosophy have justification. Philosophers have at times succumbed to the temptation to think too much about thinking and too little about life's problems. Philosophers also have often made too many mental distinctions that have little correspondence with reality. They have often been more interested in the tools of thought—logic and reasoning—than they have been with the objects of thought—the understanding and changing of human existence.

Though negative in its connotation to some, philosophy can be a fruitful and exciting human endeavor. Philosophy etymologically signifies the love of wisdom. For the ancient Greeks, who coined the word, it was the search for what is real in a world of appearances. It was the quest for the beautiful in a garish world. It was separating the good from the bad. It was searching for unity among the fragmented elements of life.

Philosophers deal in theories, a word of Greek origin suggesting a beholding, a spectacle. For the ancient Greeks to theorize was to look at, to behold, and to have a vision. For Aristotle, theorizing was the highest power of the human mind. It was the activity of persons that made them most like the gods. The theories of the philosophers are attempts to understand the world and everything in it in an active and constructive manner. Scheffler indicates this explanatory function of philosophy when he explains that

> philosophy seeks general perspective, on a rational basis. Historically, those called "philosophers" have concerned themselves with such subjects as the nature of the physical universe, mind, causality, life, virtue, law, good, history, and

community. . . The philosopher wants to see things in perspective and he wants to see things sharp and clear. He strives
for a maximum of vision and a minimum of mystery.
(Scheffler, 1960, 5)

While theory and philosophy are intellectual efforts, they are
more fundamentally efforts of feeling and imagination. Philosophers
first wonder at a work of nature or humankind; they follow this with
the effort to imaginatively understand it in some meaningful manner. Before he analyzed knowledge philosophically, Plato first pic-
tured it as the ascent from the dark shadows of the cave to a world
brightly illuminated by the sun.

Philosophy is interested in the general principles of any phenomenon, object, process, or subject matter. Principles are general
if they apply to a large number of phenomena. The philosopher of
education considers the general principles that apply to the educational process. Principles are the foundations or basic structures
by which phenomena, events, and realities are understood. The
philosopher of education is interested in certain general principles:
objectives of education, curriculum or subject matter, general methodological principles, analysis of the teaching-learning process, and
the relationship between education and the society in which it takes
place.

Philosophy as a discipline has traditionally been divided into a
number of subdisciplines. Logic is concerned with the rules for correct reasoning and thinking and the various forms of argumentation. Epistemology investigates the rules for determining whether
we have arrived at truth, opinion, or falsehood. Metaphysics searches
out the most general principles of reality. Many contemporary emphases in philosophy question the possibility of metaphysical knowledge, i.e., knowledge about reality in the most general sense that is
applicable to all reality. An important branch of philosophy is ethics,
an investigation of rules or principles of moral reasoning and conduct.

Philosophy, like most disciplines, has many divergent viewpoints
or systems. Competing schools of thought have developed approaches
to basic questions about the human person, knowledge, ethical good,
reality, and other issues. Many philosophical answers to questions
about basic issues are often contradictory. In the examination of
philosophies of adult education, some of these differences between
conflicting schools of thought will become apparent. Though some
philosophers of education approach these distinctions in an eclectic

manner and attempt to resolve them, it appears preferable to allow these differences to surface for they often involve fundamental issues that cannot be submerged.

Philosophy and Action: Theory and Practice

A major dispute among philosophers concerns the relationship between philosophy and action or between theory and practice. Some see philosophy and action as mutually exclusive concepts belonging to different realms. Others view one's practice and action as being logically derived from one's theory and philosophy. Still another approach is to attempt to synthesize the two into one view. There appears to be an emerging consensus among philosophers that both are necessary in the life of men and women. Theory without practice leads to an empty idealism, and action without philosophical reflection leads to a mindless activism. In the early 1970s, Charles Silberman lamented the lack of philosophical interest in educational practice:

> If teachers make a botch of it, and an uncomfortably large number do, it is because it never simply occurs to more than a handful to ask *why* they are doing what they are doing, to think seriously or deeply about the purposes or consequences of education.
>
> This mindlessness—the failure to think seriously about educational purpose, the reluctance to question established practice—is not the monopoly of the public school; it is diffused remarkably throughout the entire educational system, and indeed the entire society.
>
> If mindlessness is the central problem, the solution must lie in infusing the various educating institutions with purpose, more important, with thought about purpose, and about the ways in which technique, content, and organization fulfill or alter purpose. (Silberman, 1970, 11)

Silberman's indictment of mindlessness in the educational enterprise is a valid one. Many current debates in educational policy and practice would be conducted more rationally if some clarity were achieved on basic philosophic differences. The point of philosophical inquiry is to clarify issues so that decisions can be made on proper grounds. Arguments over means in education are fundamentally reduced to differences in ends to be achieved. For example, the debate over "back to the basics" revolves around what types of persons

we expect our educational system to produce. And the arguments
between the proponents of liberal arts and vocational education stem
from basic philosophic issues related to the purposes of a free society.

There is a sense in which it can be said that anyone who acts is
guided by some theory or some philosophy. We act for reasons, good
and/or bad, and generally have some understanding of what we are
doing, why we are doing it in the way we do, and the consequences
of our actions. What we have here in the ordinary course of human
activity is common sense which, though related to philosophy, can
be distinguished from it. Ancient philosophers raised questions about
common opinions and practices and demonstrated that the common
sense view of things could not always be trusted.

Philosophy is a more reflective and systematic activity than common sense. Philosophy raises questions about what we do and why
we do it, and goes beyond individual cases and phenomena to treat
questions of a general nature. When considering the interrelation-
ship of philosophy and activity, it is clear that philosophy inspires
one's activities, and gives direction to practice. The power of philosophy lies in its ability to enable individuals to better understand
and appreciate the activities of everyday life.

The theory-action split in philosophy has received treatment by
philosophers of education. Three possible relationships have been
proposed. First, there is the opposition between theory and practice
where theory achieves superiority. This tendency is found in the
philosophies of Aristotle and Plato. Second is an opposition between
the two in which practice becomes superior. Dewey's writings have
been identified with this tendency. Finally, there is a dialectical relationship between the two as is found in the work of Karl Marx and
Paulo Freire (Elias, 1982).

Philosophy of Adult Education

Philosophy of adult education has been a small but lively enterprise within the field of adult education. The past twenty years have
witnessed a modest increase in writings of a philosophical or theoretical nature in a field long dominated by practical concerns. Though
only a few persons with formal philosophical training are working in
the field, adult education has attracted its share of those interested
in probing philosophical or theoretical foundations or in presenting
comprehensive visions for adult educators.

The general discipline of philosophy of education is considered
by some to be in decline, having lost its place in many teacher education programs to courses in social foundations. The discipline is

often attacked for being far removed from educational issues, being irrelevant to teacher and administrative training, engendering skepticism about our ability to know truth and goodness, and fostering radical and destructive ideas. Scholars in the field often experience the dilemma of becoming too theoretical and thus irrelevant to practice or attempting to be relevant at the risk of abandoning philosophic rigor.

While admitting the legitimacy of some of these criticisms, we still contend that the theories reviewed in this book establish that philosophy of education is not a luxury for adult educators. We maintain that philosophy aids leaders and teachers to become more rational and critical in their thinking and acting. Philosophy's emphasis on clarity, purpose, criticism, and legitimation remains important. Philosophy of education at its best presents visions of what persons and society are capable of becoming through involvement in education. The strongest case for this is found in the earlier work of John Dewey and in the contemporary writings of Paulo Freire, both of whom consider education an essential tool for the reconstruction of both human experience and society.

The value of philosophy of adult education has been addressed in a number of publications. Merriam (1982) has edited a collection that explores ways in which philosophy can be linked to action in adult education. The authors in the collection make the case that since theoretical concerns are implicit in all practical activities, it is advantageous to make these perspectives explicit in order to promote a more reflective form of educational practice. Furthermore, Tisdell and Taylor (2001, 7) suggest five questions that can be used to guide readers in articulating their thinking about philosophy and adult education practice:

1. What is the purpose of education?
2. What is the role of the adult educator?
3. What is the role of students or adult learners in the classroom?
4. What is your conceptualization of differences among adult learners?
5. What is your worldview, or the primary lens you use in analyzing human needs?

The increasing value of philosophy of adult education has become noticeable especially in the area of ethics. Jarvis's book, *Ethics and Education for Adults* (1997), presents the argument that "there is one universal moral good which consists of being concerned for the Other, and that this is the underlying principle of all morally good actions, and it is especially important when considering the practice of education" (15). Through examining different dimensions of the teaching-learning transaction, Jarvis distinguishes between universal moral good, and moral values and ethics that are culturally situated. Brockett's (1988) collection contains a number of articles that deal with ethical issues from a philosophical perspective. Here, Brockett (1988) and Hiemstra (1988) explore the importance and relevance of personal value systems in all ethical decision making. Hiemstra makes explicit connections between these personal systems and individuals' philosophies of education. In the same volume, Cunningham (1988) draws on the ethics of critique developed by some critical theorists to make the case for a greater sense of social responsibility on the part of adult educators. Other chapters deal with ethical issues in program planning, marketing, evaluation, and research.

That philosophy and ethical issues in adult education practice continue to be important is underscored by two recent publications. In 2001, an entire issue of *Adult Learning* was devoted to "Bringing Our Philosophies into Practice" with articles on how philosophy informs practice generally, and how philosophy is specifically manifested in program development, administration, and instruction. The second publication is Brockett and Hiemstra's (2004) recent book, *Toward Ethical Practice*. The book focuses on how to promote ethical practice through the use of what they call the "Ethical Decision Making Process" or EDM process. This process is designed to help educators and trainers resolve ethical dilemmas by looking at three interrelated dimensions: the values held by the educator (personal philosophy); the obligations an educator has to various stakeholders; and reflection on the range of options available to the person and the possible consequences of each.

It is important to recognize that philosophy of education takes many forms (Powers, 1982). Some philosophies tend to be inspirational in presenting utopian ideals, such as in Plato's *Republic*, Rousseau's *Emile*, and Skinner's *Walden II*. Other philosophies are normative or prescriptive in offering clear and precise directions for educational practice, such as in Hutchins's *Higher Education in America* and Bergevin's A *Philosophy of Adult Education*. A third approach is investigative, examining educational policies and practices with a view to the justification of ideas or the reconstruction of society, such as in Dewey's *Democracy and Education* and Lindeman's *The Meaning of Adult Education*. Another approach is termed analytic because of its attempt to discover and interpret educational meaning in education, such as in Lawson's *Philosophical Concepts and Values in Adult Education.*

Another way of classifying philosophies of adult education is according to function (Broudy, 1981). Philosophy of adult education performs an *educational* function in addressing issues regarding aims, curriculum, organization, teaching and learning, methodology of research, and ethics from a theoretical perspective. In its *analytic* function, philosophy of education clarifies the language and arguments used in educational discourse. Increasingly, attention has been paid to the *critical* function which examines proposals, policies, and underlying ideologies of adult educators. What has been ignored in recent years by philosophers has been the *synthetic* or comprehensive function of providing "a synoptic, systematic, coherent set of beliefs and arguments about education that deals with the educational enterprise as a whole and that makes connection with a philosophy of life" (Broudy, 35).

Historically there has been a close connection between philosophy and religion or theology. This text points out the connection between religion and education especially in the treatment of liberal adult education. Elias (1993) has explored the works of various scholars in the field of religion who have addressed adult education, using the same classifications as found in this book. Leon McKenzie (1982) has applied his humanistic treatment of adult education to religion, showing the strong congruence between the humanistic approach and adult religious education. Norma Thompson (1984) presented five models of adult religious education: enculturation models, needs assessment and participation models, group dynamics models, sociopolitical models, and ecumenical models. Theoretical issues are competently treated in Nancy Foltz's (1986) handbook that features a succinct article by McKenzie on a religious philosophy of adult education. Linda Vogel (1991) in a comprehensive book has provided theoretical models for examining adult religious education. Most recently, Diane Tickton Schuster (2004) has presented Jewish educators and in fact all educators, with a brilliant approach to Jewish learning utilizing case studies and current adult education theories and research.

Adult Education

Although the concept of education has been analyzed extensively in recent philosophical literature, the concept of adult education has not been so clearly delineated. Even an attempt to define adult edu-

p.9

cation presupposes philosophical questions. As K. H. Lawson (1975) states

> Such a wide range of agencies engaging in such diverse fields
> of activity raises questions about the criteria which entitle
> us to bring them together in one portmanteau category. What
> is it about them that make them examples of the education
> of adults? (14)

Adulthood is another term that further confounds the defining of adult education. Age, psychological maturity, and social roles appear to be the essential variables in such a definition, but the priority of these variables often depends upon the context of the discussion. There is also the important question of whether adult education is to be distinguished from education in general. The argument between Malcolm Knowles and Cyril Houle and many others over whether there is a distinct art and science of teaching adults to be termed andragogy is an important definitional problem.

Contrary to what many believe, the problem of definition is not answered at the beginning of philosophical inquiry. Arriving at accurate and clear definitions is at the heart of philosophical inquiry and is often reached in the later part of an investigation. Also, the conclusions and definitions for one philosopher often provide the starting points and problems for the next philosopher. Thus it will be demonstrated in the course of this work that there are major differences among the various schools of thought on the important issue of definition. Liberal adult educators will view education differently from progressive adult educators. Radical adult educators will find inadequate a definition of adult education that does not include raising peoples' consciousness of the social and political contradictions in their culture.

Though definitions related to adult education are crucial philosophical issues, there are many other important questions that will surface in the treatment of various philosophers in this book. Adult educators, for example, differ in their handling of needs and interests of adult learners. As a result, there also exists among these educators contrasting approaches to content and method in instructional settings. Likewise, there is a varying emphasis upon the social and individual aims of education.

Since a great deal of adult education takes place in institutions and organizations, analysis of these is important. Again in this area we can expect to find significant differences. Radicals take one view toward institutions; behaviorists take another; those who favor a personal growth or humanistic model of adult education hold still another view.

Related to the question of the place of institutions in adult education is the issue of social change. All philosophies include social and political dimensions. The adult educator looks beyond the institution within which he or she works and sees larger social goals. In recent years, adult educators have been seriously challenged in this area by the revolutionary pedagogy of Paulo Freire. Whether one agrees with Freire's approach or not, one must concede that he has raised the social relevance issue rather dramatically.

Any number of issues in adult education might also be considered in terms of the increasingly important concept of adult development. Although extensive psychosocial research has been done in this area and, it is clear that the concept of adult development itself and its connection with education need to be explored. Most philosophical schools have not taken sufficient notice of this research and its implications for analyzing and presenting normative statements in adult education.

Finally, the curriculum of adult education usually takes the form of programs. Hansman and Mott (2001) point out "when planning programs for adults, educators' philosophies influence how programs are planned and carried out. Whether recognized and articulated or tacit and unexamined, planners' philosophical perspectives significantly impact many of the decisions in the everyday practice of planning program" (14). The development of programs can be improved if there are clear philosophical discussions about the various elements of programs. The development of program objectives and the distinction among the various types of programs is basically a philosophical matter, though certainly not detached from pragmatic considerations. The debate in adult education over the appropriateness of using behavioral objectives is fundamentally a philosophical difference among various theorists of adult education. Philosophical issues are also involved in the logical design of curricula and the evaluation of program outcomes.

Thus, within this text, issues salient to the field of adult education are explored from the perspective of various philosophical schools of thought. Needs and interests of adult learners, method and content in adult education, adult development, curriculum, institutions, and the questions of social change are better understood and appreciated by the adult educator when analyzed in light of differing philosophical approaches.

Philosophy of Adult Education for Adult Educators

As for all educators, the appealing adult education courses are usually those concerned with program planning and methods of instruction. The educator is generally more interested in skills than in principles, in means than in ends, in details than in the whole picture. Philosophy of adult education, however, does not equip a person with knowledge about *what* to teach, *how* to teach, or how to organize a program. It is more concerned with the *why* of education and with the logical analysis of the various elements of the educational process. Philosophies of education are interpretative theories, not applicatory theories. Thus this study supplies the educator with ideas and attitudes that one teaches *with,* not *to* students.

While emphasizing the theoretical nature of the discipline of philosophy of education, it is also our purpose to show how each philosophy expresses itself in a concrete type of program. The close relationship between theory and practice that we have already described in this chapter will become manifest in the investigations of educational programs. Twelve-step programs that deal with addictive behaviors as an educational experience, for example, express the philosophy of humanistic psychology. The Great Books Program captures the philosophical emphasis of liberal adult education. And Freire's literary program for adults shows clearly the radical adult educator's interest in social change.

In our presentation and analysis of these concrete educational programs which embody an educational philosophy, we believe that we add a significant dimension to the study of philosophy of education, particularly the philosophy of adult education. The philosophy will be clarified by the practice; the practice will be illuminated by the theory. In this way the particular value of educational philosophy will be enhanced for the adult educator. In doing this it is not our purpose to provide the reader with a philosophy of education, though this may happen. It is rather to encourage adult educators to ask important questions about the whole educational process. The value of a study of educational philosophy, we believe, is more in the questions asked than in the certitude of the answers given.

In writing this book it is our belief that it is the knowledge of philosophy of education that distinguishes a professional educator from a paraprofessional or a beginning teacher. True professionals know not only what they are to do, but are also aware of the principles and the reasons for so acting. Experience alone does not make a person a professional adult educator. The person must also be able to reflect deeply upon the experience he or she has had. In this manner the professional adult educator is more like the person of art who creatively combines experience and theory in the activity of teaching.

Overview of Philosophies of Adult Education

Philosophies of adult education, like all thought systems, originate within particular sociocultural contexts. Though individual philosophers are responsible for developing a philosophical approach to adult education, the development of their thought is greatly influenced by the particular problems, issues, and challenges that exist in their culture. To understand adequately a philosophy of education then, one must analyze it within the context in which it originated and developed. This does not mean that the particular theory cannot be adapted to other cultural situations with some degree of success. But there are problems with these attempts at application to differing cultural contexts, as will become clear in the course of this book.

Liberal Adult Education has its beginnings in the philosophical theories of the classical Greek philosophers, Socrates, Plato, and Aristotle. This liberal education tradition was adopted and adapted in the Christian schools in early, medieval, and modern times. It became the predominant educational theory in the Western world and is still a strong force in educational thought today. The emphasis in this tradition is upon liberal learning, organized knowledge, and the development of the intellectual powers of the mind. Philosophers who espouse this viewpoint include Mortimer Adler, Robert Hutchins, Jacques Maritain, Mark Van Doren, Allan Bloom, and E. H. Hirsch. An educational program that is inspired by this orientation is the Great Books Program.

Progressive Adult Education has its beginnings in the progressive movement in politics, social change, and education. This approach to educational philosophy emphasizes such concepts as the relationship between education and society, experience-centered, vocational, and democratic education. Leading progressive educators include William James, John Dewey, and William Kilpatrick. Philosophers of adult education with the progressive orientation include Eduard Lindeman, Paul Bergevin, Kenneth Benne, and Robert Blakely. Various educational practices in adult education are inspired by this philosophical orientation: Americanization education, English as a Second Language, and the Community School movement/ Since the beginnings of the adult education movement in this country were in the progressive period of history, this movement has been greatly influenced by this particular philosophy of education.

Behaviorist Adult Education has its roots in modem philosophic and scientific movements. Behaviorism in adult education emphasizes such concepts as control, behavioral modification, learning through reinforcement, and management by objectives. Early behaviorists include Edward Thorndike, Ivan Pavlov and James Watson. The most prominent behaviorist philosophy is that of B. F. Skinner. His ideas have permeated many disciplines and fields of study and practice. Various adult education practices are inspired by this philosophic view: programmed learning, behavioral objectives, and performance-based educational programs. Behaviorist principles are also predominant in industrial and corporate training programs.

Humanistic Adult Education is related in its development to existential philosophy and humanistic psychology. The key concepts that are emphasized in this approach are freedom and autonomy, trust, active cooperation and participation, and self-directed learning. Philosophical roots are found in such writers as Martin Heidegger, Jean Paul Sartre, Albert Camus, Gabriel Marcel, and Martin Buber. The Third Force psychologists have been equally responsible for the development of this particular approach to education: Abraham Maslow, Carl Rogers, Rollo May, Gordon Allport, and Erich Fromm. Among adult educators, Malcolm Knowles is prominent in espousing this orientation in his needs-meeting and learner-centered andragogical approach to adult learning. This philosophic orientation also permeates the research efforts of Allen Tough and his associates. There are numerous adult education practices connected with this philosophical approach: group dynamics, group relations training, group processes, self-help groups and self-directed learning. One finds elements of humanistic adult education in the works of such adult educators as Stephen Brookfield, Sherman Stanage, Jack Mezirow, and Peter Jarvis

Radical or Critical Adult Education derives from the various radical movements that have emerged in the past three centuries: anarchism, Marxism, socialism, left-wing Freudianism, critical theory and radical feminism. The radicals in education propose education as a force for achieving radical social change. Education in this viewpoint is closely connected with social, political, and economic understanding of cultures, and with the development of methods to bring

people to an awareness of responsible social action. Radical educators include George Counts and Theodore Brameld in the 1930s.
This philosophic orientation was revived during the 1960s in the
efforts of Jonathan Kozol, John Holt, Paul Goodman and Ivan Illich.
An important adult educator of this philosophic position is Paulo
Freire who has proposed radical conscientization as the true function of education among the oppressed. Educational practices inspired by this philosophy include the Freedom Schools in the South
during the 1960s, free schools, and Freire's radical approach to adult
literacy education. More recently, elements of what we are calling
radical can be seen in applications of critical theory, critical pedagogy and feminist pedagogy in the field of adult education.

Analytic Philosophy of Adult Education has made a significant
contribution to adding intellectual rigor to the philosophy of adult
education. It originated in such movements as logical positivism,
scientific positivism, and British analytic philosophy. This approach
to philosophy emphasizes the need for clarifying concepts, arguments,
and policy statements used in adult education. Philosophers of education in this tradition include Israel Scheffler, R. S. Peters, and
Thomas Green. Lawson and Paterson are two British philosophers
of adult education who have pioneered this approach. This approach
finds its practical application not in any particular educational practice or program, but rather in its attempt to establish a sound philosophic basis for the field of adult education.

Postmodern Adult Education offers a trenchant criticism of the
entire enterprise of adult education. Postmodernist critique, which
began in the arts, now permeates all academic disciplines, including
education. Based on the writings of well-known European philosophers and theorists this philosophy questions such fundamental
concepts as truth, theory, reality, knowledge and power. In questioning the modernist and Enlightenment achievement it casts
doubt on many accepted truths. A number of adult educators,
notably Robin Usher, have attempted to utilize its ideas to critique
adult education and to provide proposals for living in a postmodern
society.

We recognize the work of adult educators such as Tisdell and
Taylor (2001) who have built on and reframed the approach to philosophies of adult education used in this book. Within humanistic
adult education they have differentiated between the humanist approach of Knowles, the critical-humanist approach of Mezirow, and
the feminist-humanist approach of Belenky et al. Within radical
or critical adult education they have distinguished between the

critical-emancipatory philosophy of Freire and the feminist-emancipatory approach of bell hooks. It seems that what they have identified are not separate philosophies of adult educator but merely variations with the humanistic and radical or critical traditions.

Summary

Adult education has advanced to the point where a more systematic investigation of its philosophies is both possible and necessary. Philosophies of adult education are concerned with the most general principles of the educational process. All philosophies of adult education grapple with the important problem of the relationship between theory and practice. Philosophical issues in this field include the definition of adult education, the place of the needs and interests of adults, contrasting views of method and content, the concept and relevance of adult development, programs and objectives, the teaching-learning process, and education for social change. The value of having knowledge of philosophical theories of adult education for adult educators lies in attitudes and understandings that the educator will bring to his or her task. Finally, all philosophies of adult education originate and develop in a particular historical and sociocultural context. Seven philosophies of adult education are analyzed in this book: liberal, progressive, behaviorist, humanistic, radical or critical, analytic, and postmodern.

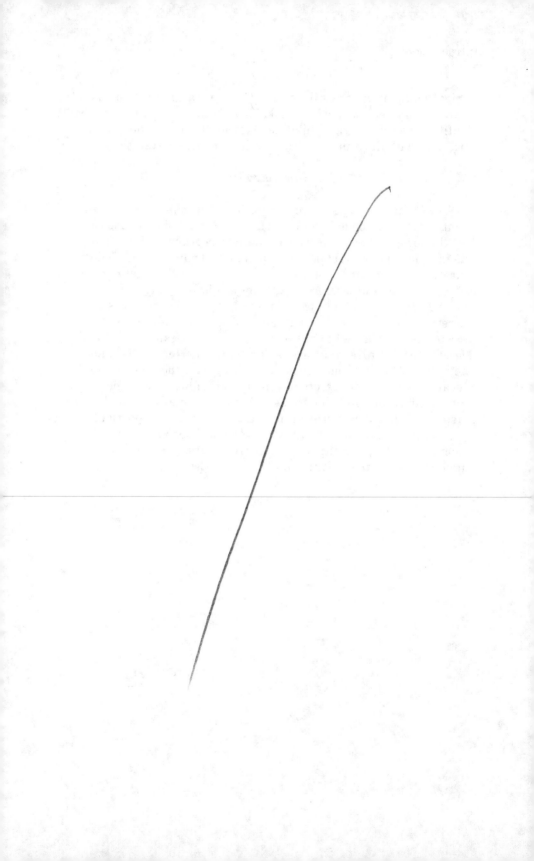

CHAPTER II

LIBERAL ADULT EDUCATION

The oldest and most enduring philosophy of education in the Western world is the liberal arts approach to education. This philosophy goes by a number of names such as classical humanism, perennialism, rational humanism, liberal education, and general education. A religious version called Neo-Thomism was named after the Catholic philosopher and theologian Thomas Aquinas. Although over a long period of time various approaches have developed, all versions emphasize liberal learning, organized knowledge, and the development of the intellectual powers of the mind.

The earliest efforts to educate adults in the Western world developed under the influence of this philosophy of education. From the Plato's Academy to the Great Books programs in contemporary America, the tradition of liberal learning among adults has persisted as an important form of learning that adults engage in either as individuals or in groups. Though liberal arts education is closely associated in the minds of many with high school and college education, this philosophy has in the past manifested itself in the education of adults and still persists in various forms in contemporary society.

This chapter will first present the historical development of the philosophy of liberal adult education. An analysis of this philosophy will clarify its various components: a particular view of human beings and society, a theory of reality, a view of knowledge, a theory of values, and an attitude toward social change. Then the educational principles of this theory will be developed, concentrating upon the aims and objectives of education, the proposed curriculum for it, and its view of the teaching-learning process. In keeping with the plan of the book to show how theories manifest themselves in practice, programs that embody this philosophy in adult education will be examined. Finally, an assessment will be made of the present status of this view and the role it might play in the movement toward lifelong education.

Historical Development of Liberal Adult Education: European Antecedents

The origins of the liberal education tradition can be seen in the contrast between the educational theory of the Sophists and the classical approaches of Socrates, Plato, and Aristotle. The goal of the Sophists was to train statesmen and politicians through a utilitarian education. These men were the first professional teachers. They proposed to produce the trained orator and politician. The means to this end were the study of rhetoric, skill in argument, and knowledge of the audience that was to be persuaded. Education was thus seen as acquiring skills and storing facts. Skills were to be public speaking, legal case pleading, and cultural information. Educators in this tradition include Protagoras, Isocrates, and Hippias in Greece. Cicero and Quintilian continued this tradition in Rome (Broudy and Palmer, 1965).

This utilitarian approach to education was strongly opposed by the three men who stand at the beginning of the liberal arts tradition, Socrates, Plato, and Aristotle. These men proposed an intellectual education for statesmen and politicians. Its aim was to produce the good and virtuous person. In the case of Plato, the highest ideal was the philosopher-king who knew both what was true and valuable and who would govern according to rational principles. The goal was to be met through a rigorous intellectual training that began with a knowledge of grammar and rhetoric, extended to the natural sciences, history and literature, and was completed with a study of logic and philosophy.

Socrates' chief contribution to this tradition was his method of exhorting his disciples to question all assumptions and to become knowledgeable, for according to him, the person who knows the truth will also do the truth. Plato's contribution lay in his portrayal of the process of learning as an individual's radical encounter with a truth that exists outside of the self. In his famous Allegory of the Cave, he taught that learning was the painful process of freeing the mind of prejudices and accepting responsibility to help others to achieve this goal. Aristotle brought to this tradition a careful investigation of the components of moral education through the formation of habits, and an intellectual education through the development of practical wisdom (art, prudence) and theoretical wisdom (knowledge of science, intelligence, and wisdom). For Aristotle, wisdom, the contemplation of truths, constituted the ideal life; it equaled happiness. It was an activity that was performed as an end in itself and not as a means to another end. This happiness was to be found in leisure and not in the conduct of the affairs of everyday life. Humans are capable of the life of contemplation because they have an element of the divine within them (Marrou, 1956).

Before passing on to other contributions to this liberal tradition, it must be pointed out that this educational theory was conditioned by the culture in which it originated. Socrates, Plato, and Aristotle proposed an education for the leadership class of a society in which a servile class did the work. John Dewey criticized their negativism toward vocational and utilitarian education for its class bias (1916). Throughout its history, liberal education has suffered from this elitist bias. Contemporary liberal philosophers of education have still been accused of it, despite efforts to shed these ancient prejudices.

The liberal arts tradition in education became enriched through its encounter with the early and medieval Christian church. The joining of Christian faith, espousing the Bible as the revelation of God, with classical Greek learning produced a struggle between competing views of life and education—the one being based upon religious faith and the other upon rational inquiry. It was the particular achievement of Augustine of Hippo to accomplish the union of ascetical and moral education in the religious tradition with the intellectual education of the Greeks, especially Plato and Plotinus. Augustine accepted liberal learning as an important component in Christian education. In his view, though, the ultimate aim of education was to prepare persons for life after death through an understanding and practice of the Christian virtues of faith, hope, charity, and humility. This aim could be advanced by the development of the intellect through classical learning (Marrou, 1956).

With Augustine's endorsement, the classical liberal arts tradition became an essential part of the curriculum of all schools in Christendom. The curriculum of these schools included the trivium (grammar, rhetoric, and logic) and the quadrivium (arithmetic, geometry, music and astronomy). Though for many these liberal arts were taught in a mechanical fashion and were subordinated to the aims of providing skills for reading and understanding the Bible, there is ample evidence that a love of learning was nicely balanced with a love of God (LeClerq, 1961).

The intellectual high point of medieval Christian thought is found in the theological and philosophical system of Thomas Aquinas. Though in his educational theory Thomas did not rely heavily on the classical literature (excepting his strong dependence on the philosophical writings of Aristotle), he did carry on and extend the decidedly intellectual approach to education found in the classical liberal tradition. Following Aristotle, Thomas argued that

> happiness is what men strive for. It is achieved in the attainment of complete truth by the intelligence and supreme good by the will. Only in the possession of the truth and the good does man attain his full liberation. Nothing less gives him complete and permanent satisfaction. (Beck, 1964, 117)

Intellectual contemplation was for Thomas the highest good because it enabled persons to gain a measure of knowledge about their true destiny and their God-given nature.

The wedding of Christian thought and liberal learning is a phenomenon that has continued to this day. Later in this chapter we will examine the religious or Neo-Thomist version of liberal education, which has influenced education both in Christian schools and in adult religious education.

The liberal arts tradition was an essential component of the classical humanist philosophy of education, which prevailed in the West from 1450 to 1850. The aim of this educational theory, as found in the writings of such humanists as Desiderius Erasmus, Thomas More, Martin Luther and Ignatius Loyola, was to produce the gentleman scholar, the cultured gentleman, fit for the demands of citizenship in the new world of commerce and the worldly court. This humanist education was also offered to a small number of women from the upper classes. This ideal also included training for service in the church. The Greek literary classics and the Latin poets and orators became the new masters, replacing the dominance and authority of Aristotle. Though education in religion for a life hereafter was stressed, an equally strong emphasis was placed on human life and nature. Renaissance humanism advocated a sensitivity to nature, and all living things, as well as a deep appreciation of the arts and culture, including painting, poetry, literature, and architecture. In the educational theory of Ignatius of Loyola was laid the foundation for Jesuit education that greatly influenced both secular and religious education in Europe and America (O'Malley, 1993).

Liberal arts education also found expression in some important Enlightenment thinkers who wrote on educational theory. Though romantics like Jean Jacques Rousseau and empiricists like Francis Bacon were not favorably disposed to liberal learning, such rationalist Enlightenment figures as Immanuel Kant and Georg Hegel saw great value in the study of liberal subjects. Their goals of developing the rational powers of the human person through mathematics and philosophy corresponded to the intellectual emphasis of the liberal tradition.

The educational theories of the humanists and rationalists contained a number of ambivalences, which have constantly plagued liberal education. The study of the liberal arts may be conducted in a formalistic, nonliberating manner. This was often an education for an elitist class, the leaders and the aristocracy. Furthermore, with the development of the natural sciences, the weaknesses of this liberal learning became clearer to such thinkers and writers as Francis Bacon, Herbert Spencer, and John Dewey. Modern efforts to promote liberal learning have taken into consideration scientific and technological knowledge that has accumulated since 1850.

Historical Developments in Liberal Adult Education in the United States

Developments in European thought and practice, especially in England and France, influenced educational theory and practice in the colonial period of United States history. It was in the colonial colleges that the liberal tradition of learning was transplanted to this country. The curriculum at Harvard at this time included the traditional trivium and quadrivium, the three philosophies (natural, moral, and mental), the ancient languages (biblical and classical), and the fine arts and religion (Cremin, 1970). All colleges imitated Harvard in providing a strong emphasis on liberal studies for the education of the future leaders for the church and the country. Those who were being prepared for the professions were expected to devote themselves to this form of learning.

The colonial period of education witnessed a struggle between two philosophies. There were those involved in collegiate educations who were committed to an elitist-classical education and others like Benjamin Franklin who pressed for a more utilitarian democratic-vocational preparation (Bridenbaugh and Bridenbaugh, 1962). This struggle has characterized American educational history at all levels. The advocates of liberal education have stressed the training of minds over the demands of preparing people for jobs and careers (Kett, 1994).

It is interesting to note, however, that even such a utilitarian as Benjamin Franklin could appreciate the value of a liberal education for adults. This "founder of American adult education" established the Junto, which in his words

> required that every member in his turn produce one or more queries on any point of morals, politics or natural philosophy to be discussed by the company, and once in three months produce and read an essay of his own writing on any subject he pleased. (Franklin, 1964, 116-117)

This particular club had ups and downs in its history and finally merged with the American Philosophical Society (Merriam, 1979). Franklin's interest in liberal adult learning also led to his encouraging the founding of libraries (Knowles, 1977, 8; Stubblefield and Keane 1994, 29-30).

In the period after the American Revolution a debate ensued in the new nation over the relationship between education and government. In the 1790s, the American Philosophical Society sponsored an essay contest on "a system of Liberal Education and Literary Instruction adapted to the genius of government" (Perkinson, 1977, 7). Thomas Jefferson, emerging as the most outstanding figure in this national debate, stressed the importance of an educated citizenry in order to prevent the abuses of government. He argued for the widespread diffusion of knowledge, the importance of self-education, and the need for education to prepare leaders for the new nation. He wanted the leaders of the country to be trained through a liberal education. In the Preamble of the *Bill for the More General Diffusion of Knowledge* he recommended that

> those whom nature hath endowed with genius and virtue should be rendered by a liberal education worthy to receive, and able to guard the sacred deposit of the rights and liberties of their fellow citizens, and that they should be called to that charge regardless of wealth, birth, or other accidental condition or circumstance. (Jefferson in Cremin, 1970, 439)

Benjamin Rush joined Jefferson in describing the liberal or learned education in a republic. Languages, including the classical languages, were to be learned. He also advocated a study of religion, eloquence, history, chronology, commerce, chemistry, and other liberal subjects. Rush was also concerned with the education of women in the new republic, whom he thought should be instructed in the principles of liberty, government and patriotism (Rush, 1786, 1969).

In the period before the Civil War, colleges and academies fostered a liberal emphasis in education. Several adult education enterprises also promoted liberal education. Institutes such as the Lowell Institute in Boston and Cooper Union in New York sponsored lectures and courses in philosophy, natural history, and the arts. The popularity of lyceums further reflected adults' interest in learning. Begun by Josiah Holbrook in 1826, the Lyceum Movement, using a national network of study groups, brought liberal learning to many American towns and cities. The movement introduced countless adults to the liberal ideas of Emerson, Thoreau, Holmes, and others (Knowles, 1977). Strong between 1820 and 1840, the Lyceum Movement eventually died out after it began to direct its efforts toward the promotion of public schools (Stubblefield and Keane, 1994).

With the emergence of science and the growth of the new industrial society after the Civil War, the debate between the defenders of liberal education and the advocates of a more progressive and pragmatic education grew more intense. Secondary education became more vocationally oriented as the curriculum expanded to include vocational and life-related subjects. At the same time progressive education began to dominate the national scene.

The most noteworthy movement to emerge at this time was Chautauqua. This program which entailed the careful, systematic, guided reading of books and other materials, combined a strong religious orientation with liberal education. The movement, founded by John Vincent, a Methodist bishop, was based upon the following assumptions: all of life is educational but the true basis of education is Christian faith; all knowledge becomes sacred by its relationship to God; those who receive no cultural education early in life desire it more avidly later in life; the intellect is to be developed through reading, reflection and production: the intellectual powers of adults need direction, assistance, and encouragement; teachers can enter the process by direct contact or through correspondence; education can occur in voluntary associations, local circles, contact with resident scholars, lectures, and in summer schools and assemblies (Vincent, 1959; Stubblefield and Keane, 1994).

For Vincent, intellectual education should continue throughout one's life. He envisioned education as being mental, social, moral and religious. His plan, in fact, sounds like a precursor to the Great Books Program:

> Let them read the same books, think along the same lines, observe the same sacred days. . . . Let the course of prescribed reading be broad and comprehensive; limited in its first general survey of the wide world of knowledge; opening out into special courses, according to the reader's development, taste, and opportunity. (Vincent, 1959, 67)

Church movements such as Chautauqua were not the only forms of adult education developed in the period after the Civil War. In 1898, Thomas Davidson, a Scottish Socialist, established a Bread Winner's College in New York (City) to bring knowledge of liberal learning to working men and women. The course of studies involved philosophy, religion, science, literature and economics. Davidson's educational ideal was to combine a strong vocational education with a broad cultural education. His experiment floundered after his death (Davidson, 1959).

Liberal adult education also developed in this period as part of the extension programs introduced at colleges and universities. In the 1890s university extensions were established at the University of Wisconsin and the University of Chicago. The extension program at Wisconsin included both vocational and liberal education (Knowles, 1977). In their early years extension programs in the United States imitated the English model, which placed emphasis on liberal learning. But by the twentieth century a distinctive American model prevailed in which service was a predominant purpose (Stubblefield and Keane, 1994).

A resurgence of interest in the liberal arts tradition after World War I in America began as a reaction against the pragmatic philosophy of the progressive education movement. From the late 1920s onwards, literary and philosophic scholars in colleges and universities called for a redirection of educational efforts toward the liberal tradition, a tradition that had been reduced in influence because of the rise of the teaching of science and other utilitarian subjects. The Carnegie Corporation fostered adult liberal education in the 1920s. For example, the corporation supported experiments in workers education that they thought would foster social stability (Lagemann, 1989).

Pratte (1971) classified the resurgent liberal tradition into two philosophical groups, neo-rationalist and Neo-Thomist. The neo-rationalist tradition was based on the religious philosophy of the human being and on a form of education that would foster this development. Major theorists in this group included Robert Hutchins (1936, 1953, 1968), Mortimer Adler (1937), Gilbert Highet (1950), and Mark Van Doren (1943).

The second wing of the liberal arts tradition was the neo-Thomist, so called because it was based on the religious philosophy of Thomas Aquinas. Most members of this wing were Catholic philosophers and educators. The most important work to appear in this tradition was Jacques Maritain's *Education at the Crossroads* (1943). Other theorists in this area included William McGucken (1942), the Anglican bishop George Beck (1964), and Robert Henle (1965).

The principles expounded by the above philosophers, though they were not expressly concerned with adult education, provided the basis for a philosophy of liberal adult education. A number of books and articles appeared in the past half century that treated liberal adult education explicitly, but these have not had the philosophical rigor of the above-mentioned theorists. In 1926, for example, Everett Dean Martin, the director of the People's Institute in New York, argued for the continued education of a liberally educated adult. While he felt that only a few could attain this goal, he acknowledged that some members of the working class could aspire to this type of education. His lectures were in fact given on Friday nights to working people at the Peoples Institute in New York where he was a director. His lectures drew an audience from 800 to 1,200 and ranged over many academic disciplines (Kett, 1994). Stubblefield's (1979) characterization of Martin's work points out one of the enduring problems of liberal education:

> Martin, in his efforts to ground adult education in liberal education, viewed the popularizing of knowledge with disdain and elevated individual development over social improvement. (5)

Stubblefield goes on to note that the liberal tradition has continued in the Great Books Program, study-discussion groups, foreign affairs associations, and other culturally oriented programs.

Martin was part of a group of adult educators who strongly opposed the trend toward vocationalism in adult education and campaigned for a decidedly liberal adult education. This group included Alvin Johnson, the director of the New School of Social Research, the Columbia University historians James Harvey Robinson and Scott Buchanan, both connected with the Peoples Institute, and Will Durant, the author of the best selling book *The Story of Philosophy*. Since these thinkers were influenced both by the ideals of liberal education and the instrumentalism of John Dewey, they attempted to find a way to utilize liberal ideas to combat the social problems of the day. The chapter on progressive adult education will address some of their contributions to adult education.

Beyond the general educational works by Adler, Hutchins, Maritain, and others mentioned previously, little writing since Martin's book in 1926 has appeared that bears directly on liberal adult education. In the 1950s and 1960s, essays on the topic were published by Houle (1955), Houle and Nelson (1956), Friedenburg (1958), and Whipple (1960).

Perhaps the strongest impetus for the study of liberal education of adults in this country came from the Center for the Study of Liberal Education for Adults. The CSLEA was established in 1951 in Chicago and was funded by the Ford Foundation. The Center had three main areas of interest: the improvement of liberal education for adults in university programs, the development of improved methods of teaching and instruction, and support for programs in liberal adult education. Important publications emanated from the CSLEA, including the Notes and Essays series which examined purposes and philosophy, Reports on methods and practices in the field, Research Reports, monographs, and journal reprints. With the closing of the CSLEA in 1961, a strong force for the liberal education of adults was lost in the United States (Knowles, 1977, pp. 162-163; Stubblefield and Keane 1994, 238-239)

In the 1950s, the Ford Foundation established the Fund for Adult Education (FAE), which provided seed money for experiments in liberal adult education in a number of American cities. Local citizens established adult education councils comprised of representatives from churches, welfare, labor, business and women's organizations. The purpose of the enterprise from the Fund's point of view was to teach people *how* to think rather than *what* to think. The program did not use Great Books but rather films, lectures, and articles. In Kett's judgment, the experiments were not successful, though some colleges absorbed the types of programs the Fund sponsored (1994).

In the 1970s the movement for the liberal education of adults received renewed interest both at the practical level and at the philo-

sophical level. At the level of practice, the increase in adult programs brought an increase in programs for the liberal education of
adults. Many of these programs existed at the college level and were
programs to reach the nontraditional student. Many colleges introduced an interdisciplinary Masters of Liberal Studies degree, which
became extremely popular with older adults. The number of such
programs went from 12 in 1975 to 120 in 1990. The motivation behind these programs was partly to attract new students to colleges
and universities and partly to meet the needs of adults in middle
and later years (Kett, 1994).

Liberal adult education received a considerable boost through
the federal infusion of funds into the National Endowment for the
Arts (NEH). The institute, begun to train teachers in the humanities, began to popularize education in the humanities for the general public. Its purpose was to make the humanities and social sciences relevant to the real interests of adults. The NEH established
state councils that attempted to broaden efforts in areas where humanities education was deficient. (Kett, 1994).

At the philosophical level, liberal adult education has received
strong philosophical support from the work of two British analytic
philosophers of education. Both Lawson (1975) and Paterson (1978)
argued for liberal adult education as the only form of education that
can fit the rigid canons of educational activity that are presented in
the analytic tradition of philosophy. The views of these philosophers
will be examined in a later chapter.

In the past two decades liberal education has been at the center
of an extensive debate in this country connected with the canon that
should be taught in schools and colleges. The traditional canon of
studies in colleges and universities has been charged with racism,
sexism, and a European bias. This debate and its relevance to adult
liberal education will be reviewed later in this chapter.

Liberal Education and the Educated Person

The purpose of liberal education is derived from a particular
conception of the human person. No matter what the changes of
time and culture have produced, the human person has remained
essentially the same throughout the history of the world. In describing this view of human nature, Hutchins wrote that

> A sound philosophy in general suggests that men are ratio-
> nal, moral, and spiritual beings, and that the improvement
> of men means the fullest development of their rational,

moral, and spiritual powers//All men have these powers, and
all men should develop them to the fullest extent. . . . (1953,
68)

A liberal education is, first of all, a *rational* or *intellectual education*. An intellectual education attempts to lead persons from information to knowledge to wisdom. Educated persons must have information and know the fundamentals of reading, writing, and compu-
tation. They should possess basic information about the world in
which they live. The mere knowledge of facts, however, does not
make one intellectually educated. A person must move to the second phase, knowledge. For the liberal educator, knowledge is the
systematic grasp of a subject matter, a discipline, or an area of study.
True knowledge also entails the ability to communicate what one
knows to others. Knowledge differs from information in that the
person who possesses it can go beyond the facts to grasp the principles or assumptions, analyze a situation, and develop an ordered
synthesis.

Though information and knowledge are necessary for a person
to be educated, it is only in the possession of wisdom that one truly
becomes educated. Wisdom is of two types—practical, and theoretical or speculative. Practical wisdom refers to the ability to apply
information and knowledge to the activities of daily life. It is
this wisdom that makes a person a good parent, citizen, and worker.
Practical wisdom is characterized by choosing the moderate
position between two extremes. This wisdom cannot be directly
taught for it demands direct experience. Theoretical wisdom is
the contemplation of the deepest principles of some reality and
the reorganization of its connection and relationship to other areas.
Theoretical wisdom is the search for truth about the human
situation and the world. It calls for study and reflection and requires
a certain amount of leisure and freedom. It results from a life
dedicated to learning for the sake of learning. Speculative wisdom
is the wisdom of the scientist, the artist, the philosopher, and the
poet.

In the liberal arts tradition it is recognized that a certain tension exists between these two types of wisdom. This tension goes
back to Plato and Aristotle. Aristotle considered speculative wisdom
the highest human achievement. While Plato put great emphasis
on this form of wisdom, he also wanted his philosophers to engage
in the work of governing. The liberal tradition recognizes that every
society must have its persons of practical wisdom as well as its per-

sons of speculative wisdom. Thus persons of action and persons of thought are both needed. What is distinctive about the liberal tradition is that it recommends that even the training of the person of action be accomplished through a strong intellectual education. Glenn Gray's (1968) attempt to resolve this tension between the two wisdoms is clear and succinct:

> The educated man is one who is either practically or theoretically wise. If such a one is not to descend the ladder, he must keep constantly educating and re-educating himself. Education is a search and not a state of being. And though wisdom is inevitably dual in nature, a new necessity is upon us. Though we cannot unite the two kinds of wisdom, they must learn to support and to supplement each other. (29)

To the intellectual education that has been proposed, liberal educators add a second form of education, *moral education.* All educators in the liberal tradition have stressed that an intellectual education must form the basis of a moral education. According to Aristotle, the moral virtues in the liberal tradition are prudence, justice, temperance, and fortitude. Plato considered these four as parts of the one virtue of justice. To these virtues Augustine added the Christian virtues of faith, hope, love and humility.

Philosophers of liberal education have consistently held to one important truth in the area of moral education. This education is to be intellectually based, and not a direct education of the will, or an attempt at direct character formation. This intellectual basis for moral education was enunciated strongly in the face of Russia's and Nazi Germany's efforts at direct character formation, which attempted to train wills and educate emotions to correct ways of action. Liberal educators today view with suspicion efforts of behaviorists to modify behavior through reinforcement and punishment, as well as the efforts of some educators to use emotional strategies to bring about value commitments.

For the liberal arts educator values come about through a careful and close study of great philosophy, literature, and works of art. The formation of character is both an intellectual and a moral task. Modern proponents of this philosophy decry the way in which the so-called liberal arts subjects are taught in schools and colleges. For Bernard Murchland, liberal education should aim to make value issues central to the intellectual life. The ultimate value questions remain essentially unchanged: what is the good life and how are we

to attain it? Murchland's (1979) program for moral education in a
liberal arts perspective had the purpose of leading

> students into a thorough investigation of freedom, into the
> requirements of a democratic ethics, into what might be
> called the rituals of a democratic faith. . . . These would
> include attitudes of sympathy and cooperation, a sense of
> restraints and limits, a sensitivity to values and discipline, a
> desire for excellence, a respect for the common good and
> attention to duties and obligation as well as insistence on
> rights. (45)

Closely connected to the moral nature of the human being is the
third dimension of liberal education, that of *spiritual* or *religious
education*. While not all liberal educators emphasize the religious
or spiritual dimension, as was mentioned earlier, a strong religious
orientation is embraced by some proponents. Jacques Maritain (1943)
gave the strongest statement of this position when he based his
philosophy on the Greek, Christian, and Jewish view of a person:

> Man as an animal endowed with reason, whose supreme
> dignity is in the intellect; and man as a free individual in
> personal relation with God, whose supreme righteousness
> consists in voluntarily obeying the law of God; and man
> as a sinful and wounded creature called to divine life and
> to the freedom of grace, whose supreme perfection consists
> of love. (7)

Consonant with this view of the human being, Maritain and other
religious educators set as the highest goal or ideal of education
fostering knowledge of God and spiritual realities along with
inculcation of Christian principles of life and a Christian view of the
world.

In his classic statement of the religious liberal arts position,
Maritain argued strenuously against the pragmatic or progressive
view of education. Since for him the prime goal of education is the
conquest of internal and spiritual freedom to be achieved in the
individual, he considered such goals as problem solving, social ad-
justment, and social change to be subsidiary goals, which should not
impede the primary goal. In keeping with this view, Maritain argued that a truly liberal education must include both morality and
religion.

(Stop 03)

The fourth and final broad ideal or aim of the liberal arts tradition, especially since the time of the Renaissance, is the development of the *aesthetic sense* in the human being. Even the ancient philosophers added the appreciation of beauty in nature and in art to the quest for the true, the good, and the holy. In the writings of such literary humanists as Mark Van Doren, this dimension of liberal arts education gets a fuller treatment. For him the Greek, Roman, and English literature classics are to be appreciated as is the beauty found in other works in the humanities and fine arts. Van Doren (1943) contends that the humanities are necessary rather than nice:

> Poetry, story, and speculation are more than pleasant to encounter; they are indispensable if we would know ourselves as men. To live with Herodotus, Euripides, Aristotle, Lucretius, Dante, Shakespeare, Cervantes, Pascal, Swift, Balzac, Dickens, Tolstoy, to take only a few names at random—musicians, painters, sculptors—is to be wiser than experience can make us in those matters that have most closely to do with family, friends, rulers, and whatever gods there be. To live with them is indeed experience of the essential kind, since it takes us beyond the local and the accidental, at the same moment that it lets us know how uniquely valuable a place and a time can be. (511)

In summary, the educated person possesses the four components of a liberal education: rational or intellectual education which involves wisdom, moral values, a spiritual or religious dimension, and an aesthetic sense.

The Broad Scope of Liberal Education

Liberal education produces a person who is literate in the broadest sense—intellectually, morally, spiritually, and aesthetically. When one reads the programs of study that liberal educators such as Hutchins, Maritain, and Van Doren propose one is staggered by the amount of reading and study that a person must do in order to be liberally educated. The demands of these educators are broad, and they clearly envisage a life of continued learning or a "learning society," in the words of Robert Hutchins. With the increase of leisure and the rapidity of change, liberal educators consider the necessity of this form of education as even more urgent today. In fact, it is argued that only adults who have the life experiences and leisure to appreciate the wisdom found in our cultural heritage can best grasp the full scope of liberal education.

Liberal educators have devoted most of their attention to the content of education. They have been severely critical of the utilitarian and vocational direction that education has taken in this country since the advent of progressive education. In their view education in the schools should be devoted to developing ability in language and mathematics at the earlier stages. At the secondary stages, literature, languages, science, history. and other liberal studies should be pursued. The ideal college for these educators is one that places the strongest emphasis on learning the arts of investigation, criticism, and communication through an intimate acquaintance with the Great Books.

A distinctive feature of the liberal arts philosophy of education is its treatment of the role of science in the curriculum. It is clear that for liberal education philosophy, religion, and the humanities are superior to science in all ways. A modern form of liberal education emerged as a separate American philosophy of education between the two World Wars when science and technology were playing (in the liberal educator's mind) a decidedly destructive role in American life and education. Liberal educators attempted to supply the values by which science and technology were to be criticized. According to both Maritain and Hutchins, if science is taught at universities, it should be done at special institutes and not as part of liberal or general education (Maritain, 1943; Hutchins, 1936).

More recent expositions of the liberal tradition seem to have recognized the place of science in the curriculum. Hutchins (1968) agrees that science and mathematics are essential to the world needs, for they are the basis of the technology that has been developed. But the questions about the uses to which science can and should be directed are philosophic questions, which demand a broader liberal education than a scientific education can provide.

Given the broad nature of the components of liberal education, the question arises regarding who should receive this type of education. Many liberal educators agree with Hutchins that the democracy in which we live requires that all be permitted to pursue liberal studies, but that "democracy does not require that the higher learning should be open to anybody except those who have the interest and ability that independent intellectual work demands" (Hutchins, 1936, 19-20). In this view, those who would not profit by all the components of a liberal education should receive technical training around the time of adolescence. This view is close to the concept of education that Jefferson proposed. It contends that people should be taught as long as possible according to the abilities they possess, but that when differences emerge, the highest training, the liberal training, should be offered only for those that intellectually deserve it.

The position of other liberal educators, such as Van Doren, is different. He contends that a liberal education is worthy of every person's study and thus he tries to avoid an elitist stance. Exposure to liberal education is demanded for all in a truly democratic society. Society needs all of its citizens to be developed to the limit of their capacities—intellectually, morally, spiritually, and aesthetically. Van Doren's (1943) sentiments on this issue are strongly expressed:

> What was once for a few must now be for the many. There is no escape from this—least of all through the sacrifice of quality to quantity. The necessity is not to produce a handful of masters; it is to produce as many masters as possible, even though this be millions.... Liberal education in the modern world must aim at the generosity of nature, must work to make the aristocrat, the man of grace, the person, as numerous as fate allows. (31)

In these words of Van Doren, the sentiments of the Jacksonian democrat are again expressed—that is, the equality principle should be applied as far as it will go in educational policy and practice.

Gilbert Highet (1950) takes a view similar to Van Doren's. The liberal curriculum for him is made up of the classics, religion, politics, art, history, sociology, and the sciences, in addition to reading, writing, and manual arts. Everyone, according to Highet, should have an equal opportunity for such study. No differentiation should be made between rich and poor. Though vocational education is included in his curriculum, the main emphasis is on the classics. In Highet's view, persons must be liberally educated, for all persons in all walks of life are teachers, in their speech, their counsel to friends, and in dealing with others (Highet, 1950, 227-229).

It is clear then that the scope of liberal education is as broad as the scope of human life itself. Central emphasis is to be given to the classics in literature and social and intellectual history. Though a number of liberal educators have conceded that science and manual training might be included in one's education, they do not usually consider these a part of liberal education. The emphasis is upon studies of an intellectual nature, and if the religious point of view is taken, then studies in religion and theology should also to be included.

The Process of Liberal Education

The process of liberal education is oriented toward conceptual and theoretical understanding rather than mere transmission and absorption of factual knowledge or development of technical skill. For Plato, the best way to achieve this theoretical understanding is through the dialectic. Through dialogues one clarifies the real meaning of concepts and can thus build syntheses of knowledge. The medieval scholastic educators also used this dialectical approach when they conducted debates on important issues.

Another process that liberal arts educators have stressed is intuition or contemplation. Augustine of Hippo first placed emphasis on this intuitive approach to knowledge. Through inner contemplation of oneself, one arrives at knowledge of many things about oneself and others (Howie 1969). In many ways, this method is similar to some modern forms of therapy whereby persons are led to a knowledge of their present situation by carefully reviewing their past life experiences. Religious persons who believe that through such contemplation of self one arrives at a truer knowledge of God and higher reality also employ this intuitive or introspective process.

The contemplation of nature and works of human art supplemented the dialectic and intuitive processes of liberal education in Renaissance humanism. For John Comenius, the great Moravian educator of the sixteenth century, and for modern-day romanticists, the contemplation of nature and beauty brings one to knowledge of self and of the world in which one lives. In its order, design, prodigality, assimilation of evil elements, and the changes through which it goes, nature holds many lessons for the learner.

An educational process that has been most appealing in the liberal arts tradition is the critical reading and discussion of classical writings. The educational program of the Great Books used in a number of colleges and among adult groups exemplifies this form of education. With experienced leadership, the reading of these books brings one to intellectual understanding and enables a person to relate the great ideas to present experience and problems. One searches for the universal ideas or truths in contemporary writings as well.

Within the processes of liberal education, a prominent place is given to the role of teacher. There are many things, liberal educators feel, that can best be taught directly by the teacher. The lecture method, if well organized and suited to the ability of the students, is recognized as an efficient instructional strategy. Since in the view of liberal educators learning through projects, insight, or discovery methods may deemphasize the directive role of the teacher, liberal educators do not generally endorse these approaches.

The fundamental process of liberal education is as old as the philosophical position of Aristotle; it is to promote theoretical thinking. Liberal learning focuses upon the operations of the intellect and attempts to promote comprehension of truth. In this perspective technical skills are of less importance, though they are not to be ignored in education. The liberal educator contends that if the mind is educated, then the person will be able to apply this knowledge to any number of areas. Skills are more easily learned through experience, and, when an intelligently formed mind gains experience, it can acquire the skills needed for particular situations.

The contention of the liberal philosopher of education is that liberal learning never becomes obsolete. Since the main thrust of liberal education is the education of the mind to a knowledge of theory, such theoretical knowledge can be applied to many different situations. The person is thus able to bridge gaps between things that are known, is able to deal flexibly with novel situations, and is capable of moving into the unknown.

While the demands of liberal education upon the student are great, the same can be said of the demands upon the teacher. Teachers must be student-scholars of exceptionally wide and lively intellectual interests. Teachers must never assume that they know all they need to know about their subject. Characterized as Socrates was by their love of wisdom, teachers derive their authority from their wisdom and their command of subject matter. The ultimate goal of teachers is that students become original or creative learners. Thus the education of teachers should be an education in the liberal arts and not training in particular skills and techniques. Liberal educators have thus been foremost in their critique of schools of education that take a narrow competency approach to teacher education.

The Liberal Education of Adults

Most of the theorizing about liberal education, in fact, most of the theorizing about education in general, has been concerned with children and youth. Yet it should be clear from our treatment of liberal education that much of what is said has applicability to adults.

In fact, a persuasive case can be made that liberal education will play an increasingly important role in the future. Arnold Toynbee looked to the affluent society of the future in which part-time adult education could be offered "to every man and woman at every stage of grown-up life" (Toynbee in Gross, 1963, 135). In the Danish high schools for adults he saw an institution that might be a forecast of the future. For Toynbee, the paradox of liberal education was that one gets it when one can least take advantage of it:

> The student has been surfeited with book learning at a stage of life at which he has not yet acquired the experience to take advantage of it, and he has been starved for book learning at a later stage in which, if he had been given the opportunity, he could have made much more of it in the light of his growing experience. (Toynbee in Gross, 1963, 134-135)

The increase in adult education at all levels in this country gives some indication that Toynbee's view of the future might still be realized.

Liberal education of adults is for Van Doren the highest level of education, following elementary, secondary schools, and college. Liberal education should be a constant study for responsible persons. The life of the mind takes on more meaning as we progress in years. Van Doren realized that this ideal was far from realized in his time, though he did recognize that a large part of adult education was liberal education:

> Whatever the reason, adult education continues to be in large part liberal education; though when Thoreau wrote that "it is time villages were universities, and their elder inhabitants the fellows of universities, with leisure—if they indeed are so well off—to pursue liberal studies the rest of their lives," he described neither his own time nor this one. Adult education is so far from universal that millions of people are unaware that it exists. (Van Doren, 1943, 104)

One of Van Doren's proposals was to give workers sabbaticals during which they could pursue studies, a suggestion which has come up again in our time. Such sabbaticals could help bring about the learning society that liberal humanists have spoken about in their writings.

Concern with the education of workers is a theme that can also be found in the philosophical writings of Horace Kallen (1962). In

Kallen's view, the aim of adult education is to liberate the mind, to bring about a synthesis of what he called a person's day-life and nightlife. The day-life is one's role as a producer in society, a worker. It is in the nightlife that one is able to enjoy the cultural benefits for which the person has worked during the day. Education, according to Kallen, should be a liberating experience. And the way to achieve this sense of liberation is through liberal studies (Kallen, 1962).

That a liberal education has a distinct function for adults was argued persuasively by Edgar Friedenberg (1956) in his article "Liberal Education and the Fear of Failure." The first function for a liberal education in his view is to teach persons the value of freedom and help them become competent to use it. Freeing persons means insuring that they have facts and the ability to deal with facts. Friedenberg wrote this article in the midst of the McCarthy hearings, thus giving his words a particular pointedness.

The second function of the liberal education of adults for Friedenberg is to help them to respond appropriately to the difference between the objective and the subjective; between the events in which they have participated and their feelings about them. A liberally educated adult is able to include feelings as the center of his or her relationship to reality. Friedenberg was also critical of the scientific approach which attempted to achieve value neutrality that excluded feelings in perceptions of truth.

Friedenberg's final purpose of a liberal education is that of increasing the range of human experience to which one could respond. In giving people a knowledge of the past, one increases the range of experience with which they can handle problems. Persons are then better able to accept and appreciate the experiences of others.

Friedenberg contended that liberal education for adults would also contribute to other goals such as improvement in the quality of citizenship and the use of leisure time, improvement of one's self-concept, and a feeling of greater human dignity. Friedenberg saw as a particularly important function of liberal adult education its potential to empower persons "to cherish dignity and not to consent to violations of it" (54). Values or virtues such as friendliness, cooperativeness, fairness, practicality, and humility can be fostered in adult groups. Human dignity was defeated in individuals who had a fear of failure. This fear of failure could be removed through education:

> Liberal education does not eradicate fear of failure by reassurance. It does so by helping people study the most significant records of human experience. This one cannot do without becoming more interested in the texture of experience

itself than in how the/story which one has impertinently interrupted, turns out. One forgets to wonder whether Destiny is going to award one some kind of a prize; whether one is going to get as rich as Mozart; as influential in the affairs of the state as Macchiavelli; as honored by a grateful citizenry as Socrates. They raise so many more interesting questions. (Friedenberg, 1956, 54)

The treatment that Friedenberg gave to the liberal education of adults was a rather broad one, concerned mainly with ideals in a rather abstract sense. At the other end of the spectrum is an evaluation study of liberal adult education by Miller and McGuire (1961). Funded by the Center for the Study of Liberal Education for Adults, they attempted to develop behaviorally stated objectives in liberal education programs for adults at college campuses. While the appropriateness of using behavioral objectives to evaluate liberal education programs might be objected to by humanist scholars, the study did reveal the scope of liberal adult education.

In their empirical examination of liberal adult education at colleges and universities, Miller and McGuire developed four categories of study. Programs existed (at the time of their study) in ethical and moral values, appreciation of the arts, political and social problems, and community participation. In their view, these four categories represented a rough approximation of the college liberal arts program: social sciences, arts, and philosophy. In the programs investigated there was a notable absence of science. The authors were surprised by this finding because of their belief that the knowledge of science among people is necessary for the survival of human existence (Miller and McGuire, 1961).

Though this scope for liberal education appears broad, it would not meet the rigorous demands of a Hutchins, Maritain, or Van Doren. This curriculum is also inadequate when compared with the Core Curriculum in the liberal arts developed at Harvard and other universities in the late 1970s. After extensive study and debate, the Harvard Task Force on the Core Curriculum, for example, decided on a core that included mathematics, natural science, literature, moral philosophy, foreign cultures, social analysis, expository writing, history, and a foreign language (Wilson, 1978). While this core might not have satisfied strict classicists, for a while it did gain acceptance in colleges and adult programs for liberal education.

The past two decades have witnessed an intense debate in higher education over a core curriculum or canon to be taught to everyone.

Critics have pointed out the Eurocentric nature of the typical curriculum of most colleges. A debate at Stanford University exposed the different ideologies of defenders of the old canon and those who sought to modify the core curriculum to include works of non-Europeans and to introduce works written by women. Acrimonious faculty debates led to the adoption of a curriculum that still gave prominence to Western Civilization but which also included the ideas of many non-Western authors (Pratt, 1992). Similar debates have taken place at many other colleges and universities. This debate also extended into the schools where debates over a multicultural curriculum still occupy many educators. Adult educators have also addressed issues concerning the multicultural adult classroom (Guy, 1999; Ross-Gordon, 1990; Tisdell, 1993b).

The Great Books Program

Probably the best known program for the liberal education of adults is the Great Books Program. Many proponents have offered this program as an adequate basis for the liberal education of both college students and adults. It was developed largely at Columbia University, the University of Chicago, and at St. John's College, Annapolis, Maryland. In 1947, the Great Books Foundation was established as an independent, nonprofit educational organization designed to provide liberal education for people of all ages. (Stubblefield and Keane 1994, 278-279). Many school systems, colleges and independent educational agencies such as public libraries have offered the program. Besides Adler, Hutchins, Maritain, and Van Doren, its distinguished list of supporters includes John Erskine, Stringfellow Barr, Scott Buchanan, Alexander Meiklejohn and Norman Forester.

Van Doren's description of this program captures its broad scope and idealistic spirit. The purpose of the program is to inculcate

> the arts of investigation, discovery, criticism, and communication, and achieve at first-hand an acquaintance with the original books, the unkillable classics, in which these miracles happen. (Van Doren, 1943, 145)

At the college level, it used to be preferred that these works be read in the original language. Nowadays, most programs deal with the classics in translation; however, an institution like St. John's College also requires the learning of Greek and French as part of the program.

For Van Doren, the Great Books embody liberal arts tradition. Selections include poets: Homer, Virgil, Shakespeare; philosophers: Plato, Aristotle, Descartes, Spinoza, Hume, and Kant; theologians: Thomas Aquinas, Augustine; scientists: Ptolemy, Galileo, Boyle, Darwin; novelists: Tolstoy, Dickens. On the list are also mathematicians, playwrights, historians, economists, political scientists, and psychologists. The curriculum is formidable, for in the view of Van Doren, education is formidable. The list does not remain static, for new books are added when they have achieved the status of classics.

For Great Books advocates there are right and wrong ways to approach the classics. The right reading of such books is not a passive but an intensely active affair. The art of discussion has to be learned before one can approach these books. But basically it is these books that are instructive; they are the real teachers in the program. Van Doren's (1943) description of the St. John's program shows the centrality of the books:

> There are no textbooks to which the great books are supplementary; the great books are the textbooks of this college, as in a sense they are its teachers. For the faculty reads them too, in preparation for seminars where they will be discussed. And since there are no departments or divisions, all of the faculty must do what all of the students do: read all of the books. (149-150)

Today, the program at St. John's College still situates the books "at the heart of learning." As stated on their website, the Great Books are

> timeless and timely; they not only illuminate the persisting questions of human existence, but also have great relevance to the contemporary problems with which we have to deal. They therefore enter directly into our everyday lives. Their authors speak to us as freshly as when they first spoke. They change our minds, move our hearts, and touch our spirits. (www.greatbooks.org)

Only a few colleges have followed the program developed at St. John's. Efforts by Harvard, Stanford, Columbia and other universities in the direction of a core curriculum indicate that the need is felt at least for core areas of liberal studies that will provide a basic and unified education.

The Great Books Foundation, based in Chicago, is currently very active in selecting and publishing soft-cover editions of the works to be discussed, providing promotional materials and organizational assistance to local leaders, and training volunteers and teachers to conduct discussion groups in their communities. As of 2004, more than 850 Great Books discussion groups sponsored by the Foundation were meeting regularly in homes and community centers. The Foundation also supports a Junior Great Books program for elementary, middle, and high school students, and an initiative called "A Latino National Conversation" that focuses on reading and discussing Latino literature (www.greatbooks.org).

That everyone can benefit from reading the classics is being demonstrated by adults in nearly a dozen states who are engaged in a college-level, multidisciplinary courses for people living in poverty. Participants' income must fall below 150% of the poverty level. Titled "The Odyssey Project," poor, low-educated adults are finding inspiration in great works of moral philosophy, literature, history and art (Perspectives, 2003). Reading and discussing "authors ranging from Plato to Shakespeare and Thomas Jefferson," the course "grant[s] students access to the nation's intellectual heritage and so to the possibilities of citizenship in its fullest sense" (Perspectives, 2003, 1).

The Great Books Program of liberal education has not been without its detractors. Many have criticized the very concept that a core of common books could provide an adequate education in contemporary society. Such a program also does not appear to allow for social and individual differences among learners. Nearly half a century ago, Kenneth Hansen (1963) in a doctoral dissertation at the University of Minnesota criticized the underlying educational philosophy of the Great Books Program. Hansen contended that the program prevented the development of a specialized or professional focus, opposed an elective system of course selection, and was presumptuous in assuming its participants could arrive at absolute, objective truth. For Hansen, the program attempted to return to a unity of knowledge through prescriptive reading, and promoted a supernatural view of the world.

In addition, Hansen considered the metaphysics of the program absolutistic, dualistic, and authoritarian. In his opinion, it placed too great emphasis on the rational mode of learning. The program manifested an antiquated view of the psychology of the person, presuming that there were separate faculties of the mind to be cultivated. He also criticized the notion that once these faculties were trained, knowledge and skills could be transferred from one area to another.

Many of the criticisms leveled against the Great Books Program have been points of difference between the progressive view of education and the liberal arts view of education. From the progressive viewpoint, the program does not take sufficient cognizance of the needs and interests of learners. It tends to dismiss present concerns in favor of past wisdom and tradition, and thus holds itself aloof from social affairs. Liberal education, which is centered on humanistic studies and intense intellectual activity and discussion, has been little accepted by progressive educators who emphasize problem solving through scientific and experimental methods.

Though some of the criticisms that Hansen and others have made of the Great Books Program and the liberal philosophy of education that underlies it are justified, something can be said in defense of this program as Hutchins, Van Doren, and others presented it. This approach to college and adult education developed when many in society feared for the very continuance of Western civilization. In the face of World Wars, the uncontrolled development of science and technology, and a vacuum in values that would hold a civilization together, Hutchins presented the liberal curriculum as a countervailing educational influence. He and others did not exclude contemporary problems from consideration, but believed that the emphasis should be placed upon the unifying factors of a common cultural tradition, much as Bloom (1987) and Hirsch (1987) have more recently argued.

Hansen's criticism that an acceptance of the Great Books program commits a person to a particular metaphysical or philosophic view does not appear correct. The program was intended as an introduction to the Western intellectual tradition with the ideal that persons would be better able to participate in self-government. The Great Books do not bring a person to transcendental truth, but rather enable persons to grapple more intelligently with present problems in light of the best thinking on human problems and existence. The very diversity of the books' historical contexts and subject matter insure that learners are introduced to a broad republic of learning.

The underlying problem with Great Books programs is not that they commit one to a particular philosophical view of the world—whether it be realism, perennialism, or idealism. Rather, one may succumb to the danger of scholasticism or Biblicism, holding too strongly to the particular views of classics and persons at the expense of examining present problems in present terms. Truths are

p43

found in the classics but often their expression and distance from present cultural patterns and concerns remove those classics from the understanding of persons today. Most of the values contained in the classics are also present in contemporary writers, who themselves are often immersed in this literature. Contemporary writers express these ideas in a contemporary idiom that speaks more to individuals of this time. What is needed is a balanced educational approach that utilizes the best of both views.

Debate over the Canon in Liberal Adult Education

The importance of liberal adult education was again recognized by Mortimer Adler (1982) in the influential *Paideia Proposal*. Though the manifesto in the main treats schooling, it begins with an important recognition that formal schooling is only part of education; as such, it is incapable of turning out educated men and women because educated persons must pass through many critical trials of adult life. Education is a lifelong process since learning never reaches an end point.

Liberal education in this proposal is presented as threefold: the acquisition of organized knowledge by means of didactic instruction in language, mathematics, and natural sciences; the development of intellectual skills by means of coaching, exercises, and supervised practice in reading, calculating, and exercising critical judgment; and enlarged understanding of ideas and values by means of the maieutic or Socratic method in the discussion of books and involvement in artistic activities.

Although the importance of liberal adult education has been recognized, a debate continues over just what should constitute the curriculum for it. While this debate has, for the most part, been restricted to undergraduate college education, the issues involved are important for liberal adult educators. Allan Bloom (1987) has argued convincingly for the continuing value of the Great Books of Western civilization to provide all of the intellectual nourishment that humans need. The purpose of a liberal education, according to Bloom, is to pose basic questions to learners as well as the alternative answers that have been offered over the ages. For him "a liberal education means reading certain generally recognized texts, just reading them, letting them dictate what the questions are and the method of approaching them—not forcing them into categories we make up, not treating them as historical products, but trying to read them as their authors wished them to be read" (344). The clas-

p. 44

sics, in Bloom's view, provide the best education possible for all persons:

> I mean rather that a life based on the Book is closer to the truth, that it provides the material for deeper research in and access to the real nature of things. Without the great revelations, epics and philosophies as part of our natural vision, there is nothing to see out there, and eventually little left inside. The Bible is not the only means to furnish a mind, but without a book of similar gravity, read with the gravity of the potential believer, it will remain unfurnished. (60)

While the university is the focus of attention of Bloom, E. D. Hirsch (1987) is concerned with the general issue of cultural literacy, especially the background knowledge necessary for functional literacy, effective national communication, and full citizenship. Although his main concern is with the teaching of cultural literacy within the schools, his ideas have relevance for adult liberal educators, especially for those involved in educating new immigrants for community life and citizenship. Bloom seems to assume a single best culture, but Hirsch's anthropological theory of education assumes a diversity of cultures in which persons can communicate effectively with one another "only by accumulating shared symbols, and the shared information that the symbols represent" (xvii).

Extending Hirsch's provocative ideas into adult education would entail attention to the learning of the national cultural language. This language includes knowledge of terms used throughout the world, a knowledge of Standard English, and information that is special to one's own country. Hirsch finds within this national culture a place for bilingualism and multiculturalism, but contends that these must remain subordinate to the development of a national culture.

These approaches to liberal education and cultural literacy (termed cultural *conservatism or* neo-*conservatism*) have met with much criticism from scholars who advocate a broadening of the liberal curriculum to include works outside the generally established canon of traditional Western education. Bloom and Hirsch along with William Bennett and Saul Bellow have been accused of creating "a narrowly specific cultural capital that will be the normative referent for everyone, but will remain the property of a small and powerful caste that is linguistically and ethnically unified" (Pratt,

1992, 15). The following argument against their stand was offered in the now famous debate over undergraduate education at Stanford:

> A "liberal education" for our time should expand beyond the culture-bound, basically colonialist, horizon that relies, albeit subtly, on the myth of the cultural superiority of the West. . . . Does the new integrated vision... entail our teaching the Greek Hermes and Prometheus alongside the North American Indian Coyote or the West African Anansi and Legba as paradigms of trickster heroes, or Japanese Noh alongside Greek drama or Indian philosophy alongside Plato? (In Pratt, 1988, 26)

Some scholars also contest the apparently value-free manner in which Bloom proposes that the classics be approached. Richard Rorty (1992) argues that we always "read books with questions in mind—not questions dictated by the books, but questions we have previously, if vaguely formulated" (32). It is not clear to him that we can totally avoid forcing books into categories we make up. There is, however, no reason to be forced to choose between these two approaches of questioning the text and allowing the text to question us, since both can be used in the educational process. Rorty's point, nevertheless, rightly discourages us from viewing the received texts as some sort of inspired and infallible literature.

Hirsch has also received criticism from many sides, notably about the existence of a national culture and desirability of focusing on it so extensively or exclusively in education. Barbara Smith (1992) argues that this approach to education would actually increase the illiteracy, economic deprivation, social marginalization, and political efficacy that Hirsch wants to eliminate. She argues that the knowledge that Hirsch wants learners to acquire belongs to a particular group and would serve to promote their interests at the expense of the interests of other groups in society. What Henri Giroux (1992) finds lacking in cultural conservatism is any notion of education as the critical reconstruction of economic, political, and social life. His call for a critical pedagogy will be explored later in this book.

The arguments of these liberal and radical critics need to be balanced by the thoughtful responses of those who offer a defense of the basic positions of Bloom and Hirsch relating to the importance of the traditional canon in Western education. Brigitte Berger (1993) argues for the continued relevance of texts that underlie the intellectual and moral values of Western societies. Arthur Schlesinger

p 46

(1992) both criticizes some of the extreme positions of multiculturalists and reasserts the necessity of focusing upon the value consensus which unites the nation. On the other hand, Henry Louis Gates (1992) makes a case against a particularism which denies the values present in all groups. Martha Nussbaum (1997) offers a defense of liberal education in which there is sufficient room for both the classics as well as a study of non-Western cultures, African American studies, and Women's studies.

The debate over the canon is part of the broader debate over political correctness, which has received extensive coverage in both the popular press and the academic and political communities. The debate is also described as one between those who propose a multicultural curriculum which takes into account ethnicity, class, gender, and sexual orientation and those who maintain that greater emphasis must be placed on transmitting the common culture that Hirsch endorses. While this debate has not engaged widespread attention from adult educators, the work of liberal adult educators necessarily deals with these issues. This may be the opportune time to engage in debates over the Great Books programs which are still offered in many communities of our nation. Questions could be raised about the goals, content, and methods of these programs.

An Evaluation of Adult Liberal Education

The continuation of the Great Books Program and the return of many schools and colleges and universities to a liberal curriculum indicate a continuing interest in this tradition in educational circles today. Liberal adult education can be found in many forms and situations. Many persons engage in programs of self-education inspired by the liberal ideal. Colleges are enrolling more and more nontraditional students and are offering them liberal studies among other programs. In addition, liberal adult education can be found in programs sponsored by churches, labor unions, evening schools, businesses, and industries.

Perhaps more than other segments of the adult population, men and women over sixty are being offered opportunities to engage in liberal studies. Several writers have in fact argued that later adulthood is a particularly appropriate time for taking up liberal studies. Moody (1976), for example, challenges educators to

> make available to older people the great ideas of the humanities and the social sciences that can nourish this psy-

chological development in old age. In the fields of philosophy, religion, psychology, and literature there are elements that can only be grasped in all their depth and richness by individuals who bring a lifetime of personal experience to their study. (11)

Colleges and universities across the United States are offering just such experiences. Programs like Fordham University's College at Sixty and Fairleigh Dickinson University's Education Program for Older Persons focus largely, if not entirely, upon liberal education. Programs associated with universities have expanded considerably since the inception in 1962 of the first Learning in Retirement (LIR) institutes, also known as Lifelong Learning Institutes (LLI). LIR organizations provide older adults with the opportunity to take part in college-level courses on a noncredit basis. The curriculum is chosen, designed, and often led by organization members, encouraging peer learning and active member participation. LIR organizations capitalize on the strengths and experiences of older adults themselves. The Learning Institute Network estimates that as of 2004, there were nearly 1000 such institutes in operation in the United States, with approximately half affiliated with a college or university (www.elderhostel.org/ein/intro.asp).

Another intriguing and highly successful program of liberal education for older persons is the Elderhostel. Inspired by youth hostels and folk schools of Europe, Elderhostel is a network of numerous colleges and universities offering special low-cost, one-week summer residential academic programs for older adults. Courses are non-credit, have no exams, grades, or required homework. The main objective of an Elderhostel program is intellectual stimulation. Participants become involved in learning for its own sake. Unlike LIRs that have an ongoing membership at the local level, Elderhostel programs are one-time offerings that draw adults from outside the sponsoring institution. Elderhostel also offers international study tours and programs. Elderhostel estimates that approximate 200,000 adults over age fifty participate annually in 10,000 programs in ninety countries (www.elderhostel.org).

Adults who are lifelong learners are often motivated by the liberal ideal. The learning efforts of two such men, Cornelius Hirschberg and Malcolm X, are described by Ronald Gross in *The Lifelong Learner* (1977). Hirschberg, a retired salesman, spent at least 20,000 hours in getting a liberal education through his own efforts. He read widely in philosophy and literature. In his memoirs, *The Priceless Gift* (1960), he beautifully expressed the values that his studies had on his life:

> I am stuck in the city, that's all I have, I am stuck in busi-
> ness and routine and tedium. But I give up only as much as
> I must; for the rest I live my life at its best, with art, music,
> poetry, literature, science, philosophy, and thought. I shall
> know the keener people of this world, think the keener
> thoughts, and taste the keener pleasures, as long as I can
> and as much as I can. (Hirschberg in Gross, 1977, 271)

While Hirschberg found personal consolation and pleasure in
his liberal studies, Malcolm X found in them a force that was truly
revolutionary. In his *Autobiography* (1964), he reports the influence
of great reading on his ideas. He read deeply in history, especially
black history and became interested in philosophy both of the West
and of the East. When asked about his alma mater, he could proudly
say that books served as his college. His writings and his life manifested the power of ideas in forging a man and a movement.

Although individuals have been inspired by liberal studies, the
overall influence of liberal education in both general and adult education in the United States has been mitigated by two factors. The
first is the movement toward career and vocational education. Since
the 1960s, funds that federal and state governments have allotted to
education have gone primarily to skill development and job-oriented
programs. The social programs of the past decades have been practical and utilitarian in orientation. It has thus been difficult for liberal adult education to get a hearing in this context.

The second development that has also gone against the liberal
educational philosophy is the strong behaviorist orientation of much
of mid-twentieth century educational theory and practice. Emphases on stating objectives behaviorally, stating outcomes in quantifi-
able terms, and developing measurable competencies mitigate humanistic thrusts in education. Liberal aims and methods do not easily lend themselves to such statements, analyses, and evaluations.
Behaviorist and progressive educational theory and practice thus
characterize the American temperament and spirit more strongly
today than does the liberal arts philosophy of education.

Nevertheless, the old and venerable tradition of liberal education is not dead. At this writing, the prospects for adult liberal education appear bright. Any strong movement for lifelong learning will
necessarily need a philosophy of education that takes seriously the
great accomplishments of civilization and the great teachers of the

past. Shorn of a number of historical biases such as elitism and antipathy toward vocationalism and specialization, this tradition can truly be a liberating force in the lives of individuals and society. Knowledge of past civilization and culture does not in itself *liberate* persons, but it can be an important step in any process of liberation. Though the world is constantly in a state of change, there are some things that do not change. People continue to search for truth, desire to develop their moral characters, strive for spiritual and religious visions, and seek the beautiful in life and nature. As long as the human beings do these things, the liberal tradition in education will be a potent force.

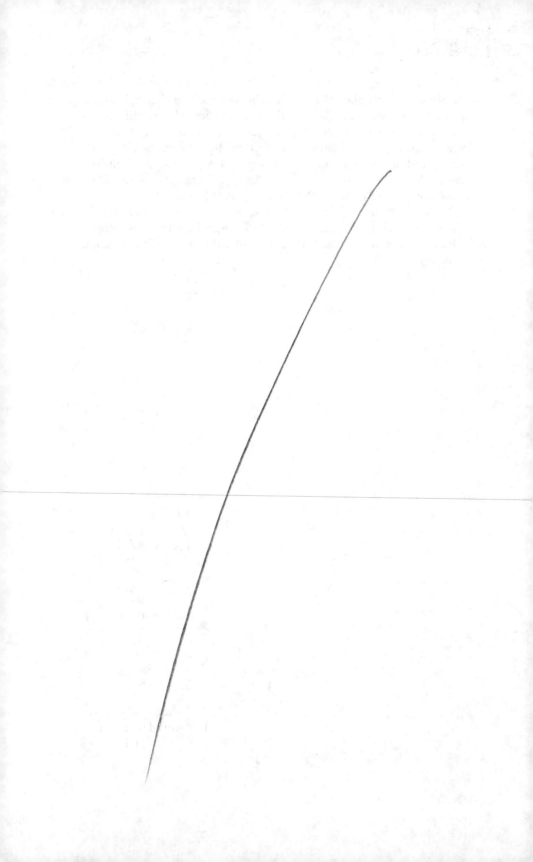

CHAPTER III

PROGRESSIVE ADULT EDUCATION

Progressivism has had a greater impact upon the adult education movement in the United States than any other single school of thought. The rapid growth of adult education occurred at a time when progressive education in varying forms was a predominant influence. In an attempt to deal with a society that was quickly becoming urbanized and industrialized, early adult educators looked to the dynamic progressive movement as an inspiration in establishing theoretical positions and practical programs.

Elements of progressive thought are found in the writings of all major theorists in the field of adult education including Malcolm Knowles, Carl Rogers, Cyril Houle, Ralph Tyler, Edward Lindeman, Paul Bergevin, and Paulo Freire. Many forms of adult education were inspired by progressive ideals: vocational adult education, extension education, education of the foreign born and citizenship education, family and parent education, and education for social action. In addition, some of the basic principles in adult education originated in progressive thought: needs and interests, the scientific method, problem-solving techniques, the centrality of experience, pragmatic and utilitarian goals, and the idea of social responsibility.

Many educators over a period of half a century contributed to the distinctive features of progressive education. The first part of this chapter will attempt to shed some light on the history of this complex movement. The historical section will be followed by a discussion of the basic principles of progressive education and their expression in adult education. A third section will examine some of the programs in adult education that have been inspired by progressive principles. Finally, an assessment of this movement in adult education will be presented.

A Historical Perspective on Progressive Education

The origins of progressive education lie in the rationalist, empirical, and scientific thought that developed first in Europe, and then became predominant in the United States. Educators who proposed new ways of seeking and applying knowledge challenged the traditional liberal education of the day. Reason, experience, and feeling began to replace tradition, faith, and authority as the chief ways of arriving at truth and value.

Progressivism's earliest threads can be traced back to the sixteenth century. Bishop John Comenius suggested allowing students to imitate nature for their education, rather than encouraging them to read books only. Jean Jacques Rousseau carried this idea to an extreme in proposing that all learning until the age of twelve should come from experience. The natural freedom and spontaneity of the child that Rousseau advocated was stressed in the practical educational experiments of Johann Pestalozzi and Fredrich Froebel. These pioneering educators advocated contact with natural objects, learning of manual skills, and incorporation of play into educational experiences. In eighteenth century England, both Francis Bacon and John Locke put greater faith in empirical knowledge instead of knowledge based on the authority of the written word.

The development of the philosophy underlying the progressive education movement owes much to the seminal ideas of Charles Darwin (1859; 2003). Darwin stressed the inductive methods of science rather than the deductive approaches of philosophy and theology. He developed a scientific method of arriving at knowledge which entailed observation and the testing of hypotheses through experience. Nature provided the context and conditions within which human persons struggled for existence. These ideas of Darwin affected not only psychology, natural sciences, social sciences and philosophy but also had an influence in shaping the new pedagogy being developed by progressive educators.

In applying Darwin's thought to a social context, Herbert Spencer (1860) also influenced progressive education. He developed a theory which, through an emphasis on science, would lead to the betterment of the human condition. Societies and cultures evolve, he reasoned, just as the human species and lower forms of life have evolved. Spencer encouraged the progressives to see in an education based on science a powerful means of advancing cultural perfection and development. Others, however, interpreted Darwin's thought in a conservative manner implying that little could be done to bring about changes for the better, except waiting for the right conditions for change to emerge naturally.

Inspired by these various intellectual developments, a distinctive progressive movement evolved by the turn of the century. At that time, the United States was undergoing great social, economic, and political changes. Mass immigration was taking place in urban areas of the country, especially in the East. The industrialization that had begun after the Civil War accelerated at the turn of the century. In the face of these social, political, and economic problems, many American thinkers expressed a great faith in the power of education for solving these problems (Perkinson, 1977). A school system from kindergarten through high school was established to socialize the new immigrants, ameliorate the social ills brought about by rapid urbanization, train workers and leaders needed for the growing industrial society, and contribute to the development of a democracy without corruption. A special teaching profession with scientific training and high ideals also emerged. Vocational education was added to the traditional liberal arts education. Although the progressive dreams were not all realized, these reforms greatly influenced the direction of American education.

The theory of progressive education developed at this time was designed to liberate the talents and gifts of individuals; thus it was learner-centered in the tradition of Rousseau, Pestalozzi, and Froebel. It was indebted to Darwin for the concept of the person as a developing and evolving organism, and its practical, utilitarian bent was influenced by the thought of Spencer. The highest ideal of the progressive movement was education for democracy, defined by John Dewey as people engaged in joint activity to solve their common problems. Thus, the goals of education as the early progressives saw them were both individual and social. In liberating the learner, a potential was released for the improvement of society and culture.

The philosophical basis of progressivism is pragmatism, a distinctively American philosophy that goes back to the 1870s and the writings of Charles Peirce, William James, and Chauncy Wright. As a philosophy, pragmatism has various dimensions. It accepts the *methods of science* for understanding human beings and solving human problems. Dewey described the inductive scientific method in his classic, *How We Think* (1910), and James (1902/1972) applied it to religious beliefs and values. Pragmatism accepts both the *relativism and pluralism* of worldviews. This attitude is most in keeping with the nature of human beings and the evolving world. The centrality of human *experience* is another dimension of pragmatic thought. Experience is placed in opposition to all authoritarian ways of arriving at knowledge. Pragmatism emphasizes the *consequences of actions* in the determination of truth or goodness. Thus, there are no absolutes in knowledge or in morality. A final characteristic of pragmatism is its emphasis on *social reform* as a legitimate concern of philosophers. In this aspect, some pragmatists were close to Karl Marx in seeing the task of philosophy as not only understanding, but also changing the world in which we live.

Charles Peirce's contribution to pragmatism was his view of how persons arrive at their ideas (Rorty, 1966). In and of themselves, ideas are little more than hypotheses until tried on the anvil of experience. Pierce attempted to balance the concept of truth as changing with the common sense awareness of stability, habit and law in human life.

William James (1909) followed Peirce in his view of the process of arriving at knowledge. For him, an idea was true in terms of its workability. Truth is neither absolute nor immutable but is made actual in real life events. James also made contributions to progressive thought in the area of psychology. He viewed the human mind as the product of the environment, an accumulation of sensory data that comes from the outside world. The task of the educator is to attend to the formation of habits in students, for once these are formed, the student has the opportunity for freedom, creativity, and progressive thought.

The chief exponent of pragmatism and progressive thought, especially as related to education, was John Dewey. This American philosopher was involved in all aspects of the progressive movement: politics, economics, social reform, and education. His writings are voluminous and have received constant evaluation and criticism. He is, without a doubt, the single most influential philosopher of education this country has produced, and his impact on all forms of education is immense. He has both defenders and detractors among philosophers and educators. But for all practical purposes, his writings represent the definitive work in the progressive philosophy of education. Three distinct phases of the progressive movement in education can be seen in the following description of his ideas.

In its earliest stages, progressive education was chiefly concerned with developing a learner-centered approach to education. Dewey's early works, *School and Society* (1900/1956), and *The Schools of Tomorrow* (1915) are classic statements of this view. Rousseau, Pestalozzi, and Froebel were most influential in these works. The primary task of education was to develop the potential of the learner.

This necessitated removing learners from the passivity and uniformity of traditional education. Manual training was introduced into the curriculum and an effort was made to begin the educational process by attending to the needs and interests of the learners. Using the lives of the learners as starting points, one could "facilitate and enrich the growth of the individual child" as well as continue to reap the benefits of traditional learning" (Dewey, 1900/1956, 70).

The germ of the second stage in the development of progressive education is also found in *School and Society* (1900/1956). Education, Dewey felt, had a role to play in social reform and reconstruction. *Democracy and Education* (1916), Dewey's most enduring and influential work, placed education at the very heart of social reform. The work explored the educational meanings of democracy, science, evolution, and industrialism. Dewey became critical of the ideas of Rousseau, Locke, Herbert, and Froebel. He also showed more awareness of contemporary developments in psychology and sociology. The social thrust of Dewey's thought at this time can be seen in his own summary of the leading ideas in his work. Three of the seven ideas involve social issues: the dependence of growth of the mind upon participation in shared activities; the influence of the physical environment on the development of culture; and the necessity of utilizing individual differences in desire and thinking to produce changes in society (1916, 377).

For Dewey, education would flourish if it took place in a democracy; democracy would develop only if there was true education. Democratic societies were intentionally progressive and aimed at a greater variety of mutually shared interests. Greater freedom was allowed its members and therefore there was a need to develop a social consciousness in individuals. Thus for Dewey a democratic society was committed to change. A democracy "is more than a form of government; it is primarily a mode of associated living, of conjoint communicated experience" (1916, 90). The goals of education in this work are expressed primarily in social terms. A democratic education will produce a society that is constantly in a state of greater growth and development.

While Dewey saw the task of the schools as important in social change, he did not go as far as radical social reconstructionists such as George Counts. As will be seen in the chapter on radical adult education, Counts called upon the schools in the 1930s to indoctrinate students with a socialist vision of society. Dewey, however, maintained that the task of the schools was to educate individuals in democratic values. Students would then work for a better society. Thus the school was only indirectly involved in social change. C. A.

p. 56

Bowers (1969) has detailed the history of the split in progressivism between liberals like Dewey and radicals like Counts.

The third phase of progressive education, experimentalism, is found in Dewey's short but influential work, *Experience and Education* (1938). By 1938 the weaknesses of learner-centered education had become apparent, and many of the goals of social reformists were being achieved through the politics and social programs of the New Deal. Dewey and other progressive educators took up the task of developing a statement of progressive education that attempted to avoid the extremes of the learner-centered and radical social action of earlier progressivism. In *Experience and Education* Dewey was critical of both the subject-centered or traditional education, and the learner-centered progressive education. He called for an education that entailed the critical and controlled type of learning exemplified in science. The methods of criticism, full public inspection, and testing became the moral principles to guide education. In this approach there is need for the guidance and direction of learning that makes the teacher more important than in the traditional education. Dewey's concept of experience is restricted to those experiences that are truly educative. Individuals achieve freedom as they master the tools of learning that are available.

Experimentation, or this third facet of progressive education, represents the mature thought of Dewey. This view took into account many of the criticisms that had been leveled against progressive education: lack of discipline, learner-centeredness, focus on trivial problems, little attention to subject matter, anti-intellectualism, and a lack of a clear definition of the teacher's role.

After the Second World War Dewey became for some the scapegoat for all that was perceived wrong in American education. In a letter to *Life* magazine (March 15, 1959), President Dwight D. Eisenhower joined the criticism:

> Educators, parents and students must be continuously stirred up by the defects in our educational system. They must be induced to abandon the educational path that, rather blindly they have been following as a result of John Dewey's teachings.

Dewey's ideas were revived, however, in the 1960s and 1970s. Significantly, this was another period of social and political change in American society. Many saw in the progressive era and its philosophy of education a suitable theory for understanding and directing education's role in social change (Holt, 1967; Herndon, 1971;

Silberman 1970). Even in these decades though, progressivism was not without its critics. Radicals charged progressives with introducing bureaucratization and fostering social control, racism, and other ills (Katz, 1968; Karrier et al., 1973). Conservatives, on the other hand, rejected progressive ideas and called for a return to traditional values and basic subjects (Conant, 1961; Kirk, 1965; Koerner, 1965). The identification of progressive thought with liberal political, social, and economic thought lies at the heart of the controversy over the impact of progressivism on American life in general, and on education in particular. Progressive education has been a target for neoconservative educators even up to the beginning of the new century (Ravitch, 2000).

Though Dewey has his critics among neoconservative educators like Ravitch and Hirsch, many liberal and radical educators still mine his writings in the areas of critical or reflective thinking, service education, scientific education, and democratic/civic education. Giroux (1988) in fact has criticized educators for ignoring Dewey's valuable ideas on democratic education. Although Giroux is indebted to Dewey for his ideas on democracy, he differs from Dewey in placing the democratic thrust not only in school, but also in the political and social struggles that occur outside school sites (Giroux, 1988).

John Dewey was also at the center of the debate in the 1990s over the nature of the good society and communitarian ethics. In his influential book, *The Good Society*, Bellah (1991) turns to Dewey's concept of the public good and Dewey's effort to enhance democracy throughout institutional life. While drawing on many observers and analysts, Bellah gives special attention to the progressive spirit found in the writings of Dewey and another progressive thinker, the journalist Walter Lippmann. Dewey's political and educational goal of liberating the potentialities of members of a group in harmony with the interests and good which are held in common, is accepted as an adequate description of balancing individual interests with the common good.

Progressive Education and the
Adult Education Movement

A comparison between Cremin's classic on progressive education, *The Transformation of the School* (1961), and Knowles's *The History of the Adult Education Movement in the United States* (1977), makes clear the intimate connection between progressive and adult education. Progressive education's emphasis upon vocational and utilitarian training, learning by experience, scientific inquiry, community involvement, and responsiveness to social problems found expression in the development of new forms of general and adult education. Both Cremin and Knowles present vocational education, university extension and cooperative extension, settlement houses for new immigrants, and Americanization education as forms of progressive education. Kett (1994) has more recently made the point that progressives did not restrict education to schooling but were concerned with educating the public which to them "meant teaching citizens to think more rationally and scientifically about their jobs, their health, the raising of their children, and community issues" (293).

Knowles's history of the adult education movement recounts the story of a movement that attempted to separate itself from the narrow focus of many schools, colleges and universities in order to develop programs to meet the needs of large numbers of people and society in general. In the period between 1866 and 1920, the "'useful,' 'functional,' 'pragmatic' became the predominant standards for knowledge and science . . ." (Knowles, 1977, 36). Agricultural education and industrial training, part of the progressive movement in both politics and education, were important developments at this time. Extension work at universities was also inspired by progressive ideals.

> A new spirit was infused into the idea of extension representing a shift away from an emphasis on academic subjects toward an all embracing concept of the role of the university in serving all of the people of the state in relation to the full scope of life problems—agricultural, political, social, and moral. (Knowles, 1977, 491)

Other common interests between the progressives and the adult educators at this time included the introduction of vocational education into the adult evening schools, the development of voluntary associations and agencies, the providing of services to the poor through settlement houses and other social agencies, and an interest in parent education programs. Knowles's (1977) characterization of this period clearly reveals the relationship of the adult education movement to progressivism:

> The general character of adult educational content shifted from general knowledge to several pin-pointed areas of emphasis—vocational education, citizenship and Americaniza-

tion, the education of women, civic and social reforms, public affairs, leisure time activity, and health. Adult education
was clearly in tune with the needs of this era of industrialization, immigration, emancipation, urbanization, and national maturation. (751)

A notable example of a progressive reformer in this period was
Jane Addams, the founder of Hull House, a settlement house in
Chicago. Addams shared John Dewey's belief that every effort had
to be made to make life educative. Her interest in educating the
public shifted from a stress on classical culture to the life of the
immigrants and their children. For her the socialization and Americanization of immigrants had to take precedence over other educational goals. To do this she made extensive use of folk dramas and
plays. She also paid particular attention to the health needs of immigrants (Kett, 1994).

The settlement house movement brings to the fore another
feature of progressive adult education, which was a stress on the
social group or community. A sense of community was needed to
deal with social unrest caused by class conflict and social problems.
Progressive adult educators joined with the new professionals in
social work to foster community, cooperation, socialization, and interdependence. The concept of community became a focal point in
adult education, leading to widespread experiments in community
schools where the education of the entire public would take place
(Kett, 1994).

When Knowles turned to the period between 1921 and 1961, the
same link between progressive ideals and adult education can be
seen. Business and industry, the broadening of the curriculum, the
growth of extension, experiments with newer methodologies, involvement with government and social agencies, and labor education are common concerns of progressives and adult educators.

During this same period, two influential books by adult educators appeared which explicitly related the two movements. James
H. Robinson in *The Humanizing of Knowledge* (1924) called for the
utilization of the new knowledge from the social sciences. Robinson
felt that this new knowledge would help free the minds of adults
from traditional ideas about religion, politics, nationalism, economics, and race. Robinson's early educational interest was in reforming the school curriculum. But in this work he recognized that "the
only effective type of instruction was that which addressed adults
rather than children and which therefore occurred outside of con-

ventional educational institutions" (Kett, 1994, 338-339).

Though Robinson's work advocated the introduction of social science knowledge into adult education, it was not until Eduard Lindeman's book, *The Meaning of Adult Education,* appeared in 1926 that the ideas of the progressives were fully applied to the field of adult education. Lindeman was directly influenced by the ideas of John Dewey and other progressives. He saw education as having as its primary aim the development of social intelligence, that is, the practical understanding of the world in which we live. Lindeman primarily identified with that aspect of progressive education that envisioned the reform of society as the principal aim of education. Like Dewey, he saw citizens involved in education as it related to their life situation:

> Every adult person finds himself in specific situations with respect to his work, his recreation, his family-life, his com- munity-life, et cetera—situations which call for adjust- ments. Adult education begins at this point. Subject matter is brought into education, is put to work, when needed. Texts and teachers play a new and secondary role in this type of education; they must give way to the primary importance of the learner. (Lindeman, 1926, 8-9)

Lindeman's influence and thus Dewey's is seen in the develop- ment of the American Association for Adult Education in 1926. Knowles reports that an early policy decision of this institution was to resist all pressures for a rigid definition of adult education and to allow a concept that included many areas of adult activity. Rejecting the narrow base of liberal adult education, early organizers recog- nized cultural, vocational, and recreational interests as legitimate facets of adult education (Knowles, 1977).

The founding of the Adult Education Association in 1951 was marked with similar debates over the nature of adult education. The impetus for the founding of the Association came from the Fund for Adult Education which, as was noted, favored the liberal arts approach. In order to receive the support of the Fund, the founding adult educators developed goals for the organization that reflected liberal adult education while at the same time responding to the more practical needs of the field (Knowles, 1977, 221-223). Over the years, the Association has broadened its base to include a wide vari- ety of educational activities in line with the broad goals of progres- sive adult education.

In its development adult education has been more faithful in many ways to the pragmatic principles that inspired its beginnings than have the public schools. Adult education, as it has been theorized about and actually practiced in this country, has been widely pragmatic, utilitarian, and, thus, progressive. This factor accounts for many of its strengths and some of its weaknesses. To better understand adult education's pragmatic orientation, the fundamental principles of progressive education and their manifestations in adult education theory and practice will be examined in the following section.

Basic Principles of Progressive Adult Education

Most of the basic principles of the progressive education movement were at least touched upon in the previous section covering the theory's historical development. Following is a more systematic treatment of this theory, drawing from Dewey and adult educators whose views are consistent with this school of thought. Some criticisms of these principles will also be offered.

1. *A Broadened View of Education.* One of the major contributions of progressive education was to expand the concept of education. The traditional or liberal philosophy of education confined the aims of education to intellectual development through a study of certain academic disciplines. Education was first of all broadened by the progressives to include what sociologists call socialization and anthropologists call inculturation. Education is thus not restricted to schooling, but includes all those incidental and intentional activities that society uses to pass on values, attitudes, knowledge, and skills. Education in this view becomes extensive. It includes the work of many institutions of society: family, workplace, school, churches and the entire community. In this scheme of things, the school is just one agency among many responsible for transmitting culture.

Second, in viewing education as socialization, the progressives took the logical step of placing some importance upon adult learning. Dewey (1916) argued for an education that was truly lifelong:

> Education must be reconceived, not as merely a preparation for maturity (whence our absurd idea that it should stop after adolescence) but as a continuous growth of the mind and a continuous illumination of life. In a sense, the school can give us only the instrumentalities of mental growth; the rest depends upon an absorption and interpretation of expe-

rience. Real education comes after we leave school and there is no reason why it should stop before death. (25)

The unfortunate thing about Dewey was that after laying the basis for lifelong learning, he devoted most of his efforts to one educational institution, the school. Thus, in the truest sense, Dewey's theory of education is a theory of schooling, though his views are were certainly applied to adult education by Lindeman and others.

A third way in which the progressives enlarged the concept of education was through advocating the introduction of the practical, pragmatic, and utilitarian into the curriculum. Their struggles in this area were long and uphill against entrenched interests in schools, colleges and universities. Dewey argued that education appropriate for American society must include both the liberal and the practical, both education for work and education for leisure, and both the humanities and the sciences (1916). He contended that Aristotle's distinction between the liberal arts and the servile arts of work was based not on philosophical grounds, but was a result of the cultural situation in Greece where slaves did the manual work. Dewey (1916) called for an education that was both liberal and practical. A broadened view of education in Dewey's view

> reconciles liberal nurture with training in social serviceableness, with ability to share effectively and happily in occupations which are productive. . . . The problem of education in a democratic society is to do away with the dualism and to construct a course of studies which makes thought a guide for free practice for all and which makes leisure a reward of accepting responsibility for service, rather than an exemption from it. (260-261)

A fourth way in which the progressives extended the concept of education was in their emphasis on the centrality of experience. Dewey defined education as the reconstruction and reorganization of experience that increases our ability to direct the course of subsequent experience. Experience for the progressives has both an active and a passive component. It is not just what has happened to a person but also what a person does. It is, more precisely, the interaction of the individual with the environment (Dewey, 1938).

The emphasis of the progressives upon experience has to be seen in relation to traditional education which centered upon books that reported the experiences of other people. The progressives felt that the learners' experiences were an equally valid center for education. Dewey was careful in his treatment of experience to point out that education and experience were not identical, for there were also experiences that were "mis-educative." Educative experiences had a special quality of agreeableness and exerted positive influences on later experiences. The role of the teacher was even more important than in traditional education, for educational experiences were likely to happen in situations where there were teacher-guided interactions between persons and the environment (Dewey, 1938).

In the chapter on analytic philosophy of adult education some British philosophers challenge the progressive expansion of adult education. In North America, however, the influence of the progressives in the theory and practice of adult education has served to widen the range of endeavors considered to be educational. One danger in this broadened view of education is that it tends to equate education with all life's experiences and thus empties the word of any normative meaning. Adult educators in this country have learned to live with the vagueness of the term adult education even though a philosophical analysis shows the theoretical weakness of our usage. The ideal of democracy thus seems to prevail over the ideal of philosophical clarity.

In summary, adult educators have adopted the enlarged view that the progressives took of education. Adult educators view education as a lifelong process and have long argued against a definition of education restricted to notions of schooling. In addition, research has shown that adults of all ages are capable of learning and do learn in a multitude of settings and programs. With regard to curriculum, adult education has always included pragmatic, utilitarian, and vocationally oriented dimensions. Finally, adult education values the experience-centeredness emphasized by progressives. Knowles (1970) has contended that the quality and volume of personal experiences of adults provide a rich learning resource that can contribute to a more mature approach to education.

2. *A New Focal Point in Education.* In broadening the view of education to include the personal experiences and interactions of students, the progressives gave education a new focus—learners with their personal needs, interests, experiences and desires. As we have seen above in the historical survey, this was the first stage of development in progressive education. Although it was somewhat modified under the attack of later criticisms, progressives have never

abandoned their original insight which they took from Rousseau, Pestalozzi, and Froebel. This view was "sloganized" into the expression "We teach children, not subjects." Though Dewey corrected this to include both children and subjects, but there was no doubt where the emphasis lay.

Besides placing the learner at the center of educational concern, the progressives also advocated a new concept of human beings. Contrary to some pessimistic religious views of human nature, progressive educators contended that persons were born neither as good as Rousseau argued, nor as evil as taught by certain forms of Christianity that appealed to an original sin. Rather, they contended that people were born with unlimited potential for development and growth. Growth for them was a series of approximations toward a final goal that is never to be reached. Humans have biological continuity with animals, but they can, within limits, adapt the environment to their own needs by the use of intelligence. Dewey and other progressives tended to be optimistic about the potential for human growth in the right environmental situations. Thus the human being could, through scientific method and experimental thinking, achieve a more satisfying life.

Dewey and other progressives criticized traditional education for being too concerned with the learning of certain academic disciplines and not attending sufficiently to the impulses, interests, and purposes of learners. The progressives were deeply committed to the insights of the newly developing psychology that explored stages in psychological development and differences among individual learners. With this information as a starting point, progressives in education attempted to make use of the interests, needs, and desires of learners in forging educational experiences. They insisted that these interests provided the energy for learning and instruction. Furthermore, the teacher's task was not just to capitalize on the interests that already existed in the learner, but also to arouse interests in those things that were educationally desirable.

Adult educators adopted this new focal point of education. As early as 1926, Lindeman spoke of the individual needs and goals that defined the adult educator's task:

> In what areas do most people appear to find life's meaning? We have only one pragmatic guide: meaning must reside in the things for which people strive, the goals which they set for themselves, their wants, needs, desires, and wishes. (13-14)

(STOP 05)

R | p.65

Emphasis in adult education upon conducting needs assessments for program development and instructional purposes gives expression to this basic progressive orientation. In addition, research efforts to determine the extent of independent learning among adults are based upon the progressive and humanist assumption that a person is "a self-directing organism with initiative, intentions, choices, freedom, energy and responsibility" (Tough, 1971, 5).

The progressives' centering upon individuals and their needs has been subject to criticism from various philosophical viewpoints. Many philosophers of education do not share the optimism of the progressives about human's natural desire to learn. Liberal educators still tend to see the primary focus in education on the academic disciplines to be taught. Behaviorists feel that since needs and interests are learned from the environment, they can be changed by manipulation of the environment. And analytical adult education philosophers like Lawson (1975), Paterson (1979), and Monette (1977, 1979), seriously question the assumption that learners can articulate and plan for their own educational needs. Radicals and critical educators would prefer that the focal point of education be upon the interests that benefit society.

3. *A New Educational Methodology.* In the popular mind, progressive education has been equated with the introduction of new instructional methodologies. The progressives attacked the rigid methods of assign, study, and recite of traditional or liberal education. They contended that only static or inert knowledge resulted from this approach. Dewey characterized traditional methods as shortsighted and faulted them for bringing about "a deliberate closing-in of surroundings upon growth" (1916, 49).

Progressives approached the question of method at both the theoretical and the practical level. At the theoretical level, they pointed to the inherent unity between method and subject matter. How we teach is intimately related to why we teach and what we teach. Although progressives saw value in learning the methods that have been used by others, they laid more stress on the individual teacher developing his or her own method of teaching suitable for the group being taught.

A method of teaching given prominence by progressive educators was the scientific method of arriving at knowledge. This can also be termed the problem-solving method, the project method, or the activity method. This method, as described by Dewey and others, entailed the clarification of a problem to be solved, the development of ideas or hypotheses about this problem, and the testing of these hypotheses by an examination of empirical evidence. Progressives felt that this method could be used in most subject areas and that it was based on the natural inclination of learners to grapple with problems. This experimental method was an attempt to discover truths about the world in which one lives.

Adult educators have, for the most part, accepted the methodology proposed by the progressives. Bergevin (1967), for example, called for adult education to be problem-centered or situation-centered. "Programs of learning for adults must," he emphasized, "be adjusted to the learners, to the problems they need solved, to the situations confronting them. Adult education must start there." The alternative—the subject-centered approach was, in Bergevin's words, "a wasteful procedure" (1967, p. 149). Broudy (1960) made a similar observation noting that since adult education was not a preparation for the future, a more creative problem-solving curriculum was needed.

Clearly, Lindeman (1956) incorporated progressive ideas about method into his concept of adult education:

> I am conceiving adult education in terms of a new technique for learning, a technique as essential to the college graduate as to the unlettered manual worker. It represents a process by which the adult learns to become aware of and to evaluate his experience. To do this he cannot begin by studying subjects in the hope that some day this information will be useful. On the contrary, he begins by giving attention to situations in which he finds himself, to problems which include obstacles to his self-fulfillment. Facts and information from the differentiated spheres of knowledge are used, not for the purpose of accumulation, but because of the need in solving problems. (160)

While Lindeman seems to equate the two terms, methods and techniques, Coolie Verner made an important distinction between the two. Method for him is "the relationship that exists between the learner, the knowledge, and the institution which has knowledge to diffuse" (Verner, 1959). Verner considers techniques to be the various devices that are used in learning: role playing, symposiums, forums, buzz groups, panels, etc. Other adult educators (Knowles 1970, Kidd 1973; Houle 1972; Bergevin and McKinley 1965) have given extensive attention to describing and promoting methods that are largely in keeping with the progressive approach to education. In an introductory essay tracing various systems of thought, Houle

(1972) notes Dewey's permanent influence on methodology and program planning in adult education. Some later systems, Houle points out, have not had the openness and fluidity of Dewey's thought (1972, 13).

Other adult philosophers of education who have taken a progressive or experimental view of methodology include Paul Sheats and Kenneth Benne. Sheats (1938) attempted to forge a middle path between those who want to impose a definite curriculum and those who want education to bring about radical social change. He advocated an experimental attitude toward the work of adult education. Benne (1957), in arguing the merits of various philosophical approaches to adult education, concludes, "a broadened method still must be an experimental method, rather than a method of authority, of intuition, of deduction, or of induction. Rationality, for our time at least, must be defined in experimental terms" (79). In this experimental view, learning is a "series of experiments with respect to problems encountered and constructed" (77). The preferred methodology in adult education, according to Benne, is problem solving, for "programs of learning for adults must be adjusted to the learners, to the problems they need solved, to the situations confronting them" (1957, 149).

The chief criticism leveled against progressive methodology is that it tends to minimize the importance of subject matter or content in education. Obviously progressives have countered that they are interested in both content and methods but they feel that a rigid approach to teaching academic disciplines leads to a stultifying education. Whether or not progressives actually were able to change educational methods is a matter debated to this day by historians (Cuban, 1984; Tyack and Cuban, 1995).

Though progressive education has left its mark through the introduction of a new methodology, in the last analysis it is not in this area that its greatest impact on adult education lies. Its greatest influence is found in the new relationship between teachers and learners.

4. *A Changed Relationship Between Teachers and Learners.* The broadened view of education, the new focal point, and the new methodology that the progressives proposed led logically to a new role for the teacher in the educational process. Progressive educators opposed viewing the teacher as the sole source of knowledge whose task was to put, or as Freire would have it, "bank" knowledge into the minds of students. In an educational theory that values the learning of subject matter or academic disciplines as the heart of the educational effort, the transmission conception of education is use-

ful/ But if education is seen, as the progressives viewed it, as the reconstruction of experiences through interactive processes with one's environment—then the traditional view of the teacher-learner relationship is inadequate.

Learning, according to Dewey, is primarily something that students do for themselves. The teacher's responsibility is to organize, stimulate, instigate, and evaluate the highly complex process of education. The teacher provides a setting that is conducive to learning. In so doing, the teacher also becomes a learner, for the relationship between teacher and learners is reciprocal. Both should plan and learn from each other.

Dewey's earliest writings tended to downplay the role of the teacher. At that time he was perhaps overreacting against the traditional authoritarian stance of the teacher. In *Democracy and Education,* he stated that:

> When the parent or teacher has provided the conditions which stimulate thinking, and has taken a sympathetic attitude toward the activities of the learner by entering into a common or conjoint experience, all has been done which a second party can do to instigate learning. The rest lies with the one directly concerned. (1916, 160)

Dewey, however, rejected the view that the teacher merely stands off and looks on. He wanted teachers to participate and share in all the learning activities:

> In such shared activity, the teacher is a learner, and the learner is, without knowing it, a teacher, and upon the whole the less consciousness there is, on either side of either giving or receiving instruction, the better. (1916, 160)

By the time that Dewey wrote his most mature statement on educational theory in *Experience and Education* (1938), this view was modified and developed further. By then progressive education had come under severe criticism both for the learner-centeredness of its approach and its apparent denial of any real role and authority for the teacher. In this work Dewey gave a more sophisticated appraisal of the teacher's role and tried to avoid the extremes of permissiveness and manipulation. Dewey, however, still saw learning as based in the personal experiences of the student. The important tasks of the educator were to guide, direct, and evaluate experiences in terms of their educational component. Teachers were also to share with learners insights that came from their own experiences. Dewey admitted that to do this without imposing one's own views upon learners made the teacher's role more difficult than in traditional education.

Another task that Dewey allotted the teacher in *Experience and Education* was that of exercising social control or discipline without violating the freedom of the learners. When teachers exercise control, it is not a matter of personal power, but of acting in behalf of the group (54). Dewey observed that the primary source of discipline should be found in the work itself. This work must be thought out and planned:

> The educator is responsible for a knowledge of individuals and for a knowledge of subject-matter that will enable activities to be selected which lend themselves to social organization, an organization in which all individuals have an opportunity to contribute something, and in which the activities in which all participate are the chief carriers of control. (1938, 56]

Thus it is clear that for Dewey the term social control meant both classroom discipline and the discipline of learning. Since progressive education was considered weak in discipline, Dewey felt it necessary to defend the purposes and methods of discipline in progressive schools.

Though Dewey stresses at length the role of the teacher in exercising social control, perhaps his most adequate description of a teacher was that of leader of group activities:

> The educator must survey the capacities and needs of the particular set of individuals with whom he is dealing and must at the same time arrange the conditions which provide the subject matter or content for experiences that satisfy these needs and develop these capacities. The planning must be flexible enough to permit free play for individuality of experience and yet firm enough to give direction towards continuous development of power. (1938, 580)

Though progressives recognized the difficulty of this proposed balancing act, such a view was necessary both to safeguard freedom and to ensure that genuine educational experiences resulted.

Dewey wanted learners to have freedom. But he also criticized the attitudes of some progressive teachers who would put materials before learners and then not even suggest what should be done with them (1938, 71). Dewey argued that suggestions from teachers with varied experiences and wider horizons were more valuable than suggestions from incidental sources. But still, Dewey wanted only suggestions for students in planning and carrying out their learning experiences.

Dewey recognized the weakness of the progressive theory when it came to the learning of subject matter. He contended that improvisation in education could not take the place of selection and organization of subject matter. He called for the organization of curriculum around problems that would relate to experiences of the learners. In discussing this issue, Dewey used the learning of science as an example. It would have been more telling if Dewey had chosen other fields like history, languages, humanities, mathematics, and skills learning. Progressive educators tended to see scientific learning as the ideal form of learning. It is because of this approach that critics tend to see the progressive theory as best adapted to science learning and less suitable for other forms of learning.

It should be clear to anyone familiar with the work of adult educators in the past half century that the progressive view of the teacher has greatly influenced the descriptions of the role of the adult educator. Lindeman incorporated the progressive view of the teacher into his theory of education. He stated that in adult education

> The teacher finds a new function. He is no longer the oracle who speaks from the platform of authority, but rather the guide, the pointer-out, who also participates in learning in proportion to the vitality and relevancy of his facts and experiences. (1956, 160)

Lindeman goes on to give a definition of adult education that is truly Deweyan and progressive, and that underlies the theoretical and practical thinking of many adult educators today. The following is his conception of adult education:

> A cooperative venture is nonauthoritarian, informal learning, the chief purpose of which is to discover the meaning of experience; a quest of the mind which digs down to the roots of the preoccupations which formulate our conduct; a tech-

nique of learning for adults which makes education coterminous with life and hence elevates living itself to the level of adventurous experiment. (1956, 160)

Knowles is also indebted to this progressive concept of the role of the teacher. He characterizes the role of the adult educator as that of a "helper, guide, encourager, consultant, and resource, not that of transmitter, disciplinarian, judge and authority" (1970, 34). Knowles's description of the adult educator as andragogue rather than pedagogue is in reality a contrast between the view of the teacher of traditional education and that proposed by the progressives (Elias, 1979).

Benne (1957) has presented a view of the teacher-learner relationship that is clearly in the progressive spirit. He prefers to view the teacher as a helper in the learning process. The teacher as helper must not only possess knowledge, but must also evaluate the knowledge that the learner acquires. The teacher-helper is a resource person who knows more about what is being studied. It is also the task of this helper to aid the learner in removing some of the emotional blocks to learning. Finally, the role of the teacher-learner is to establish the appropriate methodology for learning, which for Benne is the experimental method (1957). Benne is truly a progressive educator when he discusses the source of the teacher's authority. Rejecting views that place educational authority in a mandate from God, the content of the Great Tradition or Great Books, the dominant ideology of a society, or the realities of the situation, Benne locates the educator's authority in "the widening of a community of shared and evaluated experiences" (Benne, 1957).

Another educator who has also been greatly influenced by the progressive description of the relationship between teachers and learners is Paul Bergevin. Although Bergevin in his influential *A Philosophy for Adult Education* (1967) gives no reference to John Dewey and the progressives, his indebtedness to this tradition is clear in many areas, but especially in the role that the teacher plays in the educational process. Bergevin argues for full participation of the learner in the teaching-learning process. He does not elaborate on the role of the teacher or the learning process except to say that both must carry out the program.

Critics of progressive education have leveled many charges against the progressives' role for teachers. They contend that the teacher's role is to teach and the learners is to learn. To expect significant learning to take place without direct instruction from teachers is, in the critics view, an unrealistic expectation. They also contend that a stronger role for the teacher leads to a more efficient educational process. Although there are areas where learners' experiences are helpful, there are even more areas in which learners' experiences are not relevant or significant. While the progressives did modify their views in the face of exaggerated claims for student-directed learning, they maintained that the traditional view of the teaching-learning process too often led to unengaged and consequently irrelevant learning.

5. *Education As an Instrument of Social Change.* From the historical perspective presented in this chapter, it might be recalled that progressive educators placed a strong emphasis upon education's role in promoting social change. Progressives believed that the function of education was not merely to prepare learners for fitting into the existing society, but also to educate persons who would be interested in changing society. For the progressives education was to be directed at fostering creativity and stability, as well as individuality and social consciousness.

As in other areas, the ideas of the progressives were brought into adult education through the powerful influence of Lindeman. The relationship between education and social change and action was a special concern of Lindeman, a professor of social philosophy at the New York School of Social Work. Lindeman believed that in a democratic society education and participation were necessary for bringing about change. In his view:

> Adult Education turns out to be the most reliable instrument for social actionists. If they learn how to educate the adherents of their movement, they can continue to utilize the compelling power of a group and still remain within the scope of democratic behavior. When they substitute some thing other than intelligence and reason, social action emanates as sheer power and soon degenerates into habits which tend toward an anti-democratic direction. Every social-action group should at the same time be an adult education group, and I go even so far as to believe that all successful adult education groups sooner or later become social-action groups. (Lindeman in Kidd, 1973, 154)

Lindeman was also deeply involved in The Inquiry, an organization founded by members of the National Conference on the Christian Way, which created programs for social change and for dealing with social conflicts. Lindeman considered this project essential to the mission of adult education (Stubblefield and Keane, 1994).

Although Lindeman was adult education's most eloquent spokesman for the progressive point of view, two other adult educators writing from a progressive orientation addressed the issue of social order and social change. Bergevin (1967) saw adult education as essential in contributing to what he called "the civilizing process." The civilizing process had an individual and societal dimension, each having responsibility for the other. At the individual level, the civilizing process referred to a person's "maturing" from a "mere survival" level to a "responsible member of social order" (7). From the societal perspective, the civilizing process was a "corporate, social movement involving the whole of society, as it moves from barbarism toward refinement in behavior, tastes, and thought" (8). Adult education, then, consists of a

> consciously elaborated program aiding and reinforcing the civilizing process. The over-all aim of the professional or lay adult educator, then, will be to bring each of us into some kind of constructive relationship with the civilizing process, always remembering that this process should represent those positive elements in environment and society that help us develop mature rationality in our lives and institutions. (1967, 9-10)

For Bergevin, the continuing education of adults was essential in preserving and enhancing a democratic way of life. It was a necessity, a "built-in requirement of a society emerging from control by the few to control by the many" (p. 35). Speaking of the progressive's view of human nature as being neither inherently good nor inherently evil, Bergevin presented adult education as a most serious and urgent matter-"a determining factor in the race between building and destroying, between the civilizing process and barbarism. We adults are capable of either and both" (14).

Robert Blakely (1958, 1965) also explored the role of education in social change. Learning, especially adult learning was, in his words, "fundamental to the solution of all social problems" (1965, 54). Like Bergevin, Blakely ascribed both an individual and a social purpose to adult education. Education would lead to a better, more fulfilling personal life, while at the same time making a better citizenry and a better world (1958). While Bergevin spoke of the "civilizing process," Blakely wanted to see education working toward a "homeodynamic" society, that is, a society in which a balance could be achieved between cultural components that imitated the past, and components that were inventive of the future. Survival of individuals and society depended upon achieving this balance (1965). Other than to mention the value of group process, Blakely offers little in the way of specific suggestions for achieving a homeodynamic society.

The social action thrust in adult progressive education inspired the founding of Myles Horton's Highlander Folk School in Tennessee. Although considered by some to be an example of radical adult education, as Adams (1972) describes the Highlander idea, Horton drew his inspiration from both Dewey and Lindeman in generating the adult residential center for the development of community leaders among school, church, civic, labor, and farm groups (520). Participants in the Highlander School have been involved in worker education, civil rights struggles, and other liberal social causes. Adams judges the Highlander School as committed to democracy, mutuality, and united social action. The school's governing concepts are deliberately vague, "letting the people it serves and the times they live in define precisely what they mean" (520). This is a good description of the progressive ideal in social action: education for social change, but always respecting the freedom of individuals to be true to their own convictions and commitments.

In summary, until recently only a few adult educators have taken up the social thrust of the progressive education movement. The learner-centeredness and methodology of the progressives have had a much greater impact upon the field of adult education. It was left to the radicals, treated in the chapter on Radical and Critical Adult Education, to highlight the social change dimension of adult education. The work of Paulo Freire in particular has raised the consciousness of many North American and European adult educators about the potential of adult education for social and political change. The chapter on radical and critical adult education will treat those adult educators who in the past twenty years have continued the social thrust of progressive education in the Lindeman tradition. Thomas Heaney (1996) has been particularly influential in keeping this tradition alive in the field of adult education.

Programs Inspired by Progressive Adult Education

In previous sections of this chapter the influence of progressive ideas on contemporary adult educators has been indicated. There is scarcely an adult educator whose ideas cannot be traced at least in some indirect form to the seminal ideas of Dewey and Lindeman. It could be argued that humanistic, radical, and behavioristic adult educations are all in some ways dependent upon progressive education for some of their chief ideas. Humanism took hold of the learner-centeredness of this approach, radicalism carried to further lengths the social change impulse of progressivism, and behaviorism placed an emphasis on the experimental and scientific dimensions of progressive thought.

Besides inspiring contemporary forms of adult education theory and practice, progressivism's influence can be seen in a number of programs currently in operation in adult education. Three of these programs—Americanization education, the National Issues Forum program, and the Community Education Movement will be discussed in the following section.

Americanization Education. Americanization education or Schools for the Foreign Born arose at a time when progressive ideas permeated educational circles. The great influx of immigrants in the early decades of the twentieth century led to social concern for their welfare as well as fear that their numbers would produce an unstable political condition. Adult education's role in the "civilizing process" was enthusiastically put into practice by the adult evening schools primarily, but also by churches, factories, settlement houses, the YMCA, and other organizations. Seller (1978) reviewed the curriculum of these programs:

> Their major emphasis between 1914 and 1924 (even more than in the earlier years) was English lessons for all. For men, they stressed citizenship training (with emphasis upon the virtues of democracy and capitalism) and instruction in the factories in work habits and safety. For women, they stressed lessons in hygiene, childcare, and American-style cooking and homemaking. (85)

Such campaigns were failures in the sense that only a small percentage of the target population was involved. Immigrants desired literacy in their own native language as well as opportunities to develop cultural and intellectual interests. As a result, organizations within ethnic communities more effectively met the educational needs of immigrants (Seller, 1978). Adult ethnic schools located within immigrant communities today offer a wide variety of classes and activities for their members including English classes.

Lee (2001/2002) notes that with their bilingual staff and sensitivity to cultural norms, these adult ethnic schools "create a unique learning space for immigrant learners whose cultural values, experiences, and methods of understanding are viewed as the norm" (p. 7).

Today, Americanization education or civics education programs exist in communities throughout the United States. The emphasis in these programs is upon preparation for citizenship. The U.S. government defines civics education as follows:

> An educational program that emphasizes contextualized instruction on the rights and responsibilities of citizenship, naturalization procedures, civic participation, and U.S. history and government to help learners acquire the skills and knowledge to become active and informed parents, workers, and community members. (Tolbert, 2001, p. 9)

Americanization education includes learning the basic skills to pass the INS exam as well as learning "how to be active community members and why they should be active by providing them with a comprehensive understanding of the U.S.'s culture, government, and educational system" (Tolbert, 2001, p. 10). English as a Second Language (ESL) and civics instruction are often linked together in these programs. According to Tolbert (2001), the U.S. government budgeted $70 million dollars for ESL and civics education in the year 2002.

National Issues Forums. The National Issues Forum is a program supported by the Kettering Foundation. The Kettering Foundation itself is devoted to the single question of "What does it take to make democracy work as it should?" Much of the foundation's work in the 1990s was based on commissioned studies, the most notable being Citizens and Politics: A View from Main Street America. "The study concluded that while Americans feel alienated from the political process, they are not apathetic; they will participate when they feel that they can make a difference. Helping citizens make a difference, here and elsewhere, is central to all of the foundation's efforts."(www.Kettering.org).

The National Issues Forum (NIF) is a network of community and educational organizations that makes space for citizens to come together to discuss, deliberate, and analyze contemporary issues facing communities. Individuals, libraries, churches, senior centers, colleges, schools, and extension services can organize NIFs. The Kettering Foundation puts together materials on different issues such as the health care crisis, immigration, terrorism, news media and so on, for use in these forums. Typically, the material presents an overview of the issue with several possible solutions, each of which reflects different values. Led by trained discussion leaders, participants weigh the costs and consequences of different solutions, eventually identifying common ground that can form the basis for action steps. "Reports on the outcomes of the forums are shared with local, state, and national officeholders to give them insight into what the public is thinking" (www.nifi.org). Forums can range in size from small study groups to large town meetings.

As an example of how the NIF works, in 2002 nearly 2000 people in forty states participated in forums on terrorism. The materials presented three approaches—The Swords of All-out War, The Shield of Homeland Security, and The Battle for Hearts and Minds. An overview of each approach was presented, followed by possible action steps, their tradeoffs, and opposing voices (www.nifi.org/terrorism.html). An analysis of what happened in forums is available in the report, "Terrorism: What Should We do Now?—Results from Citizen Forums" (www.nifi.org/terrorism_02.pdf).

Community Education. The origin of the Community Education movement can be found in the ideals of early progressive educators. Dewey, in his attempt to shift education's focus from subject matter to learner needs and experiences wrote:

> From the standpoint of the child, the great waste in school comes from his inability to utilize the experiences he gets outside the school within the school itself; he is unable to apply in daily life what he is learning at school. That is the isolation of the school—its isolation from life. (Dewey, 1900/1956, 75)

Community Education as it has developed since the early decades of the twentieth century can be characterized by its two major thrusts more easily than by a single definition. The two thrusts are (1) the enhancement of school programs by involving the community in the schools; and (2) the enhancement of the community through providing educational experiences for all people of all ages in the community.

Numerous programs in diverse settings developed in the first years of the movement. Welser (1978) points out that the movement had rural beginnings in Kentucky and Tennessee, and urban forms which sought to deal with community problems of crime, unemployment, delinquency, etc. It also thrived in times of social calm and times of great social upheaval, such as during the Great Depression (Welser, 1978). Welser's conceptualization of community education could have been written by Dewey:

> Education is a natural community process, of which the traditional school system is but a single component. In every community, all of the people are being educated all the time by everything that is happening in that community. It is both the amount and the overall quality of education that distinguishes one community from another. (1978, 544)

Today the National Community Education Association serves 1,350 members and 37 state community education associations, and continues to train approximately 800 national and international educators annually.

A discussion of community education, no matter how brief, cannot overlook the importance of the Mott Foundation's contribution to the Community Education Movement (Hiemstra, 2000). In 1936, Charles Mott supported the opening of five school buildings as community centers in Flint, Michigan. Still thriving, the Flint Community Education Program has served as a model for countless other programs. In addition, the Mott Foundation currently supports a number of programs designed to address community-level issues. Among these programs are 21st Century Community Learning Centers (CCLC) which focus on underserved children and their families. In 2001, these centers operated in 6,600 schools and served 1.2 million children and youth, and 400,000 adults (www.mott.org/21/history.asp). Other Mott-funded programs include, Adolescent Pregnancy Prevention Centers, Pathways Out of Poverty programs that wed community organizing, education and economic opportunity, an Environmental Program that strengthens partnerships between individuals and communities to protect and conserve the environment, and Civil Society programs to support institution building, equitable access to resources and strengthening of the nonprofit sector both in the United States and internationally (www.mott.org).

Although community education has developed as a movement somewhat separate from adult education, the connections between the two are clear. Both are interested in lifelong learning and in the continuing education of adults. In an analysis of the concept of the learning society, Holford and Jarvis (2000) point out that various models of the learning society all incorporate some notion of community/society and its relationship to adult learning. For example, the learning society as a consumer society is highly responsive to learners' needs; the learning society as reflexive, enabling people "to live in a rapidly changing society" (p. 646) depends on the creation, rather than acquisition of knowledge through problem-centered and experiential approaches.

Assessment of Progressive Adult Education

When one looks for recent developments in the philosophy of progressive adult education, one encounters an initial sense of disappointment. While progressive is not often used as a category to define a particular philosophical stance in adult education, except among British authors, the ideas of the progressives are still alive in general education, as well as in adult education. Also, there has developed in the past decade a more sophisticated interpretation of progressive education which needs to inform historical thinking about progressive philosophy in adult education.

The history and meaning of progressive education have generated a great deal of discussion. The standard history of progressivism, Cremin's *The Transformation of the School* (1961), no longer stands uncontested as a definitive study. Cremin's thesis that progressive education was an enlightened and praiseworthy effort to respond to the problems of American society and education has been criticized by scholars who object to both the motives of the reformers and the effects of their reforms (Lazerson, 1971). Radical revisionists have condemned the movement as one enormous effort aimed at the social control of immigrants and the children of immigrants. (Bowles and Gintis, 1976; Hogan, 1985). Furthermore, writing in an anti-progressive tenor, Ravitch (1982; 2000) has challenged the educational and intellectual implications of progressive education.

For a balanced treatment of the philosophy and aims of progressives as well as today's educational issues, Fass's (1989) work is relevant. In her view, progressive reformers thought education and schooling

> were to be at once instruments of remedial socialization and primary agents of culture; they were to connect the democratic potential of an enormously diverse population to the unities of an ancient citizenship; they were to educate for future success but be attentive to present needs. (34)

It took great faith in the power of education, which the progressives certainly possessed, to assign it this paradoxical philosophy.

There is no doubt that the main ideas of Dewey and the progressives (student-centeredness, social reform, scientific method) are still influential today among philosophers of education. Dewey's continued relevance to the issues of developing a public philosophy of education and democracy has been admirably argued by Westbrook (1991). But what has not yet been developed within education is the type of neo-pragmatic philosophizing that is engaged in by Richard Rorty (1992) who sees in the basically optimistic American pragmatic tradition a counteractive force to the excessive pessimism of much of Continental philosophy.

As in general education, there has been some discussion about the meaning of a progressive orientation in adult education. This discussion has been in reference to Knowles's (1980) concept of andragogy. Although primarily humanistic in its grounding, andragogy also rests upon Knowles's firm belief in "the ideals of a democratic citizenship and the belief that civic and democratic virtue would arise out of natural self-fulfillment through adult education" (Pratt, 1988, 20). Discussions and critique of the progressive underpinnings of andragogy have been advanced most recently by Pratt (1988), but also by Carlson (1989) and Podeschi (1987).

In one sense it is possible to speak of progressive education as a theory of the past. The Progressive Education Association died in the 1950s. No contemporary philosophers of education would align themselves totally with this movement. No major adult educator is clearly a progressive in the sense that Dewey and Lindeman were progressives. The strength of the movement may have been in its particular response to social conditions that were present in this country between 1890 and 1950.

But to consider progressive education a theory of the past is to miss the powerful influence that this theory has exercised to this day, both in general and adult education. Silberman (1970) showed that reforms in American education in the sixties were partly inspired by the philosophy of John Dewey. Many reforms of this period—open classrooms, renewed interest in moral education, student-centered learning, intelligent use of the environment, schools without walls, the introduction of creative methods, the emphasis on the role of education in social change, the reintroduction of the problem or situation curriculum—these are all elements of progressive education that were rediscovered by such reformers as John Holt, George Dennison, Jonathan Kozol, Joseph Featherstone, and

Paulo Freire. In fact, a strong case can be made that the reform movements of this time were led by neo-progressives, some of whom read their Dewey, and others of whom arrived independently at similar conclusions and suggestions for educational reform.

As has been pointed out in this chapter, the distinctive features of progressive education have been incorporated in one fashion or another into the theory and practice of adult education. Learner centeredness, the experimental method, and social activism are part of the legacy that the progressives have left to American education. In varying degrees, these elements are found in the philosophies of adult educators. All adult educators accept the basic progressive premise that education is a process of reflective inquiry.

In the passage of time, however, some of the weaknesses of progressive education have come to light, especially those pointed out by liberal educators. This philosophy at times emphasizes science at the expense of the humanities, history, literature, and the arts. Progressives have often replaced the fixity of ideas with the fixity of the problem. Too great an influence has been ascribed by this theory to the power of education to bring about social change. The view of education and human life appears too optimistic in its failure to take account of the tragic in life. In placing the learner at the center of the process of education, at times insufficient attention is given to the role of the teacher and to the importance of subject matter.

It is not only the liberal educators who have criticized progressive education. In the next four chapters we shall see four contemporary philosophies of education that have been inspired in some form by progressive principles, but are also critical of this philosophy at certain points. This pluralism of philosophic viewpoints is to be expected in such an endeavor as education which is closely related to both individual and social goals.

// p.82 is blank

(STOP 06)

CHAPTER IV

BEHAVIORIST ADULT EDUCATION

Probably no other system of psychology has had as much impact on general and adult education, or had its principles be the cause of as much debate, as behaviorism. Founded by John B. Watson in the 1920s, behaviorism focuses upon the overt, observable behavior of an organism. Animal and human behavior is studied in laboratory settings employing scientific principles and methodology used so successfully in the "hard" sciences such as chemistry and physics. The intellect, feelings, emotions, and a person's "inner" life are not observable or measurable and therefore not investigated in and of themselves. Behaviorists from Watson through Skinner believe all human behavior is the result of a person's prior conditioning and is determined by external forces in the environment over which a person has little or no control.

Although behaviorism is ordinarily considered a psychological system, the fundamental questions raised by this approach are clearly philosophical in nature. Are people more than complex machines? What differentiates humans from animals? To what extent are men and women free agents? What is the relationship between education and the shaping of culture? Is education no more than training, than arranging certain stimuli to elicit predetermined responses? As will be seen in the next chapter, humanism and humanistic psychology grapple with these questions and provide an alternative to a behaviorist view of the world.

This chapter will begin with a brief discussion of the historical antecedents of philosophical and psychological behaviorism and its major contributors in the twentieth century. A second section will examine the application of behaviorism to education—the roles of the teacher and learner, accountability, behavioral objectives, pro-

grammed instruction, etc. Behaviorism's impact on adult and continuing education will also be examined through analyzing its manifestation in continuing professional education, business and industry, and adult literacy programs.

Not all books in philosophy of education view behaviorism as a
distinct philosophy of education. Yet a case can be made that education in the United States and elsewhere draws extensively both on
the psychological research and philosophical assumptions of behaviorism. Behaviorism rests on certain philosophical assumptions about
human beings, the society for which they are educated, as well as
the aims, content, and methods of education. This is true not only
for the education of children but also for that of adults. The philosophical aspects of behaviorism are seen especially in the later writings
of B. F. Skinner. It is our belief that many adult educators and many
adult education practices are rooted the philosophy of behaviorism.

Philosophical Antecedents of
Twentieth Century Behaviorism

Though modem psychological behaviorism has arrived at its conclusions through scientific research, it is clear that behaviorism as a
system of thought has its roots in a number of philosophical traditions in European philosophical ideas. The first of these traditions is
materialism, the theory that the laws of matter and motion can
explain reality without any appeal to mind or spiritual reality. In the
materialist viewpoint humans are part of nature, though they are
complex parts. Materialism entails some form of determinism of
human actions. This materialist point of view is found in the writings of Thomas Hobbes who was both a materialist and a determinist. This British philosopher contended that the psychological make-
up of persons could be explained in mechanistic terms. For materi-
alists there is no internal reality; what is real is external, factual,
and observable.

A second philosophic tradition to which modern behaviorism is
allied is *scientific realism and empiricism*. Francis Bacon introduced
into Western thought the inductive method by which one arrived at
truth through an examination of information gained from the
senses alone. John Locke who denied the innateness of ideas and
explained human knowing through empirical processes of association followed Bacon in this viewpoint. Bertrand Russell contributed
to this tradition by his preference for the "hard" data of science over
the "soft" data of the humanities.

Positivism is the third philosophic tradition to which modern behaviorism is allied. Philosophical positivism was proposed by Auguste Comte who contended that one arrived at knowledge not through theology or traditional philosophy, but through scientific observation and the measurement of facts. Logical positivism, prevalent in Germany and England, placed greater emphasis on developing a language that corresponded to reality and that did not go beyond reality that could be experienced. Finally, the British philosopher Gilbert Ryle (1943) developed a philosophical behaviorism through an analysis of language. In his thought, the causes of behavior can be explained by the behavior itself and not by any concept of self, mind, consciousness, or "ghost in the machine."

A distinctive psychological orientation toward the study of human behavior is rooted in the thought of the seventeenth century French philosopher René Descartes. He viewed behavior systematically when he suggested that all instances of behavior could be classified as voluntary or involuntary. The involuntary or automatic behavior identified by Descartes led to the development of the "reflex" concept in the eighteenth and nineteenth centuries.

Charles Darwin's work provided another impetus for the emergence of behaviorism. The instinctual behavior in animals delineated by Darwin was viewed as involuntary, reflexive, and dependent upon internal stimuli. His *Origin of Species* (1859) also proposed the notion of biological continuity, which implied that humans were more intelligent, perhaps, but not separate from other species. The idea that humans are in continuity with the animal world led to an examination of the similarities between humans and animals, and the beginnings of animal psychology. Humans were thus at the mercy of their environment and if humans thought they could plan their behavior and affect their environment, then so could animals. Such ideas gave rise to research into animal intelligence in the late nineteenth and early twentieth centuries.

Early Behavioral Psychologists

The reflexology implied in the writings of Descartes culminated in the work of Sir Charles Sherrington and Ivan Pavlov. Sherrington demonstrated the usefulness of the experimental scientific method in revealing lawful properties of behavior, specifically reflex action in animals. Pavlov, through his famous experiments with salivating dogs, explored mechanisms for the acquisition and extinction of conditioned reflexes. The concept of classical conditioning emerged from his work. Classical conditioning emphasizes the importance of controlling behavior by controlling the stimulus. It differs from B. F. Skinner's operant conditioning, to be explained later in this chapter, which involves control of both the stimulus before the behavior and the environmental contingencies after the behavior is exhibited. Pavlov rejected the Freudian theory of human nature that posited internal forces or drives as determinants of human behavior. Pavlov posited an explanation of human behavior based on controllable external conditions, which require no inner source of action.

With the publication of two important texts, *Behavior—An Introduction to Comparative Psychology* (1914/1930) and *Psychology from the Standpoint of a Behaviorist* (1919), John B. Watson became the acknowledged leader of behaviorism. Watson adamantly endorsed the idea that psychology was a science of behavior, not a study of the mind or mental activity. The way to understand humans, he insisted, was through observing their behavior, not exploring the inner, unobservable recesses of mind and emotion. Emotion he defined as a hereditary pattern of response and rejected entirely the concept of instinct. For Watson, "the genesis of behavior, from the squirming and squalling of the new-born child to the complex skills and language responses of the adult, he ascribed to Pavlov's principle of conditioning" (Keller, 1977).

Using Pavlov's techniques, Watson, in a famous experiment with an eleven-month-old child, successfully conditioned the boy to fear a white rat. Watson argued that emotional responses together with motor reflexes could be conditioned to evoke reflexes. All behavior, from the fear response of the rat to the most complex activity of the adult, could be explained in terms of conditioning. As an extreme environmentalist, Watson maintained that he could take any healthy infant and through environmental conditioning produce anything from a doctor to a beggar.

Through books, articles, and lectures, Watson brought the science of behaviorism to the attention of the American public and other psychologists. Childrearing practices of rigid feeding schedules and strict discipline reflected his influence. Classical conditioning, although considered today to be inadequate to explain all behavior, is still a useful strategy for reversing inappropriate fear responses such as fear of crowds, snakes, or darkness (Herman, 1977).

Watson's work established the legitimacy and value of experimental or behaviorist psychology. In a famous article in the *Psychological Review* in 1913, "Psychology as the Behaviorist Views It," he

p. 87

called for a revolution in psychology and according to many gave birth to psychological behaviorism:

> Psychology as the behaviorist views it is a purely objective experimental branch of natural science. Its theoretical goal is the reduction and control of behavior. Introspection forms no essential part of its methods, nor is the scientific value of its data dependent upon the readiness with which they lend themselves to interpretation in terms of consciousness. The behaviorist, in his efforts to get a unitary scheme of animal response, recognized no dividing line between man and brute. (Watson, 1913/1948)

Between the 1920s and 1950s other behaviorists expanded upon the work of Watson and Pavlov and attempted to explain, control, and predict more complex behaviors. E. R. Guthrie proposed that contiguity was important; that is, the only significant aspects of a response were in what it made the organism do next. Tolman investigated latent learning and the intervening variables between a stimulus and a response. Hull, and his colleague Spence, considered drive, habit, strength, and motivation as salient aspects of response behavior. Important as the work of these researchers was, behaviorism received its greatest boost from the successor to Watson, B. F. Skinner.

Another early behaviorist, E. L. Thorndike, a psychologist and contemporary of Watson, investigated both animal and human intelligence. Using animals in controlled laboratory experiments, Thorndike explained learning as a process of association. An organism, when presented with a stimulus, formed a connection or bond with a response. Hence, his work became known as "connectionism" or the "S-R" theory of learning. Thorndike's laws of learning were major contributions to the psychology of learning and have long been viewed as applicable to learners of any age. According to Thorndike, organisms acquire and remember those responses that lead to satisfying after-effects (law of effect); repetition in itself does not establish a connection, but repetition of a meaningful bond will strengthen the learning (law of exercise); and a pleasurable bond, hence maximized learning, occurs if the organism is ready (law of readiness) (Thorndike, 1932).

For Thorndike, human learning precedes in much the same manner as animal learning. The evolution of mind from animal to humans has no essential discontinuity or break. Thinking is the result of the tremendous increase in the number and complexity of stimulus-response bonds. Human nature is purely mechanical; connections can be stamped into the human person.

Thorndike et al.'s book, *Adult Learning*, published in 1928, was in fact the first major report of research on learning with adults. While Thorndike's timed experiments with adults up to the age of forty-five seem rather quaint by today's standards, he did conclude that "teachers of adults of age twenty-five to forty-five should expect them to learn at nearly the same rate and in nearly the manner as they would have learned the same thing at fifteen to twenty" (p. 177), and "adult education suffers no mystical handicap because of the age of the students" (p. 179). He also determined that amount of schooling was a better predictor of progress than age, and that "other things being equal, the best time to learn anything is just before you have to use it" (191).

The Behaviorism of B. F. Skinner

Burrhus Frederick Skinner became known in psychological circles in the 1930s with his book, *The Behavior of Organisms* (1938/ 1999). As a radical determinist and behaviorist, Skinner firmly believed that their environment, the conditions of which can be studied, specified, and manipulated, controls humans. An individual's behavior is determined by the events experienced in an objective environment. "The effects of exposure to various events during one's life-span are critically important . . . and it is assumed that only knowledge of the relationships between such events and the resultant behaviors will allow an adequate account of a person's functioning . . . it is psychology's business to investigate these relationships" (Nye, 1975, 39). Through refined research techniques and an amassing of experimental data, Skinner and his followers have made significant theoretical contributions to understanding human behavior. Following is a brief discussion of several principles of modern behaviorism.

Skinner's major contribution has been to distinguish between classical and operant conditioning. In classical conditioning, responses are conditioned or unconditioned reflexes. The stimuli that evoke the responses are all that matter; reward, reinforcement, and feedback are not necessary. In operant conditioning the response is as important as the stimulus and, if reinforced, will solidify the bond to the stimulus. According to Skinner, the behavior is *"strengthened* by its consequences, and for that reason the consequences themselves are called 'reinforcers'." He goes on to point out that "the standard distinction between operant and reflex behavior is that one is voluntary and the other involuntary" (Skinner, 1974, 39-40).

The principle of reinforcement is essential to understanding operant conditioning. If a behavior is reinforced, the response is more likely to occur again under similar circumstances. Behavior that is not reinforced or rewarded is likely to become less frequent and may even disappear. Even something as complex as personality can be understood in terms of operant conditioning. Personality, according to Skinner, is a "repertoire of behavior imported by an organized set of contingencies"—in effect, a personal history of reinforcements (1974, 149). Reinforcements can be both positive and negative:

> Positive reinforcement involves the *addition* of something (a positive reinforcer) to a situation when a response is made. For example, a response may be positively reinforced if the obtaining of food, water, sexual contact, money, or praise is a consequence. Negative reinforcement involves the *removal* of something (called either a negative reinforcer or an aversive stimulus) from a situation when a response is made. For example, a response may be negatively reinforced if the removal of extreme cold or heat, a loud noise, a threat, a tedious task, or a headache is a consequence. In short, much of our behavior is conditioned because it gains us something (in the case of positive reinforcement) or because it allows us to escape or avoid something (in the case of negative reinforcement). (Nye, 1975, 48)

Reinforcement, in the behaviorist view, can both explain our own behavior and be used to modify another's behavior. Particular reinforcers might be difficult to identify, but that doesn't mean they aren't there. They might, in fact, be intrinsic rather than extrinsic. That is, the behavior itself is rewarding. The key to controlling behavior is being able to identify the most effective reinforcers, the amount they should be employed, and the timing of their use.

The timing of reinforcements has been another area of experimentation by Skinner and modern behaviorists. Skinner distinguishes between continuous and intermittent reinforcement schedules. In continuous schedules, a response is reinforced each time it is made. Behavior that is maintained by continuous reinforcement has been found to extinguish rapidly when reinforcement is not forthcoming. On the other hand, behavior that is only intermittently reinforced is likely to be maintained longer. Intermittent reinforcement schedules can be fixed, that is, occurring not continually but regularly in relation to time or number of responses, or variable, having no set pattern. Knowing the most effective scheduling of reinforcements for eliciting desired behavior has been a continuing area of interest of behavioral psychologists. Educational settings, where certain learning behaviors are desired, are but one area of application of such knowledge.

Skinner differentiates between negative reinforcement and punishment, two forms of aversive control. A negative reinforcer is something a person tries to avoid or escape; it generates behavior in the same way as a positive reinforcer does. For example, people pay taxes because they want to avoid a fine or going to jail; a student memorizes spelling words to avoid a failing grade. Punishment, on the other hand, is used to *eliminate* a specific behavior. Skinner opposes the use of both negative reinforcement and punishment.

Operant conditioning, positive and negative reinforcement, extinction and avoidance behavior, and reinforcement schedules are Skinner's experimentally derived contributions to better understanding human behavior. It is the philosophical assumptions underlying his approach, however, that have brought much criticism and debate from nonbehaviorists.

While philosophical assumptions are implicit in most of his writings, *Beyond Freedom and Dignity* (1971) squarely established Skinner as a philosopher in general and as a philosopher of education. In this work of radical behaviorism, he confronted the role of humans, human will, freedom, dignity, and the concept of self-determinism in a behaviorist society. The work is considered an attack on the doctrine of the autonomous person; that is, the person who possess freedom, dignity, and destiny.

The purposes of psychology according to Skinner are to understand, predict, and control human behavior. Since most of the problems of any society involve the behavior of humans who live in that society, controlling human behavior can result in a better society. If we want to improve our society, Skinner reasons, we must first give up the notion of personal freedom and its accompanying sense of dignity and personal worth. Personal freedom is, in fact, an illusion. "Man's struggle for freedom is not due to a will to be free, but to certain behavioral processes characteristic of the human organism, the chief effect of which is the avoidance of or escape from the so called 'aversive' features of the environment" (Skinner, 1971, 42). The task for society, according to Skinner, is "not to free man from control but to analyze and change the kinds of control to which they are exposed" (Skinner, 1971, 43).

For Skinner the autonomous person becomes a scapegoat for behavior that we do not yet understand. The role of environment in shaping and maintaining behavior is in its nascent stages. Skinner is convinced, however, that a "technology of behavior" is the only means of solving social problems and ensuring survival of the human species. "The task of parents and professional educators and society at large, according to Skinner, is to define the kinds of behavior wanted in their societies and then to produce people who will behave in those ways" (Kolesnik, 1975, 106). *Walden Two* (1948/1960) is Skinner's fictional account of a utopian society based upon behavioral engineering. At least one community, founded in 1967 and still in existence, has attempted to put Skinner's ideas into practice (Kinkade, *A Walden Two Experiment: The First Five Years of Twin Oaks Community,* 1972). Currently, approximately 80 adults and 15 children are members of the Twin Oaks Community (www.twinoaks.org). The community is dedicated to nonviolence, egalitarianism, and sustainability and "the last several years leading up to the millennium have seen the blossoming of an increased ecological orientation" (www.twinoaks.org).

It is difficult to argue with a behaviorist worldview. Skinner is a competent philosopher who gives a well-reasoned defense for his theories and assumptions. Instances of puzzling human behavior, consciousness, feelings, mind, notions of free will, dignity, and freedom are at least potentially explainable if, according to behaviorists, one looks long and hard enough for determinants of reinforcement in the environment. The more unanswerable questions have to do with the mechanisms of control in a society. The potential for misuse of a technology of behavior exists. Skinner himself notes the question of "values" involved in designing a society. "Who," he asks, "will use a technology and to what ends?" (Skinner, 1971, 25).

Over the years many criticisms have been leveled against Skinner's radical behaviorism. Many consider Skinner's view of science as rather narrow since many scientists, even physicists, develop hypotheses about unobservable phenomena. Many approaches to psychology such as Gestalt, psychoanalytic theory, and constructivism have operated on a broader view of the human being and human consciousness. Also, Noam Chomsky, the Harvard linguistic scholar, has shown that Skinner's theories do not account for how children learn their native language. Reinforcement seems to be an inadequate explanation for this complex phenomenon. Furthermore, many working in animal psychology believe that the behavior of animals can be explained by some sort of mental map that guides animals in their behavior. This implies that learners may form some sort of mental structure of their knowledge, and it is this that allows them to perform or to behave correctly. (Phillips and Soltis, 1991, 30-31).

Regardless of the extent to which one concurs with Skinner's underlying philosophical assumptions or plans for restructuring society, one can make use of the techniques and principles of behaviorism proposed by this school of psychology. Behaviorism has, in fact, had a significant impact upon various facets of our society. The following section deals with behaviorism's influence upon education.

Behaviorism Applied to
Education and Adult Education

The educational patterns of any society reflect the underlying values of that society. According to Skinner (1974), survival is the fundamental value for individuals and societies:

> What is good for the species is what makes for its survival. What is good for the individual is what promotes . . .well being. What is good for a culture is what permits it to solve its problems. There are . . . other kinds of values, but they eventually take second place to survival. (205)

An educational system can ensure the survival of individuals and of society by carefully arranging the contingencies of reinforcement to meet these ends. On the individual level, behaviorist education emphasizes the acquisition of job skills so that a person can "survive" in our society. Learning how to learn is also an important skill needed if one is to adapt successfully to a changing environment. Behaviorists would also deemphasize competition and individual success. Education, they feel, should reinforce cooperation and interdependence on a global level in order that the world's problems can be addressed. Education should produce people who can work with one another to design and build a society that minimizes suffering and maximizes the chances of survival.

In *The Technology of Teaching* (1968), Skinner addresses the issues of who and what should be taught as well as the administrative concerns of student control and individual differences. In his view, "that culture is strongest which educates as many of its members as possible" (233). Thus, both school entry age could be lowered and opportunities for adults extended. With regard to what should be taught, Skinner advocates allowing for novelty and diversity for "both cultures and species increase their strength with respect to a far wider range of contingencies when subject to variations and selection" (1968, 235). The diversity should be carefully planned, however, and not left to accident or chance. Finally, teaching should take place under favorable conditions, student behavior can and should be controlled through positive rather than negative reinforcement, and individual differences need to be more efficiently dealt with.

The roles of teacher and learner are quite defined in the behaviorist framework. The ultimate goal of education is to bring about behavior that will ensure survival of the human species, societies, and individuals. The role of the teacher is to design an environment that elicits desired behavior toward meeting these goals and to extinguish behavior that is not desirable. The teacher, then, is a contingency manager, an environmental controller, or behavioral engineer who plans in detail the conditions necessary to bring about desired behavior.

The student role in behavioral education is active rather than passive. The environment is arranged in such a way that certain student behaviors are emitted. It is essential that students act so that their behavior can be reinforced. A student has learned something if there is a change in behavior, and if his or her response occurs again under similar circumstances.

Behavioral psychology applied to the educational context has also resulted in several policy emphases and specific instructional practices. Following is a brief discussion of behavioral objectives, accountability, competency-based education, and instructional strategies.

Behavioral Objectives

The use of behavioral objectives in educational settings, particularly in the 1960s and 1970s, was a direct outgrowth of behavioral psychology. Behaviorism focuses upon the measureable, overt activity of an organism. Learning, in behavioral terms, is a change in behavior. Behavioral objectives, then, specify the behavior to be exhibited by learners after completing a unit of instruction. Also called "instructional objectives," behavioral objectives contain three components: (1) the relevant *conditions* or stimuli under which a student is expected to perform; (2) the *behavior* a student is to perform, including a general reference to the product of the student's behavior; and (3) a description of the *criteria* by which the behavior will be judged acceptable or unacceptable, successful or unsuccessful.

Advocates of behavioral objectives maintain that learning outcomes could be measured objectively and precisely, thus revealing how much progress has been made on the part of the learner. Evaluation based on behavioral objectives eliminates subjective, capricious estimates of student performance. Behavioral objectives also provide teachers with a means of clarifying just what is going to be taught, and hence, what a student is supposed to learn. Advocates further claim that using behavioral objectives leads to more effective teaching and learning.

The criticisms of behavioral objectives appear to cluster around the concept of learning. Opponents argue that learning is a complex phenomenon, that many kinds of behaviors might reveal that learning has occurred, that outcomes can be creative and unpredictable, and that learning can be unstructured or latent and approached from the whole rather than bits and parts. Also, say opponents, behavioral objectives are more appropriate for certain subjects and types of learning than others, and they do not ensure that what is learned in one situation will transfer to a new situation.

Whether or not one supports the concept of behavioral objectives, they are still used by teachers, curriculum designers, administrators, and adult educators in a variety of settings. Adult basic education, continuing professional education, and training in business and industry are three program areas that make use of behavioral objectives.

The use of behavioral objectives reflects the demand at all levels of education for accountability—the idea that all those involved with the educational process must be held accountable for bringing about what education is designed to accomplish. The link between behavioral objectives and accountability is expressed by Popham (1971): "Those who discourage educators from precisely explicating their instructional objectives are often permitting, if not promoting, the same kind of unclear thinking that has led in part to the generally abysmal quality of instruction in this country" (78).

Accountability

Behaviorist education, with its emphasis upon arranging the contingencies of learning and then measuring the change in behavior, provides a basis for the notion of accountability. According to Popham

the concept of educational accountability involves the teacher's producing evidence regarding the quality of his or her teaching, usually in terms of what happens to pupils, then standing ready to be judged on the basis of the evidence. Any accountable teacher, therefore, takes *responsibility for* the results his or her instruction produces in learners. (41)

Other educators hold a somewhat broader view of accountability in that all the professionals involved in an educational activity should be held responsible for its outcomes. The taxpayers' concern with making education cost effective, the inevitable evaluations that accompany such a demand, the need to effectively reach disadvantaged groups, and a drive to be responsible to individual needs are forces that have led to attempts to make education more accountable. The current No Child Left Behind (NCLB) federal mandate is a good example of efforts to make education accountable. Enacted in 2001, NCLB has said that students, schools, districts, and states must be evaluated each year; those schools that fail to meet certain standards will be penalized. Furthermore, school districts that receive federal Title I funds "face potential sanctions that include takeover and replacement of administrators and school board members if they don't make adequate yearly progress for several years in a row" (DeMao, 2004). A recent *TIME* magazine article reported that "No Child Left Behind has declared more than 6,000 schools failing and, the states say, imposed on them millions in costs to create new tests and accountability systems" (Feb. 23, 2004, 14).

The recent federal push to "scientifically based" or "evidence based" practices in research and education is another example of the behaviorist notion of accountability. Scientifically based research in education "means there is reliable evidence that the program or practice works. . . . It moves the testing of educational practices toward the medical model used by scientists to assess the effectiveness of medications, therapies and the like" (http://www.ed.gov/offices/OERI/whatworks). Eisenhart and Towne (2003) provide a history of the hotly "contested" idea of scientifically based research in education, and trace how public input has had some impact in broadening the law from its original narrow conception.

Evidence-based practice has found its way into adult education and in particular adult basic education (ABE), adult English for speakers of other languages (ESOL), and adult secondary education (ASE). For the most part, these are publically-supported programs that must be "accountable" to funding sources. A recent report titled "Establishing an Evidence-based Adult Education System" defines evidence-based as "The integration of professional wisdom with the best available empirical evidence in making decisions about how to deliver instruction" (Comings, 2003, 2). The proposed model consists of three components—(1)basic and applied research upon which to build programs which are then (2) evaluated for their effectiveness in conjunction with (3) the practitioner's knowledge in improving implementation. A hierarchy of five program evaluation models positions experimental and quasi-experimental at the top, followed by correlational with statistical controls, correlational without statistical controls, ending with case study at the bottom of the hierarchy (Comings, 2003).

Performance contracting and educational vouchers are two of the more intriguing ways in which school systems have sought to deal with accountability. In performance contracting, businesses or industries using modern technology and principles of behavioral design contract to bring about better student performance more efficiently than the public school system. Perhaps because the results of such attempts have been inconclusive, business to school performance contracting is not as prominent as it was in the 1970s and 1980s. Currently, teachers' pay is being linked to student performance and skills. At least nine states have "enacted laws authorizing various types of merit or performance-based pay for educators" (Gleason, 2000, 1). Educational vouchers essentially present an economic incentive for bringing about quality education. Although various plans exist, each provides a process for allocating funds through a governmental agency to parents of school children. Parents then "purchase" education for their children at a school of their own choosing. This would then force schools to provide quality education in order to remain solvent (Caire, 2002).

In adult education, educational vouchers and entitlement programs have been proposed for consideration as one means of implementing lifelong learning (Lifelong Learning Act, 1976). The G.I. Bill is an example of a voucher-like method of financing adult education. The educational section of the Bill allows service personnel to receive a fixed sum of money if they are enrolled in an accredited or degree-granting program more than half time. A veteran enrolled in a course of study less than half time can be reimbursed for the cost of the course. Each state has a State Approving Agency which "approves" programs for which veterans can be funded.

Employer tuition-aid programs in business and industry also allow adults to purchase education, thus causing deliverers to be more accountable. Fortune magazine's survey of the 100 best companies to work for found that "53 offer on-site university courses, and 91 have tuition reimbursement, with 24 reimbursing more than $4,000 a year" (Levering and Moskowitz, 2000, 84). The number one ranked company, Edward Jones, "spends 3.8% of its payroll on training, with an average of 146 hours for every employee (Harrington, 2003, 128). Most programs, however, require that the courses be job-related, reimburse according to completion and/or grade obtained, and have a low rate of participation (4 to 5 percent). Companies experimenting with more liberal policies have had better results.

A systems approach to administration and planning for schools and adult education activities is yet another manifestation of the accountability movement. Systems is a way of looking at the educational organization, its various components, and how they fit together to bring about a specified end product. The three basic components of any systems model are the input, that which enters the system to be processed to bring about the desired results; throughput, the heart of the system where the inputs are processed in an orderly fashion; and output, the end result of the inputs being processed. The systems approach includes a flow chart that visually represents the structure of the subsystems. including elements of directionality, time allotment, and decision points.

Although new tools have been developed for its implementation, the concept of accountability is not a recent phenomenon in adult education. The voluntary nature of most adult education has mandated that teachers and programs of study effectively meet the needs of students. Programs have also had to be cost effective to justify continued support from parent institutions or public funds. The issue of accountability is, in fact, philosophical as well as economic. In a society that emphasizes preparatory education of youth and values education for becoming a more productive member of society, most adult education has had to be remedial or job-oriented. Activities focusing on personal growth and development, leisure and recreation, have also had to be "accounted" for largely because of adult education's structurally and financially subordinate position in the educational hierarchy.

Instructional Methods

Behaviorism's impact on instruction can be seen in programmed instruction, computer based-or computer-assisted instruction, and contract learning. These instructional methods

> are based on the principles of operant conditioning and on the assumption that learning is acquired through repeated reinforcement of behavior. They all define learning in *be-*

> *havioral terms,* and almost all shape the student's behavior
> through a *gradual progression* toward the goal. They pro-
> vide for *constant and immediate feedback, liberal positive
> reinforcement, and self-pacing* insures that no student must
> fail just because he learns less quickly than others. (Herman,
> 1977, 93)

Building upon the work of Sidney Pressey, B. F. Skinner is accredited with developing programmed instruction. Programmed instruction, originally via teaching machines and now through com-
puter-based programs, is simply a "device which arranges contingencies of reinforcement" (Skinner 1968, 65). According to Skinner
(1968), there are four types of programming designed either to (1)
generate new patterns of behavior, (2) alter properties of behavior,
(3) bring behavior under control of stimuli, or (4) maintain behavior
under infrequent reinforcement. Programs can be linear in which
material is broken into small units leading towards a final goal, or
branching, which allows students to explore wrong answers and skip
sections already understood. As with other aspects of behavioral
education, programmed instruction has its advocates and its opponents. The controversy centers on two points—student satisfaction
with the method, and acquisition and retention of material. Some
students respond well to this form of instruction, but others find it
too confining. In a review of the research on computer-assisted instruction (CAI) compared to non-CAI in adult basic and secondary
education settings, Rachal (1993) found mixed results across the
twelve studies reviewed. He concluded that "CAI has earned a place
in the ABSE setting. But at the same time, expectations of it becoming a miracle cure for the adults in these educational programs are
naïve and unrealistic" (171-172).

Many adult educators would like to see more emphasis on educational activities that foster self-directed learning. Knowles's *Self
Directed Learning* (1975) advocates a process wherein students determine the behavior to be performed and criteria and mechanisms
for evaluation. These criteria are spelled out in a learning contract
in which the objectives, activities, resources, and criteria for evaluation are identified. In reality, formal instruction in adult education
is more likely to be individualized through joint teacher-student contracting or teacher determined tasks. In an analysis of individualized instruction, Herman (1977) has delineated the following steps
by which educators and learners at all levels can utilize principles of
behaviorism for designing individualized instruction:

(STOP 07)

Step 1: Specify Behavioral Goals.

Step 2: Analyze the Learning Task—sequence material in a logical progression.

Step 3: Assess Entry Behavior—identify what your students or you already know.

Step 4: Plan Presentation—provide cues, feedback, reinforcement, and self-pacing.

Step 5: Evaluate, record, and adjust. (126-128)

Behaviorism in Adult Education

As in other areas of education, behaviorism in terms of behavioral objectives, accountability, and instruction undergirds, at least partially, a number of practice areas in adult education. Vocational education, human resource development, continuing professional education, and literacy education all exhibit, to some extent, a behavioristic orientation as does program planning models that span each of these areas.

Adult Vocational Education

Behaviorism grounds vocational education or what is now more commonly called career and technical education. The emphasis in vocational education is on identifying the skills needed to perform in an occupation, teaching those skills, and requiring a certain standard of performance in those skills. Education in this arena of practice is concerned with the outcomes rather than the process of learning, on exit rather than entrance requirements, and on criterion-referenced evaluation rather than norm-referenced evaluation. Criterion-referenced evaluation is an important concept in behavioral psychology. In criterion-referenced evaluation, the learner's progress or accomplishments are compared to a fixed standard or criterion of mastery rather than to the performance of other students. It is based on the assumption that learning objectives can be predetermined, and that given sufficient time and proper reinforcements nearly all students can meet the objectives.

Historically, vocational education has been associated with competency-based education. To begin with, the *competencies* (knowledge, skills, behaviors) to be demonstrated by the learner are derived from analysis of worker roles, stated in behavioral terms, and made public in advance. Second, the *criteria* to be used in assessing student competency are direct outgrowths of the competencies them-

selves, stated explicitly and in advance, including specified conditions for mastery. The *assessment* of a student's competency uses
performance as the primary source of evidence, while at the same
time taking into account evidences of a student's knowledge. Student progress is determined by demonstrated competency rather
than in time periods or course completion. Finally, the individual's
learning experience is guided by *feedback.*

Since the mid-1990s, the "competency" idea of vocational education has been eclipsed by the notion of "standards-based" or skill
standards. The "fixed standard" for workforce education is via skill
standards set up by the National Skills Standards Board (NSSB).
Established in 1994, the NSSB has as its mission to develop skills
standards in each of the 15 industry sectors, and to establish assessment and certification systems (http://www.nssb.org/). In a work
environment where skills are complex and workers highly mobile,
"certification based on industry-validated skill standards provides a
portable credential and communicates mastery of job skills required
by employers" (Brown et al., 2001, 1). There are two dimensions to
these skill standards. One is "the Work-Oriented Component that
describes what needs to be done on the job and how well, including
critical work functions, key activities, and performance indicators;"
the second component is Worker-Oriented "that describes the skills
an individual must have to perform the work competently, including
academic knowledge and skills, employability knowledge and skills,
and occupational/technical knowledge and skills" (Brown et al., 2001,
3).

Developing a curriculum or course for skills-based vocational
technical instruction begins with detailed job descriptions which include location and general working conditions, job functions, general duties, contingent responsibilities, and so on. The job description provides the basis for a detailed task analysis, a process that
breaks the basic job down into successively more detailed components. For many occupations, task analyses are already in existence
and can be obtained through various vocational-technical publications, the U.S. military, and business and industry. A detailed task
analysis of a specific job is then used as a basis for developing instructional objectives and materials. Finally, criterion-referenced
measures are developed and used to evaluate student performance
on each task.

Standards-based vocational education or instruction is well suited
to adult vocational education for several reasons: it allows for individual differences in terms of the starting point for instruction; the

time it takes a student to master competencies is flexible and dependent upon individual ability; learning specified competencies may be done in a variety of ways from formal class activities to life or work experiences; criterion-referenced evaluation is nonthreatening; it is an ideal vehicle for a self-directed individual learning experience.

These advantages would appear to outweigh their problems. There are, however, constraints or at least potential pitfalls when standards-based concepts are applied to vocational training. Such an approach depends on an accurate identification of tasks performed in thousands of occupations and the availability of such task inventories to curriculum developers. Also, some competencies desirable for certain occupations might be difficult to specify from task inventories and, if identified, difficult to perform. For some tasks, identifying what constitutes minimum performance standards for mastery might be difficult. Further, this approach predetermines the end product of a learning experience. Other learning that may occur during the process or shifting to different outcomes as a result of formative evaluations are changes not easily accommodated in the behaviorist framework. These drawbacks are in addition to basic philosophical differences between a behaviorist and humanistic orientation. Standards-based education has been criticized because it has been seen as dehumanizing or nonhumanistic, lacking in concern for the student, and inhibiting creativity. It has also been attacked for forcing all students into the same mold, and fragmenting curriculum into bits and pieces while overlooking the whole.

Human Resource Development and Continuing Professional Education

Probably the most visible articulation of a behaviorist orientation is in the area of human resource development (HRD). This form of adult education is organizationally based, especially in business and industry, where employees are "trained" to enhance their on-the-job performance. Within the last several decades a large number of books, monographs, and journals have been published reflecting a growing interest in HRD by both practitioners and academicians. Like adult education, HRD defies simple definitions but the following certainly conveys the nature of the endeavor:

In the U.S. the scope of definitions is somewhat narrower [than in the UK] and organization-focused, to the exclusion of concerns for national or global needs, Nadler's definition of HRD as a "series of organized activities conducted within a specific time and designed to produce behavioural change" (1970:3), McLagan's definition of HRD as the "integrated use of training and development, career development, and organization development to improve individual and organizational performance" (1983:7) and Swanson's definition of HRD as a "process of developing and unleashing human expertise through organization development and personnel training and development for the purpose of improving performance "(1995; 208) are . . . functional in scope. (Kuchinke, 2003, 286)

Performance or performance improvement is how some conceptualize HRD. Jacobs (1987), for example, weaves instructional technology into his concept of HRD, which he renames as human performance technology. This approach uses systems theory "to ensure that the right individuals have the knowledge, skills, motivation, and environmental supports to do their jobs effectively and efficiently" (13). He also presents this very behaviorist definition: "Human performance technology is about engineering human performance. Thus, the technologies involved are based on what is known about the principles to change the outcomes of behavior" (19). In this orientation, "subsystem performance measures" are "central to performance improvement research: it is impossible to implement research or discuss performance improvement from an organizational perspective without some form of measurement" (Torraco, 1999, 98).

In the 1980s, the American Society for Training and Development (ASTD) commissioned two major studies in an attempt to define the field of HRD (Patricia McLagan, 1983; Patrick McLagan, 1989). The second study (which sought to update the 1983 study) "summarizes 74 work outputs of HRD, more than 500 quality requirements linked to the outputs, 35 competencies necessary to achieve the outputs, 11 roles that may be enacted by HRD professionals, 5 role clusters that link, related roles, and 19 possible uses of the study's results" (Rothwell and Sredl, 1992, 87). Several authors, such as Gilley and Eggland (1989) and (Dubois & Rothwell, 2004), have drawn heavily from this competency-based model of HRD.

Others in HRD also draw from a behaviorist orientation. Carnevale, Gainer, and Villet (1990), whose emphasis is on "the bottom line," present an instructional systems design model derived from the military. They point out that employers are anxious to return to "needs-driven education and training and away from providing a patchwork of unconnected training courses covering topics recognized as "nice to know' but not immediately germane to the jobs at hand" (31). Sleezer, Conti, and Nolan (2003) note that "HRD professionals who rely on behaviorism and cognitivism emphasize rewards, the stimuli that learners receive from the environment, the systematic observation of behavior, and relating new information to previous learning" (26).

Company executives see the majority of employee education and training as necessary to carrying out company goals. As in other areas of education, accountability is an important facet of corporate programs. Concerned with the most economic and efficient way to accomplish a task, corporate training makes use of competency-based concepts and modern instructional technologies. Indeed,

> in deciding whether to implement an HRD program, decision makers can rely on negotiations, explanations of how the program will instrumentally improve performance, and forecasts of costs and benefits. After a program has been implemented, measures of satisfaction, learning, and performance are common. Individual workers also measure program quality when they determine their level of commitment to an HRD program. (Sleezer, Conti, & Nolan, 2003, 29-30)

Continuing education is another area where behaviorism has had an impact. While career and technical education prepares people to enter a job or occupation, continuing education takes place after one is employed and reflects the need to remain current with developments in the field. The companies through their HRD programs offer some of this continuing education, but as in vocational education, independent or self-directed learning modules are also a means for continuing education. In the areas of health, education, and business, for example, self-directed modules follow the same steps of task analysis, development of behavioral objectives and instructional materials, and criterion-referenced measures of performance as in standards-based vocational education.

Professionals in particular engage in continuing professional education (CPE) to "provide higher quality service to clients by improving their knowledge, competence, or performance" (Cervero, 1989, p. 518). Indeed, much of CPE is mandatory; that is, in order to maintain one's license and therefore ability to practice, annual participation in continuing education is required. Concern with certification and licensing requirements of professional associations and state and federal bodies drives much formal CPE. Professional knowledge and accountability to clients is updated and sustained through on-going learning. As Sleezer, Conti, and Nolan (2003) observe, "In CPE, certification reflects judgments of quality. Certification can assess individual learning and a CPE program's contribution to that learning. It can also reflect on the entire profession because it communicates the profession's required standards for learning" (29).

Of course it is oversimplified to say that the theoretical orientations of HRD and CPE are behavioristic alone. Although certainly aspects of behaviorism can be seen in both, both also draw from other theoretical frameworks. In an entire issue devoted to exploring the connections between HRD and CPE, the editors point out that "over the last few years, trends in the professions, the workplace, and society have affected both fields" and that "debates flourish within both communities of practice regarding the role, processes, ethics, and scope of certification" (Daley & Jeris, 2003, 5).

Adult Literacy Education

Adult literacy education is a function of the "evolving concept of literacy that over time has moved from a school-based model . . . to a functional set of skills or competencies to be mastered, the more recent social and cultural notion of multiple literacies" (Askov, 2000, 248). Underlying literacy education are behaviorist and cognitivist learning theories. "These two theories align with the double thrust . . . toward an education for 'workers' (behaviorist) and one for 'leaders' (cognitive), the former being taught to behave without thinking, the latter to think without any resulting praxis or action" (Askov, 2000, p. 255). Sparks and Peterson (2000) suggest that Adult Basic Education (ABE) is perhaps too behaviorally driven:

> The preoccupation with technique in adult education is informed by a scientific and technical rationality which privileges a globalized capital economy. As the link between education and the economy tightens, corporate demands refocus the goals and purposes of education. ABE has become a system designed to meet the economic imperatives where a premium is put on technical knowledge that, in the end, deskills learners and practitioners. Moral and ethical issues are neglected for the sake of efficiency. (265)

Historically, adult literacy instruction has been skill and compe-
tency-driven. Many states have competency-based high school
completion programs which emphasize the mastery of basic requirements rather than the number of hours of instruction or the number of courses completed. Assessing literacy from a competency perspective has been an effort to demonstrate the effectiveness of a
complex and often times costly investment. As a manifestation of
the behaviorist orientation to education, competency-based education emphasizes setting behavioral goals, objectives, or outcomes,
demonstrating behavioral change, and measuring the amount of
change against predetermined criteria. The 1970s Adult Performance
Level (APL) Study conducted by the University of Texas and funded
by the U.S. Office of Education was a major impetus towards the
development of a competency-based high school and curriculum in
adult basic education. The purposes of this study were to (1) define
adult literacy in terms of the competencies needed to function successfully in today's society, and (2) to assess those competencies in
the adult population of the United States.

The APL study proved foundational to the 1980s and 1990s National Assessment of Adult Literacy Survey (NALS) which "assessed
literacy by analyzing the tasks and skills that comprise literacy behaviors in the prose, quantitative and document domains. It was
assumed that "skills and competencies that are assessed and mastered in one context are transferable to other contexts" (Askov, 2000,
249). From a different starting point—the perceptions of literacy
participants themselves—a study titled "Equipped for the Future"
identified four literacy needs: to gain information, to express oneself, to take independent action, and to continue further education,
and three social roles for adults—worker, family member, and citizen. In addition, the 1998 Adult Education and Family Literacy Act
set in motion yet another program, this time one "preoccupied with
isolated skill attainment, the public domain of work, and technical
efficiency" (Sparks & Peterson, 2000, 263-264). All of these initiatives have led to what Sparks and Peterson term "the crisis of accountability" in adult basic education.

Program Planning in Adult Education

Behaviorism has perhaps had its greatest impact in adult education in curriculum design and program development. Although no
single individual can be singled out as the major proponent of this
philosophical orientation, Ralph Tyler can be credited with having a

major influence on the program development models proposed by Cyril Houle (1972), Malcolm Knowles (1970) and others.

In *Basic Principles of Curriculum and Instruction* (1949), Tyler presents a generic model for designing an educational activity whether it be a single instructional unit or a comprehensive program. Tyler bases his model upon the assumption that "education is a process of changing the behavior patterns of people" (5). Each educational program should have clearly defined purposes. Defining these purposes is the first step in program design. Purposes can be derived from many sources including the learners themselves, contemporary life outside of school and subject specialists. Information derived from these sources is then filtered through the philosophical orientation of the designer and institution, and through psychological findings related to learning. This process should lead one to formulate specific objectives that would guide in the selection of learning activities.

Writing specific objectives that can be used to guide learning experiences is the second step in planning. The nature of these objectives is identical to behavioral objectives discussed earlier in this chapter. Tyler (1949) reminds his readers that "since the real purpose of education is not to have the instructor perform certain activities but to bring about significant changes in the students' patterns of behavior," an objective should be "a statement of changes to take place in students." Each objective should specify "both the kind of behavior to be developed in the student and the content or area of life in which this behavior is to operate" (44).

Learning experiences are then selected that will facilitate attaining the objectives. Tyler defines a learning experience in behavioral terms as "the interaction between the learner and the external conditions in the environment to which he can react" (63). The role of the teacher is that of a contingency manager who sets up the environment or structures the situation to elicit predetermined responses. Tyler states "the teacher's method of controlling the learning experience is through the manipulation of the environment in such a way as to set up stimulating situations—situations that will evoke the kind of behavior desired" (64). It is not enough to select appropriate learning experiences. They must also be organized so as to reinforce each other. Tyler posits three major criteria for organizing a group of learning experiences. The experiences should be (1) continuous—provide recurring opportunities for experiencing particular elements, (2) sequential—each successive experience builds up the preceding so as to increase the learner's depth and breadth of understanding, and (3) integrated—arranged so that the segments of learning experiences can be united into the learner's behavior (84-86).

The final step in Tyler's model is evaluation. Evaluation is based upon the educational objectives that specified the behavioral change desired. Specifically, it is "the process of determining the degree to which these changes in behavior are actually taking place" (106). According to Tyler, evaluation must be based upon overt behavior since that is the only way one "can tell whether students have acquired given types of behavior" (111). Methods of evaluation can be varied, however, including tests (written and oral), questionnaires, observations, and samplings of a student's work. Evaluations should be used for both individual and program assessments. Tyler points out that curriculum planning is a continuous process in which evaluation leads to re-planning and redevelopment (123).

Tyler's thought can be readily seen in most program planning models in adult education. Houle, whose philosophical orientation draws from several schools of thought, credits Tyler with having the primary influence on his system for planning and implementing adult education programs (Houle 1972). Houle's "fundamental system" begins by identifying an educational activity and deciding to proceed. General and specific objectives are identified and refined. Once objectives are put into some hierarchy, the most suitable learning format and its accompanying activities are designed for carrying out the objectives. The program is then put into effect. Finally, the results are measured and appraised. Ideally, the evaluation influences future planning. Similarities between Houle's "fundamental system" and Tyler's principles of curriculum design are obvious. Objectives, a measurable form of evaluation, and manipulation of environmental factors to carry out a program are important components in Houle's model.

Although Malcolm Knowles clearly identifies with humanistic psychological principles when proposing an andragogical approach to adult education (1970), his program planning model nevertheless reflects Tyler's influence. His model begins with a needs assessment. Sources of identifying needs are adult learners themselves, organizations, and communities. Tyler, it might be remembered, suggests identifying "purposes" from learners, contemporary life, and specialists. Purposes for Tyler become objectives after considering them in terms of philosophy and psychologically based learning theories. Needs in Knowles's scheme become objectives once they are filtered through institutional purposes and philosophies, and feasibility, which, Knowles notes, include "the psychology of learning" (125) and the interests of the clientele.

Knowles divides objectives into operational—things to be done to improve the quality of resources for meeting needs, and educational—"the kinds of behavioral outcomes that participants are to be invited to seek in specific areas of content" (126). Knowles's model proceeds to the selection of a learning format "that will most effectively accomplish the objectives of the program" (133). Implementation and evaluation are the final steps in the model.

Other program planning models (see for example, Boone, Safrit, and Jones, 2002; Cookson, 1998; Nadler and Nadler, 1994; Rothwell and Cookson, 1997) draw at least loosely from Tyler's design for curriculum and instruction. That is not to say that the authors of various models are behaviorist adult educators. Rather, some of the basic concepts of behavioral psychology are particularly appropriate to situations where a person or agency wants to bring about certain behaviors. Thus, behavioral terminology has found expression in the design and implementation of educational activities ranging from a single unit of instruction to more comprehensive programs. While these models based in what Sork (2000, 173) terms the "technical-rational tradition" have "continued to dominate into the 1990s," there have been a number of critiques that when applied to conventional planning theory, reveal its "flaws" (174). Sork singles out feminism, postmodernism and critical theory as perspectives that have challenged the traditional program planning models.

The Impact of Behaviorism on Adult Education

Estimating the extent of behaviorism's impact upon adult education has been a difficult undertaking. Aside from B. F. Skinner who has attempted to transfer psychological concepts into educational practice, there is no adult educator or specific educational program that espouses a philosophy drawn exclusively from behavioral psychology. Rather, one must look to policies, programs, and practices in education and in adult education in particular to detect behaviorism's influence. Behavioral objectives and accountability are two concepts soundly based in behaviorism and permeating all levels of education. Competency or skills-based education has become popular in adult vocational education, human resource development, continuing education, and adult basic education. Program planning and instructional methods in adult and continuing education also contain concepts from behavioral psychology. The diverse and wide-spread manifestations of behaviorism in education perhaps speak to the desire on the part of all educators to know better the nature of the impact one has in the learning process. That's not to say that other perspectives can't be incorporated. Matuszowicz (2001, 17) in fact makes a case for "building a program" based on " variety of philosophies."

Recent philosophical literature in adult education tends to be highly critical of the assumptions behind behaviorism. This is especially true of those philosophers who make use of critical theory or phenomenology in investigating aspects of adult education (Collins, 1991, 1998; Griffin, 1983; Stanage, 1987). Behaviorism has been dismissed as cold, inhumane, devoid of feeling, and ignorant of the subjective, creative, and intuitive dimensions of human behavior. Collins (1991) also points out that often the literature on program planning, design, and evaluation tries to have it both ways by modifying the language of behaviorism with that of humanistic psychology. Collins (1995) is especially critical of the Competency Based model and the Human Relations Development model so prevalent in adult education. In his view CBE diverts learners from careful reflection on their work, involves them in busy work and "imbues them with narrow expectations about education and about the world of work" (85). Collins is equally critical of the HRD model which he considers a management tool to serve bureaucratic interests and fails to "engage with the moral-political problem of what gets in the way of ordinary men and women realizing the potential which resides in the collective *competence which they already possess*" (1995, 88-89). Collins (1998) further points out that "the behaviorist viewpoint is entirely antithetical to the aspirations for voluntary, autonomous, learning that sustains any reasonable notion of self-directed learning within the context of lifelong learning" (p. 116). And when an educational system is tied to measurable outcome statements, we know little about "the nature and quality of learning" (117).

Some postmodern adult educators, interestingly enough, have come to the defense of the behaviorist mode at least in its focus on empowering teachers and learners through competency based education. In their view such an educational approach might actually empower both teachers and learners. They call for a competency-based approach that combines tenets of behaviorism with those of humanism. Their description of this type of competency education argues that

p. 110

> Learner-centredness is part of the rationale, evoking the
> need for individuals to become active, to take responsibility
> for their own learning in order to become 'competent', to
> 'own' what they learn and do and to show what they know
> through behaviourist outcomes. (Usher, Bryant, and Johnson
> 1997, 84)

One can speculate on the persistence of the behavioral paradigm in adult education, as well as in general education. This paradigm, based as it is on logical empiricist philosophy of science, satis-
fies the quest for certainty in many educators since it bases education on explicit, scientific-technical procedures. Logical empiricism
and behaviorism have devoted great energies toward accounting for
method, justification, and procedures of verification (Kaplan, 1964).
These philosophies have identified causal elements that might account for, predict, and control human behavior. Furthermore, behaviorism sets before teachers, aims, objectives, and criteria which
are standard and fixed. And finally, behaviorism's appeal is that
funding and other forms of support for adult education can be linked
to measurable outcomes constituting "success," "competency," "increased productivity," and "concrete results."

(STOP 08)

// CHAPTER V

HUMANISTIC ADULT EDUCATION

Humanism is a broad philosophical point of view that holds sacred the dignity and autonomy of human beings. As a philosophy, humanism is as old as civilization and as modern as the twentieth century. Its roots can be traced back to classical China, Greece, and Rome; historically it has found expression in religion, literature, education, and psychology.

Humanistic adult education draws from some of the same sources as liberal adult education. The emphasis of the humanistic educator, however, is not upon the works of the past and the values these possess, but upon the freedom and dignity of the individual that is highlighted in this tradition. Humanistic adult educators are concerned with the development of the whole person with a special emphasis upon the affective dimensions of the personality. In taking this particular stance, humanistic adult educators are more closely allied with some existentialist and phenomenological philosophers.

This chapter will first follow the threads of humanism as it has surfaced at various points and in various contexts throughout history. Second, the general principles gleaned from humanism's many expressions and which most humanists would ascribe to will be presented and discussed. A third section will be devoted to an exploration of humanism as it manifests itself in modern general and adult education. The chapter concludes with a discussion and analysis of humanistic adult education, its major proponents and applications.

Humanism in Historical Context

Humanism as a philosophy can be traced back to Confucius and Greco-Roman thinkers, especially Plato and Aristotle. The Italian

Renaissance, however, is most often pointed to as the first full expression of this philosophy. The term itself derives from the fifteenth-century Italian *humanista* meaning teacher of the humanities. The term developed to distinguish certain studies in philosophy, literature and the arts from theology or the study of divinity. In its strictest sense, humanism referred to a Renaissance literary cult or Renaissance Humanism, which spearheaded an awakened interest in Greek and Roman literature. Studying such works for their own sake, it was believed, would develop autonomous and responsible individuals. The so-called "New Learning" movement was a revolt against the stultifying authority of a church-dominated world in which the Greek and Latin Classics were read for the edification of Christians. The emergence of humanism in Renaissance Italy as a revolt against a dehumanizing force begins a pattern repeated several times.

Italian humanism, despite some repression from the Church which at times supported it, introduced the study of Greek, translated Plato's writings into Latin, and produced work in historiography. A belief that humans had great potential and an innate ethical sense is clearly reflected in humanist writings. Not so clear is their image of the human. Castiglione's *Courtier,* for example, presents a worldly, cultured gentleman which contrasts with Machiavelli's evil, though rational, Prince.

The influence of Italian humanism was pervasive. It eventually molded the worldview of many Europeans and resulted in diminishing the powerful grip of the Church. The humanists' fascination with classical scholarship was equaled by an interest in Hebrew and Christian writings. Erasmus, the best known of the Christian humanists, propounded a resolute faith in reason, popularized the new learning of the humanist tradition, and worked for reform from within the Church. Martin Luther was also committed to many of the ideals of Renaissance humanism. In retrospect, the Renaissance humanists left a legacy of principles adopted by humanists from then on: the revolt against a force such as the Church which tries to control knowledge; emphasis on intellectual capabilities; the ideal of a gentleman-scholar; and the promotion of a good-life for all humanity.

Humanism was identified to some extent with the Enlightenment of the eighteenth century. The Enlightenment's interest in works of antiquity, confidence in human intellect and reason, and its appetite for learning were endeavors highly compatible with a humanistic worldview. An even greater resurgence in humanism occurred in the late nineteenth and early twentieth centuries. As with Renaissance humanism, modern humanism developed as a pro-

p. 113

test against forces viewed as threatening to humanity—the industrial revolution with its pursuit of wealth and material goods, the advance of natural science which had given vogue, some felt, "to a mechanistic philosophy or destroyed the philosophical pursuit altogether," and the spread of communism which promoted atheism and materialism (Perry, 1956, 5). In more recent years, humanism has been a protest against behaviorist psychology and the dehumanizing potential of nuclear power.

Humanists' reactions to these forces have taken many forms. To deal with the problem of science, Scientific Humanism evolved to propose using science to enhance human life. Christian Humanism rejects traditional concepts of God and devotes its attention to promoting the well-being of humanity. A myriad of other movements and philosophies have espoused a humanistic component including Marxism existentialism, phenomenology, and pragmatism.

Existential Humanism. Existentialism is a modern expression of humanistic thought that has had great influence on a number of adult educators, especially Carl Rogers. Existentialism is a broad term that embraces the thought of a rather diverse group of thinkers: Soren Kierkegaard, Fredriech Nietzsche, Martin Heidegger, Karl Jaspers, Albert Camus, Gabriel Marcel, Paul Tillich, Martin Buber, Jean Paul Sartre, and Simone deBeauvoir. This philosophical movement is deeply concerned with the freedom and integrity of the individual in the face of increased bureaucratization in society and its institutions, as well as the whole gamut of human relations. Existentialists stress awareness, consciousness, perception, the total meaning-structure of individuals, their visions of life and death, their work choices, and other aspects of their lives.

Pratte (1971) briefly summarizes a number of common philosophic themes in existentialism that have some influence upon existential and humanistic educational theory. Existentialists contend that existence precedes essence in the sense that persons are not ready-made, but are rather the designers of their own being or essence. Second, essence is contingent or superfluous for, in the words of Sartre (1949), "every existing being is born without reason, prolongs life out of weakness, and dies by chance" (18). Third, human existence is fundamentally absurd or irrational for no reason can be given for a thing being one way rather than another. Fourth, persons are destined to choose and bear responsibility for their choices. Fifth, meaningful human relations are the very substance of human life.

Humanism and Education. As a means of obtaining its goals of developing the individual and promoting the well-being of humanity, humanists have always placed great value upon education. Although the process of education proposed by Aristotle would hardly be humanistic by today's standards, much from his philosophy can be construed in a humanistic light. For Aristotle, the goal of all human striving is the attainment of the highest or supreme good, which is often synonymous with happiness. Moral and political action and intellectual activities are the best ways to achieve the ultimate goal. Striving for this goal is a self-actualizing activity. The goal of education, Aristotle felt, was "to cultivate the disposition that will lead people to be ready, able, and willing to engage in the excellent activities that constitute or which lead to happiness" (Patterson, 1973, 34).

The humanists of the Renaissance taught in schools and universities as well as actively participated in affairs of state, thus exemplifying the well-rounded educated person. Erasmus, already mentioned as an influential humanist who sought to reform the Catholic church, wrote a work called "The Education of a Christian Prince." In it he recommended that virtue be the highest quality to be obtained. Montaigne, another Renaissance scholar, thought a youth should seek learning "not so much for external advantages as for his own good, to enrich and furnish himself within," and that a tutor should be selected for character and intelligence (Montaigne in Noll and Kelly, 1970, 72).

Humanistic values underlie the educational thought of such important thinkers as John Comenius, Jean Jacques Rousseau, and Johann Pestalozzi. Comenius in his book *The Great Didactic* (1649) set forth a methodology of teaching for leading the learner toward a maximum attainment in knowledge, virtue, and piety. In keeping with the Renaissance ideal of the well-rounded citizen, Comenius proposed a system of education that would enhance social, emotional, spiritual, and intellectual development.

Rousseau's *Emile* (1762) is perhaps one of the best known treatises on education. Written to a parent who was concerned about her son's education, Rousseau describes the ideal education of a fictitious boy, Emile. Believing in the natural goodness of human nature and deploring the corrupting forces of society and its institutions, Rousseau felt education should strive to preserve the naturalness of human beings. The humane and sensitive teacher would allow the learner to become self-sufficient, to develop all his/her potentialities, and to learn naturally. Rousseau is quite modern in his advocacy of the learner as starting point, of problem-posing and discovery techniques, and of a warm and relaxed teacher-student relationship (Noll and Kelly, 1970).

Like Comenius and Rousseau, Pestalozzi emphasized the total development of the learner and the need for education to be as natural as possible. The growth and development of learners was to be brought out by love in a loving environment. The result of the educative process would be humanist persons who were emotionally secure, intellectually alive, and socially active.

Thus, the essential principles of humanistic education have been enunciated by many thinkers since Aristotle. Patterson (1973) identifies two major principles inherited from earlier educators: "(1) the purpose of education is to develop the potentials—all the potentials— of humans as a whole; (2) the essential method for achieving this is providing a good human relationship between the teacher and the student" (44).

In the past two decades a number of educational theorists have attempted to apply various themes of existential philosophy to the traditional components of educational philosophy (Kneller, 1958; Morris, 1966; Greene, 1973). The overly pessimistic themes of some existentialists have in these writings been abandoned, with emphasis being placed upon the educational task of assisting a feeling, suffering, rejoicing free person to fashion an essence or character. The primary task of the existentialist educator is defined as assisting in the development of responsible selfhood in the face of the complexities and problems of modern life.

Humanistic psychology. Humanistic psychology has also had a significant impact upon educational theory and practice. As with the earlier humanist "revolts," humanistic psychology developed from a reaction to behaviorism, the predominant psychological orientation in the United States in the first half of the century. Commonly referred to as the "third 'force" in psychology, humanistic psychology rejected the view of humans espoused by both behaviorists and Freudian psychologists. While humanists could accept Freud's and behaviorists' contributions to understanding human nature, and behaviorists' efforts to make psychology an exact science, they were distressed by the lack of concern these two theories had for the complexity of human beings. What was lacking, they felt, was a recognition of the individuality, potentialities, creativity, and freedom of the person.

The common point of reference for all behaviorists, as was discussed earlier in the previous chapter, is their attempt to explain behavior in terms of the connection between stimuli and observable responses. This largely mechanistic and piecemeal approach to human behavior and learning was first challenged by the introduction of Gestalt psychology to America in the 1930s. Gestalt theorists proposed looking at the whole rather than individual parts and at the total structure of learning rather than one incident. The major proponents of Gestalt psychology, Koehler, Koffka, and Wertheimer, broadened the investigation of learning to include notions of understanding, insight, and problem-solving. The individual, however, was still primarily at the mercy of a configuration of external forces. Not until the mid-1950s with the writings of Maslow, Rogers, Buhler, and Bugental was a humanistic psychological position clearly delineated. Bugental succinctly stated the difference between the behaviorist and humanist view of human nature. According to Bugental (1967), the behaviorists see the human being as

> an object acted upon from the outside by various forces or driven from within by other forces which are to be characterized by their relation to the outside (e.g., thirst, hunger, sexual appetite). The regularities in man thus most attract the mechanomorph: instincts, reflexes, conditional responses, habits, learning. (8)

In the humanistic psychologists' model the human being

> is viewed as a subject in the midst of his own living, acting on the world, changing himself and all about him. While man's reactiveness is certainly recognized, the humanistic psychologist regards this as less distinctive of the human experience and tends to look to those ways in which humans distinguish themselves from objects, from lower animals and from one another. (8)

An understanding of the humanistic orientation toward human nature can be gleaned from noting the general differences with respect to research between behaviorists and humanists:

1. scientific versus intuitive: behaviorists use rigorous scientific methods and precise language in their experimentation; humanists are more concerned with intuition, understanding and subjective experience than objectification.
2. means versus ends: behaviorists are more concerned with the means of changing behavior; humanists emphasize the ends toward which change should be directed.

3. external behavior versus internal emotion: behaviorists are concerned with observable external behavior as opposed to internal and often not clearly discerned emotions.

4. behavior change versus insight: in learning situations as well as in therapeutic treatment, behaviorists look for changes in overt behavior whereas humanists aim for achieving insight into problem-solving.

5. manipulation versus humanization: behaviorists manipulate people or the environment to produce an effect; humanists "attempt to sensitize people to their uniquely human characteristics and possibilities." (Wandersman et al., 1976, 24)

Other dichotomies that have been used to characterize their differences in approach to humans include pessimistic versus optimistic, reductionist versus holistic, objective versus subjective.

The humanistic psychologists have done much to establish their form of humanism as a major force in the United States. In a later section of this chapter the humanistic psychologists' impact upon educational theory and practice will be discussed. Modern humanists, whether they identify themselves as psychologists, philosophers, or theologians, share certain fundamental beliefs and values. The following discussion elucidates these basic tenets.

Basic Assumptions of Humanistic Philosophy

Humanism is a philosophy broad enough to encompass many individual variations and manifestations. Each age has sought to define what its basic values are, what it holds as irreducible, what it seeks to accomplish. In 1933, thirty-four humanists in the United States met for the purpose of defining humanism's fundamental principles. The result of their meeting was the *Humanist Manifesto I*. In this short document, any notion of a dogmatic or deterministic control over human beings is firmly rejected. Instead, human beings themselves are held responsible for bettering the state of human affairs:

The quest for the good life is still the central task of mankind. Man is at last becoming aware that he alone is responsible for the realization of the world of his dreams, that he has within himself the power for its achievement. He must set intelligence and will to the task" *(Humanist Manifestos I and II,* 1973, 10).

In 1973, forty years after *Humanist Manifesto I* appeared, a second and more comprehensive document was written and signed by 114 prominent individuals. Since 1973, the document has been endorsed worldwide by countless others representing many disciplines. As with the earlier version, the starting point for *Humanist Manifesto II* is the preservation and enhancement of all things human. The document then addresses itself to religion and ethics as well as the issues of civil liberties, equality, democracy, the survival of human kind, world economic growth, population and ecological control, war and peace, and the building of a world community. The statement presents a vision of faith in the human potentiality of each person and in humanity as a whole.

As was noted earlier, the humanistic psychologists have had a great influence on the establishment of humanism in the United States. The Association for Humanistic Psychology lists four characteristics with which most humanists would agree. These tenets, when considered in conjunction with Humanist *Manifestos I and II,* provide a foundation for uncovering the basic assumptions of humanism. Protagonists of humanistic psychology would agree to

> A centering of attention on the experiencing person and thus a focus on experience as the primary phenomenon in the study of man. Both theoretical explanations and overt behavior are considered secondary to experience itself and to its meaning to the person.
>
> An emphasis on such distinctively human qualities as choice, creativity, valuation, and self-realization, as opposed to thinking about human beings in mechanistic and reductionistic terms.
>
> An allegiance to meaningfulness in the selection of problems for study and of research procedures, and an opposition to a primary emphasis on objectivity at the expense of significance.
>
> An ultimate concern with and valuing of the dignity and worth of man and an interest in the development of the potential inherent in every person. Central in this view is the person as he discovers his own being and relates to other persons and to social groups. (Misiak and Sexton, 1973, 116)

These common elements of humanism that psychologists propose and the underlying assumptions of the *Manifestos* are complementary. These documents as well as other humanistic writings are predicated upon the following principles of humanism. These presented are not meant to be exclusive; major points have been selected for discussion.

Human Nature Is Naturally Good. Many humanists believe that humans are naturally, inherently good. Given a loving environment and freedom to develop, human beings will grow in a manner beneficial to themselves and to society in general. It is partly due to this assumption that humanists are considered by some to be romantics. Humanists, however, support their view by pointing out that humans and societies have continually striven toward a better and more ideal society. "If there were not an inherent drive toward good in man," they argue, "it is difficult to understand how the human race could have continued to survive; men would long ago have killed each other off" (Patterson, 1973, 65).

The view that human nature is inherently good corresponds to many humanists' rejection of a religious force that has power over the lives of men and women. Many religions are predicated upon the depravity of humans. Hence, according to some humanists, these religions stress that persons are in need of a god to save them from annihilation. In believing that humans are naturally good and therefore not automatically doomed, there is little need, in the view of some humanists, to ascribe to a traditional theism. Faith is not placed in a force outside individuals but within individuals themselves.

However, not all humanists and existentialists see an incompatibility between affirming the autonomy and dignity of humans and the existence of God. A group of religious existentialists that includes Marcel, Jaspers, Buber, and Tillich have attempted to develop a concept of God that is consonant with and not contradictory to full human autonomy and integrity. Their religious philosophies downplay the traditional emphasis on human depravity and put stress on the basic goodness and power of humans as God's creatures to cooperate with God in fashioning a more perfect human society.

In many ways the humanistic view of human nature stands in contrast to both the Freudian and behaviorist view. Freud portrays the majority of individuals as antisocial, destructive and hostile. The id, or emotional core of one's personality, has instinctive tendencies toward gratification, aggression, destruction, and death. These impulses are to be checked by the more rational ego and societal superego, but they nevertheless constitute the essence of human nature.

The behaviorists do not see humans as either inherently good or bad. For them, all behavior is learned. Humans are controlled by forces in the environment and are in essence programmed to respond in predetermined ways. It might be recalled that the humanistic psychology movement was begun as a protest against both the Freudian and behaviorist positions.

Freedom and Autonomy. Again in contrast to the behaviorist position that "free inner man . . . is only a prescientific substitute for the kinds of causes which are discovered in the course of scientific analysis" (Skinner in Rogers, 1965, 396), humanistic educators believe that humans are truly free creatures. A person's behavior is not determined by external forces or internal urges; rather, behavior is the consequence of human choices which individuals can freely exercise.

This notion of freedom and autonomy does not mean that behavior is totally random, uncontrolled, and unaffected by heredity or environment. Rather, human beings are capable of making significant personal choices within the constraints imposed by heredity, personal history, and environment. Not all is predetermined. Persons can be proactive rather than reactive and, in so being, exert an influence on their situation. The force of persons who are free to act can bring about change for the betterment of their lives and humanity in general.

Individuality and Potentiality. In humanistic philosophy the individuality or uniqueness of each person is recognized and valued. Behavior, then, is not as predictable as some would desire. Likewise, it is important to promote one's individuality by nurturing each person's special talents and skills. The potentiality each person possesses for growth and development is unlimited. Humanism places unlimited faith in the individual and believes that human beings possess the power or potentiality for achieving the good life, for solving their own problems, and for developing into the best persons possible. Reason and intelligence are the most effective tools humans have in this process, but they are not to be depended upon solely. Intuition and emotions are important components of the whole person. As expressed in *Manifesto II* (1973), "critical intelligence, infused by a sense of human caring, is the best method humanity has for solving problems. Reason should be balanced with compassion and empathy and the whole person fulfilled." (18)

Self-Concept and The Self. Humanism has been criticized on occasion as devoting too much time to the self. The humanistic emphasis on the self, however, does not mean to promulgate a self-centeredness that excludes others. In fact, an important assumption of humanistic philosophy is one's responsibility to others and working for the good of humanity in general. For humanists the self is the heart of the person, the enhancement of which is possible through actualizing individual potentialities.

As defined by humanists, the self consists of the sum total of everything that distinguishes one person from another—attitudes, body, values, feelings, intellect, etc. This brings one back to the humanists' emphasis on the uniqueness of each individual, for each "self" is like no other.

The notion of self-concept is also fundamental to the humanistic position, especially the psychologist's. Briefly defined, the self-concept is a person's subjective evaluation of who he or she is. The self is what a person really is; the self-concept is a determiner of behavior and has a great influence on one's ability to grow and develop.

Self-Actualization. Growth, self-actualization, or self-transcendence are innate human characteristics according to humanistic philosophy and psychology. Men and women continuously strive toward personal growth and toward realizing their unique potentialities. Although a number of humanistic psychologists have written of human striving for self-actualization, Abraham Maslow's *Motivation and Personality* first published in 1954, popularized the term. In this work Maslow offers a theory of human motivation based on a hierarchy of needs. The needs at the lowest level of the hierarchy are physiological, such as hunger and thirst and must be attended to before a person can cope with safety needs—those related to security, protection, etc. The next three levels on Maslow's hierarchy are belongingness, love needs, and esteem needs—to feel that one is useful and one's life has worth and finally, the need for self-actualization. The needs are hierarchical but at the same time "people who are normal are partially satisfied in all their basic needs and partially unsatisfied at the same time" (Maslow, 1954, 94). Self-actualization manifests itself in a desire for self-fulfillment, for becoming what one has the potentiality to become.

Perception. Another important concept of humanism is that behavior is the result of selective perception. The world is known and stimuli, external and internal, are reacted to as a result of one's individual perception. The same seemingly objective stimuli can be perceived differently by different persons. It is at this juncture that the philosophy of phenomenology intersects with humanism. For both phenomenologists and humanists, reality is what one believes it to be, not necessarily what actually exists.

Perception is a key concept in humanism for it explains behavior. A person's overt behavior as well as attitudes, feelings, beliefs, and values are all a product of personal perceptions. In order to understand another's behavior one must enter that person's world. An empathic identification with other human situations lays the foundation for the humanist goal of promoting a better world for all of humanity.

Responsibility and Humanity. Humanism's emphasis upon the self, the individual, and the free autonomous person carries with it a strong sense of responsibility both to the self and to other people. Individuals are charged with the task of developing their potentialities to the fullest, of striving toward self-actualization. In becoming a better person, individuals contribute to the betterment of humanity.

Interaction with others is essential because humans are not only by nature social beings, but need others in order to satisfy drives for love, recognition, esteem, etc. The growth of self does not occur in isolation from others; neither is the welfare of humanity advanced by ignoring the humanness of all peoples. Although each person is unique, the humanist vision is predicated upon the recognition of the common humanity of all people. Much of the 1973 *Manifesto* is devoted to promoting a world community and an ideal vision of human potentiality.

In a recent analysis of the tension in humanistic philosophy between the individual and society, and in particular in Maslow's work, Pearson and Podeschi (1999) point out that

> whereas there is a core U.S. value of individualism that is girded by beliefs in self reliance and self-motivation, this core value also is a collective individualism involving association with others and belonging to organizations. (44)

Pearson and Podeschi go on to say that Maslow was quite aware of the tension between self and others and the struggle of a self-actualizing individual to resist "social conformity" (44). In fact, his writings "make clear that he became increasingly preoccupied in the 1960s with social and political forces, concerned with shortcomings in his own theoretical framework, and was putting increasing emphasis on social psychology" (51).

This tension was also explored by Jansen and Wildemeersch (1998). They point out that adult education's tendency to promote individualized self-actualization is at the same time in the context of valuing labor participation "as an indispensable condition for both self-actualization and social integration" (216). For them, the key question for adult education is "how to enhance people's opportunities to participate in social contexts and be present in social places that enable them to connect personal qualities and desires to their competency to experience responsibility and togetherness with others" (226).

Delineating "basic assumptions" of any philosophy leaves one open to criticisms of omission and selectivity. The ones that have been presented here represent a synthesis of humanists" philosophical and psychological position statements. They are also logical derivations from the historical evolution of humanistic thought. A faith in basic human goodness, for example, underlies Rousseau's *Emile*. Individual freedom in lieu of obedience to an oppressive religion was embraced by Italian Renaissance humanists. And the importance of perception, self-concept, and self-actualization have been emphasized by twentieth century psychologists. Many of these same assumptions are found in the application of humanism to an educational setting.

General and Adult Humanistic Education

Education in the United States has been affected by humanistic philosophy and psychology. Since the mid-twentieth century, humanistic education has exerted an influence comparable to that of behaviorist education. All levels of education, from preschool through adult, have modified both theory and practice in accordance with humanistic principles.

Historically, the purpose of education has been the transmission of cultural heritage and the perpetuation of existing society. This concept is based upon the assumptions that society will remain pretty much the same from generation to generation and that society's elders know what knowledge and skills are necessary for maintaining the cultural status quo. This view also assumes that there is an identifiable body of knowledge that can be packaged and passed on to new learners. Even in the area of adult education, it has been assumed that adults need to know certain basic skills for functioning in society (Adult Basic Education), and need to acquire certain values and attitudes (Americanization Education), if they somehow missed them in earlier schooling. There is much that can be said in support of the transmission of cultural heritage to a society's new learners, and humanists would not exclude this as an objective of the educative process. However, humanistic educators see the purpose of education as being considerably broader, not limited to a particular culture or historical pattern.

Simply stated, the goal of humanistic education is the development of persons—persons who are open to change and continued learning, persons who strive for self-actualization, and persons who can live together as fully functioning individuals. As such, the whole focus of humanistic education is upon the individual learner rather than a body of information. That is not to say that humanistic education lacks substance. It is the approach to material and persons within the educative process that is emphasized. Patterson (1973) noted that there are really two aspects of humanistic education: "The first is that of teaching subject matter in a more human way, that is, facilitating subject matter learning by students. The second is that of educating the nonintellectual or affective aspects of the student, that is, developing persons who understand themselves, who understand others, and who can relate to others" (x).

Several components of humanistic education find expression in both general and adult education. In both educative settings, the student is the center of the process, the teacher is a facilitator, and learning is by discovery.

Student-Centered. Humanistic education is student centered. In this orientation the teacher does not necessarily know best, especially when working with adult learners. Philosophical assumptions of individual freedom, responsibility, and natural goodness underpin the student-centered emphasis in humanistic education. Arbitrary curriculum and methodological decisions violate the student's ability to identify his or her own learning needs. Humanistic education places the responsibility for learning with the student—the student is free to learn what he or she wants to learn and in a manner desired by the learner. A teacher can guide or facilitate the process, but the emphasis is upon learning rather than teaching and on the student rather than the instructor.

Humanistic education is student-centered not only with regard to the responsibility for learning but in terms of the self-development of each learner. The student is viewed as a unique individual in whom all aspects of the person must be allowed to grow in the educative process. Emotions, attitudes, physical aspects are as important as intellectual development. The whole personality, all the dimensions of humanness that differentiate human beings from animals, are deemed the important areas of development in humanistic education. Education's assistance in the development of persons leads to a better society, one of the philosophical goals of humanism. A society of self-actualizing or fully functioning, thinking, feeling, active individuals will result, humanists feel, in the betterment of humanity as a whole.

Both Abraham Maslow and Carl Rogers see education as a means of fostering self-actualizing and fully functioning individuals. The goal of education according to Maslow, is self-actualization, or "helping the person to become the best that he is able to become." Educationists should think in terms of bringing about intrinsic rather than extrinsic learning,"that is, learning to be a human being in general, and second, learning to be this particular human being" (Maslow, 1976, 120-121). While Maslow felt that self-actualization did not occur in young people, education at all levels could assist in bringing about its development. Given that being a self-actualized person is an adult phenomenon, however, a humanistic approach to adult education would seem to be essential. It was, in fact, Maslow's study of extraordinary adults such as Lincoln, Beethoven, and Schweitzer which led to the following personality characteristics of self-actualized persons:

— they are realistically oriented
— they accept themselves, other people, and the natural world for what they are
— they are spontaneous in thinking, emotions, and behavior
— they are problem-centered rather than self-centered in the sense of being able to devote their attention to a task, duty, or mission that seems cut out for them
— they have a need for privacy and even seek it out on occasion, needing it for periods of intense concentration on subjects of interest to them
— they are autonomous, independent, and able to remain true to themselves in the face of rejection or unpopularity
— they have a continuous freshness of appreciation and capacity to stand in awe again and again of the basic goods of life, a sunset, a flower, a baby, a melody, a person
— they have frequent "mystic" or "oceanic" experiences, although not necessarily religious in character

— they feel a sense of identification with mankind as a whole in the sense of being concerned not only with the lot of their own immediate families, but with the welfare of the world as a whole

— their intimate relationships with a few specifically loved people tend to be profound and deeply emotional rather than superficial

— they have democratic character structures in the sense of judging people and being friendly not on the basis of race, status, religion, but rather on the basis of who other people are as individuals

— they have a highly developed sense of ethics

— they resist total conformity to culture. (Maslow, 1954, 203-208)

Similar to Maslow's self-actualizing person is Rogers's fully functioning individual. The emphasis upon the student is obvious in Rogers's question, "If education were as complete as we could wish it to be in promoting personal growth and development, what sort of person would emerge?" His answer is that it is the person who

> is able to experience all of his feelings, and is afraid of none of his feelings; he is his own sifter of evidence, but is open to evidence from all sources; he is completely engaged in the process of being and becoming himself, and thus discovers that he is soundly and realistically social; he lives completely in this moment, but learns that this is the soundest living for all time. He is a fully functioning organism, and because of the awareness of himself which flows freely in and through his experiences, he is a fully functioning person. (Rogers, 1969, 288)

For Rogers, the emphasis upon the student in the learning process is essential. It is also a principle that can be applied to any student in any setting. In *Freedom to Learn* (1969), for example, Rogers shows how humanistic student-centered education has been employed in a sixth grade, a college psychology course, and a graduate seminar. For humanists, a student-centered approach is more than taking into account the individual learning style, needs, and interests of students. Rather, these formulate "the starting point and guiding principles of the entire educational process" (Kolesnik, 1975, 55).

(STOP 09)

R p.127

Teacher As Facilitator. The role of the teacher in a humanistic setting is that of facilitator, helper, and partner in the learning process. The teacher does not simply provide information; it is the teacher's role to create the conditions within which learning can take place. In order to be a facilitator one must trust students to assume responsibility for their learning. This is a most difficult stance for the traditional teacher for it necessitates abdicating the authority generally ascribed to the teacher role. The truly humanistic teacher respects and utilizes the experiences and potentialities of students. Ideally, the humanistic teacher is a self-actualized or fully functioning individual. That this applies to an adult educational setting as well as any other is obvious. An adult instructor dealing with adult students can hardly ignore the wealth and variety of individual experiences as a foundation for facilitating learning.

Carl Rogers worked extensively with adults in both counseling and educational settings, and set forth guidelines characterizing the qualities and methods of a facilitator. These guidelines reflect many of the philosophical assumptions underlying humanism presented earlier in this chapter:

1. The facilitator sets the initial mood or climate of the group or class experience.
2. He/she helps to elicit and clarify the purposes of the individuals in the class as well as the more general purposes of the group. Diversity of purpose is permitted to exist.
3. The facilitator relies upon the desire of each student to implement those purposes which have meaning for him, as the motivational force behind significant learning.
4. He endeavors to organize and make easily available the widest possible range of resources for learning.
5. He regards himself as a flexible resource to be utilized by the group.
6. In responding to expressions in the classroom group, he accepts both the intellectual content and the emotionalized attitudes, endeavoring to give each aspect the approximate degree of emphasis which it has for the individual or group.
7. As the accepting classroom climate becomes established, the facilitator is able increasingly to become a participant learner, a member of the group, expressing his views as those of one individual only.
8. He takes the initiative in sharing himself with the

group—his feelings as well as his thoughts.
9. Throughout the classroom experience, he remains alert to the expressions indicative of deep or strong feelings.
10. In his functioning as a facilitator of learning, the leader endeavors to recognize and accept his own limitations. (Rogers, 1969, 164-166)

The Act of Learning. Humanistic educators view the act of learning as a highly personal endeavor. As mentioned earlier, perception is an important concept in humanistic thought and it bears upon the notion of learning. One perceives selectively what accounts for individual behavior. Perception also accounts for differences in what is "learned" in an educational setting. A student "learns" what he or she perceives to be necessary, important, or meaningful. The meaning one gleans from a subject depends upon personal goals, interests, attitudes, beliefs, etc. The importance of self-concept also has a bearing on learning. A positive or negative self-concept can promote or inhibit learning respectively. Rogers also feels that there is a real and an ideal self, that which the person would like to be. The discrepancy between the two can provide a stimulus for learning.

Individuals differ; therefore perception is selective and self-concepts vary. Because of this, the most effective learning takes place in discovery. Learners are encouraged to bring all their uniqueness to a situation or problem, grapple with it, and in so doing discover or learn whatever is most meaningful. Learning through experimentation and discovery is that learning which will become a part of the person. Information and knowledge that are given to a student in a traditional instructional situation (called the "banking concept" by Paulo Freire) may be meaningful to a teacher, but will not necessarily be perceived as such by a learner.

In the humanistic learning process, motivation is intrinsic rather than extrinsic. As one writer put it, it is learning "from the inside out" (Weinberg, 1972, 123). For humanists, motivation is not something put upon learners, it emanates from the learner. A facilitator need only provide a number of options from which a student might choose. Perhaps more than any other characteristic of humanistic education, intrinsic motivation characterizes adult learners. In most adult educational settings, the adult learners are there, not because they have to be, but because they want to be. Most adult students engage in learning activities under no compulsion except that which is generated from within.

Evaluation is an integral part of the learning process. For humanistic educators, self-evaluation is the only meaningful test of whether learning has taken place. Students themselves are thought to be the best judges of whether learning has met their needs and interests. Educators have experimented with various methods of self-evaluation including student reporting, learning by student-designed objectives, pass-fail grading, and concept mastery learning.

Thus, self-evaluation, intrinsic motivation, self-concept, perception, and discovery are all important components in the learning process for learners of any age. Rogers calls meaningful learning "experiential" and sums up the process in the following principles of learning:

1. personal involvement—the affective and cognitive aspects of a person should be involved in the learning event;
2. self-initiated—a sense of discovery needs to come from within;
3. pervasive—the learning makes impact on the behavior, attitudes or personality of the learner;
4. evaluated by the learner—the learner can best evaluate if the experience is meeting a need;
5. essence is meaning—when experiential learning takes place its meaning to the learner becomes incorporated into his total experience. (Rogers, 1969, 5)

Curriculum. The goal of humanistic education is the development of self-actualizing persons. The selection of content is subsumed under the goal of assisting learners to grow and develop in accordance with their needs and interests. Humanistic education is a process. It is a stance assumed by the teacher who respects learners as unique individuals, motivated to learn and anxious to grow. Curriculum becomes a vehicle, not an end in itself for achieving humanistic goals.

Historically, the classical humanistic curriculum consisted of the study of Greek and Roman literature and later Judaeo-Christian works. Through the centuries the term "humanities" has been broadened to include philosophy, literature, history, ethics, language, and social sciences. The humanities as a curriculum are compatible with humanistic education, for the humanists "have traditionally been concerned with the person—the individual—and the eternal, existential questions of relationships among persons, universes, gods and dreams" (Simpson and Gray, 1976, 6). The humanities are also at the essence of liberal education.

Modem humanistic education, which draws more on humanistic psychology than on classical and Renaissance humanism, includes much more than the humanities. While studying the social, political, religious, and philosophical values of other ages and cultures might contribute to the development of the self, an equally valued source of curriculum is the examination of one's *own* values, attitudes, and emotions. With youth this emphasis finds expression in the evaluation of moral dilemmas and in courses designed to develop empathic attitudes toward others. Adult education has embraced this emphasis through values clarification workshops, encounter groups, transactional analysis, and human potential workshops.

Teaching a prescribed curriculum, then, is not the goal of humanistic educators. The curriculum functions as a vehicle which, if creatively employed, can promote the real goal of humanistic education—the development of self-actualizing individuals.

Cooperation and Groups. Humanistic educators strive for self-actualization. But self-development and growth do not occur in an individual isolated from others. Growth is best fostered in a cooperative, supportive environment. In an educational setting, humanistic educators attempt to attend to the affective and emotional dimensions of a learner as well as the intellectual. This is best achieved through improving interpersonal relationships in a cooperative, oftentimes group learning experience. Humanistic educators thus stand in opposition to the notion of competition as a motivating force in education.

First, if one adopts the humanistic assumption that motivation is intrinsic to the learner, then one need not construct an artificial motivating force such as competition. Second, competition is threatening; learning that is threatening tends to be resisted (Rogers, 1969). Combs (1971) notes the relationship between competition and threat:

> Competition has motivating force only for those persons who believe they have a chance of winning. . . . Persons who are forced to compete and who do not believe they have a chance of success, are not motivated by the experience; they are threatened by it.... When competition becomes too important, any means becomes justified to achieve the ends. (110-111)

One of the best ways to foster growth and cooperation amongst learners is through groups. Discussions, small group projects, committees, and teams as instructional techniques are not new to education. Dewey and other progressive educators, including adult educators Lindeman and Bergevin, gave their support to group activities as a means of promoting learning and preserving democratic ideals. Groups as an outgrowth of the humanistic psychological movement of the mid-twentieth century took on a meaning different from the progressive education movement. The primary purpose of the encounter groups, training groups (T-groups), or sensitivity groups of the 1960s was to foster personal growth and development through an experiential process. The goal of what Rogers called a "basic encounter group" was to "enable the participants to become experiencing persons capable of choice, creativity, valuation, and self-actualization" (Misiak and Sexton, 1973, 121).

It is interesting to note that the encounter group movement was a largely adult activity. At its height of popularity in the 1960s and early 1970s, large numbers of educators, businesspeople, executives, criminals, housewives, single and married men and women met in homes, churches, business, and growth centers (such as the Esalen Institute in Big Sur, California) for the purpose of experiencing and interacting with other people. What one learned in an encounter group varied. Patterson (1973) found that from an encounter group experience one might learn such things as to accept and respect others, to express one's own feelings, and "to change oneself in the direction of being more the self one wants to be" (195). Overall, it was a direct approach to promoting affective growth, an important component of a humanistic education.

The commercialization and sensationalization of personal growth groups resulted in a cautious use of them in educational settings. Rogers, considered to be the founder of encounter groups, pointed out the possible disadvantages: behavior changes if they occurred in the group were not necessarily lasting; a person may "become deeply involved in revealing himself and then be left with problems which are not worked through"; the surfacing of marital tensions; and complications related to liaisons which develop between group members (Rogers, 1967, 272-274). These criticisms notwithstanding, groups have filtered into more liberal, less tradition-bound school systems and they continue to be employed by counselors and adult educators in a variety of settings. From continued professional training to academic settings to human potential seminars in business and industry, groups remain a major manifestation of adult humanistic education.

Humanistic Adult Educators

Humanistic adult educators share the basic tenets of humanistic education explored in the foregoing section of this chapter. What they provide for the most part is an application of humanistic philosophy and psychology to an educational setting. As the major theoretician and spokesperson for humanistic education, Carl Rogers articulated and popularized many of the practical applications of a humanistic philosophy to education. His emphasis upon self-initiated learning that is relevant to the learner, student participation in planning and evaluation, the teacher as facilitator, and group methods has served as a model for adult educators. In this section will be described some adult educators who can be classified as humanistic in their philosophical orientation. It is recognized that classifications are not perfect since many theorists tend to be somewhat eclectic in their theoretical orientation.

Adult Education As Andragogy

That a humanistic orientation is particularly suited to the education of adults was espoused by Malcolm Knowles. Considered one of the most influential adult educators in the United States, Malcolm Knowles attempted to translate humanistic goals into a theoretical framework for adult educators. Calling for a technology for teaching adults that was distinguishable from teaching children, Knowles popularized the European concept of *andragogy* to characterize the education of adults. Knowles felt that andragogy, the art and science of helping adults learn, could be contrasted to pedagogy, the education of children.

While trying to propose andragogy as a rubric for adult education, Knowles recognized that it meant more than helping adults learn. "It means," he says, "helping human beings learn, and . . . it therefore has implications for the education of children and youth" (Knowles, 1970, 38-39). With its emphasis upon the learner and the development of human beings, andragogy is basically a humanistic theoretical framework applied primarily to adult education. An examination of what Knowles considers to be the five underlying assumptions of andragogy reveals the humanistic foundations of what he called the "new technology."

The first assumption centers on the notion of self-concept, a basic emphasis in humanistic psychology. Knowles notes that as persons mature, their self-concepts move from being dependent personalities toward being self-directed human beings. Learning that is most meaningful capitalizes upon the self-directed, autonomous nature of adults. Assuming that adults are self-directed has implications for educational practice. The learning climate must be supportive, cooperative, informal, and in general, cause adults to feel accepted and respected. Because adults are self-directed they are able to, and do, determine their own educational needs. Self-diagnosis of learning needs and self-evaluation of the learning that has taken place are important components of adult educational practice based upon the self-concept assumption of andragogy.

The self-concept of adults with regard to learning, Knowles feels, is a particularly delicate matter. Adults who have experienced failure in earlier schooling and who have little confidence in their ability to learn will find their negative self-concept a barrier to success in adult education.

This first assumption of andragogy, then, incorporates many of the basic principles of humanistic educational thought such as the importance of self-concept, self-diagnosed learning and evaluation, a cooperative rather than competitive atmosphere, and the necessity for respecting and trusting the adult learner.

The second assumption underlying andragogy is that the adult defines him-or herself in terms of the accumulation of a unique set of life experiences. Although children also have had experiences, an adult has had many more which have had more time to become integrated into a unique personality. Respect for an individual's uniqueness and experiences is a basic humanistic concept. Knowles proposes using the adult's experiences as resources for learning and advocates an emphasis upon experiential, participatory learning. In particular, Knowles recommends sensitivity or human relations training, at least in the early phases of an educational activity. Reflecting his own humanistic orientation, he states:

> One of the almost universal initial needs of adults is to learn how to take responsibility for their own learning through self-directed inquiry, how to learn collaboratively with the help of colleagues rather than to compete with them, and especially, how to learn by analyzing one's own experience. Since this is the essence of the human relations laboratory,

it is coming to be used increasingly as an orientation activity in a long-run program of adult education. (1970, 45)

The third and fourth assumptions upon which andragogy is based place the emphasis in the learning process where humanistic educators believe it should be—with the learners themselves. The third assumption holds that an adult's readiness to learn is linked to developmental tasks unique to a stage in life. The implication of this assumption is that adults will not learn what is not relevant to their stage in life. What is relevant depends upon their particular needs and interests of a particular life stage. These needs and interests give rise to an intrinsic motivation to learn. And as all humanistic educators believe, intrinsic rather than extrinsic motivation is an integral part of the learning process.

The fourth assumption—that adults desire an immediate application of knowledge as contrasted to postponed application of much youth learning, has implications for a curriculum that is decidedly humanistic. Knowles advocates an adult educational curriculum that subsumes specific subject content under general problem areas. The real and immediate needs of adult learners are more effectively met through problem-solving group techniques in which traditional curriculum content is a by-product.

Finally, the fifth assumption underlying andragogy that Knowles added at a later date, is that adults are internally rather than externally motivated (Knowles and Associates, 1984).

Thus Malcolm Knowles is indeed a humanistic adult educator. For him, the learning process involves the whole person, emotional, psychological, and intellectual. It is the mission of adult educators to assist adults in becoming self-actualized and mature adults. Andragogy is a methodology for bringing about these humanistic ideals.

It is in the assumptions underlying andragogy, that Knowles's allegiance to humanism is unabashedly clear. In his autobiographical "journey," Knowles (1989) cites Carl Rogers as a major influence on his thinking, and lists "learning to be authentic" and "learning to make things happen by releasing the energy of others" as two of eight episodes that changed his life. Pratt (1988), in a provocative analysis titled "Andragogy After Twenty-Five Years," concludes that "andragogy is saturated with the ideals of individualism and entrepreneurial democracy" (p. 21). It is also based on five humanistic values including placing the individual at the center of education, believing in the goodness and potency of each person, in each person's potential to grow toward self-actualization, and in autonomy and self-direction as "signposts of adulthood" (21).

Knowles's philosophy of adult education also incorporates elements of the humanistic revolt against a behaviorist and determinist view of human nature and education. His "democratic philosophy" of education is characterized

> by a concern for the development of persons, a deep conviction as to the worth of every individual, and faith that people will make the right decisions for themselves if given the necessary information and support. It gives precedence to growth of *people* over the accomplishment of *things* when these two values are in conflict. It emphasizes the release of human potential over the control of human behavior. (Knowles, 1970, 60)

It is interesting to note that some research on adult learning tends to support humanistic and andragogical notions that adult learners are self-directed and intrinsically motivated. Allen Tough (1971), an adult educator, studied individual adult learners and discovered that 90 percent of the adult population conducted at least one major learning effort per year, and 73 percent of the projects were self-planned. Especially intriguing in Tough's work are the "high learners"—those who spend perhaps two thousand hours a year at learning and complete fifteen or twenty projects in one year. "In their lives," Tough says, "learning is a central activity; such individuals are marked by extraordinary growth" (Tough, 1971, 28). These "high learners" exhibit characteristics similar to Rogers's fully functioning individuals or Maslow's self-actualizing adults.

As most adult educators are aware, Tough's 1971 book on *The Adult's Learning Projects* followed by Knowles's *Self-Directed Learning* (1975) inspired a major thrust in adult learning research and theory building. Subsequent to these publications, the area of self-directed learning became a popular research topic resulting in a plethora of books, monographs, articles, and conference proceedings Much of this literature is reviewed by Caffarella (1993), Merriam and Caffarella (1999), and Candy (1991). Underlying all of this literature is a humanistic philosophy. Caffarella (1993) notes that this is the "predominate" orientation and that

> from this perspective, the focus of learning is on the individual and self-development, with learners expected to as-

sume primary responsibility for their own learning. The process of learning, which is centered on learner need, is seen as more important than the content; therefore, when educators are involved in the learning process, their most important role is to act as facilitators, or guides, as opposed to content experts. (26)

Debate Over Andragogy. According to its advocates andragogy is a popular as ever, adopted by legions of adult educators around the world (Pratt, 1988, 21). Despite this assertion a debate over the validity of andragogy began shortly after Knowles book was published. Houle (1972) was critical of the distinction Knowles made between the andragogy and pedagogy. McKenzie (1977) attempted to give the concept of andragogy a more solid philosophical basis in existentialism. Andragogy as an overarching adult education theory was later criticized by many others including Elias (1979), Cross (1981), and Brookfield (1986).

In 1980, the second edition of Knowles's *The Modern Practice of Adult Education* was published, only this edition's subtitle read, *From Pedagogy to Andragogy,* rather than the 1970 version which read, *Andragogy Versus Pedagogy.* This shift in subtitles reflects the lively debate the field engaged in as to whether andragogy was exclusively for adults, and whether andragogy constituted a theory of adult learning. Knowles became persuaded that andragogy could be seen as being on a continuum with pedagogy at the other end, and that each orientation would be at times appropriate for both adults and children, depending upon the instructional situation. In this work, Knowles considered andragogy and pedagogy as "probably most useful when seen not as dichotomous but rather as two ends of a spectrum, with a realistic assumption in a given situation falling in between the two ends" (Knowles, 1980, 43). Further, most have conceded that rather than a learning theory, andragogy is a set of assumptions that delineate characteristics of adult learners, and thus best functions as a guide to instructional design. However, as Brookfield (1986) noted, "attempts to erect a massive theoretical edifice concerning the nature of adult learning on the foundations of a set of empirically unproved assumptions are misconceived" (91) In a recent review of the research on andragogy, Rachal (2002) concludes that while "nearly all adult educators would be sympathetic to the view that as much of the spirit of andragogy as possible should infuse adult learning situations," research of the 1980s and 1990s relative to andragogy's effectiveness in both achievement and satisfaction provide mixed results and often "no significant differences" emerging from variegated methodologies, and thus reveal an unstable theoretical foundation upon which to prescribe practice. (224)

Rachal goes on to say that "if andragogy is to be . . . more than a slogan, . . . it must coalesce into some form of roughly agreed-upon testable hypothesis" (224-225).

Adult Education As a Humanistic-Existential Enterprise

Another attempt to present a philosophical framework for the field of adult education was offered by Leon McKenzie (1978). His vision, which he hoped would give meaning to adult educational practice, drew from both humanistic and existential orientations. McKenzie felt that adult education should foster a courageous spirit among individual learners. Prometheus, who defied Zeus by stealing fire and giving it to humanity, is the prototype of the adult to be formed through education. McKenzie proposes seven principles of adult education, most of which are humanistic in orientation. Education, for example, should facilitate in adults a rejection of a determinist and behaviorist worldview. It should also facilitate the development of proactive, self-directed adults who would be responsible for evolving into a more enlightened human existence. It is the adult educator's role to foster a concern for human welfare, a spirit of interdependence and cooperation, and courage among adult learners. In discussing the "how" of putting the principles into practice, McKenzie advocates such humanistic educational techniques as self-directed learning in group situations guided by a facilitator.

In a later work McKenzie (1991) presented a comprehensive or transcendent goal for all of adult education, the construction of a worldview. Worldview construction involves "the ongoing development and maturation of understanding: understanding of the world, of others, of self, of understanding itself" (p. vii). Drawing on the thought of Martin Heidegger, McKenzie presents worldviews as vantage points in time and culture that condition persons' experience of the world and provide an understanding of the self. In this view, the primary goal of adult education is the search for personal meaning.

McKenzie makes use of the work of Hans-Georg Gadamer to show how worldview construction is related to tradition. Early socialization provides us with ready-made worldviews. Through education, persons can be led to an understanding of their prejudices, assumptions, and beliefs and to a realization of how these affect interpretations of new experiences of thinking and knowing. Thinking and knowing need to be systematic, that is, balanced, orderly, informed, self-referencing, and productive. Thinking and knowing should lead to understanding, and to "insight that integrates experiences, ideas, judgments, and beliefs into a meaningful whole" (x, xi). All thinking develops in a particular social and cultural context. This analysis is informed by the work of the philosophers Ludwig Wittgenstein and Bernard Lonergan.

McKenzie makes a strong case that adult educators have an ethical responsibility to examine their own worldviews so they may avoid imposing them on students. He is strongly critical of how adult educators on both the political right and left have imposed their ideologies on their students rather than facilitate the emergence of the learners' own worldviews. While those on the right impose the classic wisdom of the past, those on the left indoctrinate with the political utopias of the future. Although McKenzie argues that adult educators should be impartial in all controversial areas and only attend to the unveiling of the truth, he recognizes that it is often not possible for educators to remain neutral in their teaching. McKenzie is particularly critical of radical adult educators for their politicizing the educational process. Informed by the philosophical work of Richard Rorty, he contends that there are no absolute truths and that the educational process is an ongoing conversation and dialogue in which positions can often change.

McKenzie acknowledges that his own philosophical assumptions are eclectic, drawing as he does on various philosophers. Although he remains committed to many Enlightenment prejudices and assumptions, he has come to place higher value on tradition. He remains committed to many of the values of existentialism, phenomenology, and humanistic psychology. What he does not make clear are his own political, social, and economic commitments and how these have influenced his criticisms of radical adult education, liberation theology, and attitudes toward activism among adult educators.

Adult Education As Phenomenological Analysis

Stanage (1987) has provided the field of adult education with a difficult and challenging approach to the philosophy of adult education. Though he is aware of and makes use of elements of various philosophical approaches to adult education, he prefers to investigate various phenomena of adult education and learning according to the philosophical methods of Edmund Husserl and other continental philosophers. Stanage also suggests that the works of Dewey, (1939) especially *Logic: The Theory of Inquiry,* are particularly useful in examining adult education from a phenomenological perspective.

Stanage offers the reader an introduction to phenomenology (an investigation of human consciousness including feelings, experiences, ideas, hopes, problems, etc.), as well as a phenomenological investigation of the adult world and of the components of adult education (assumptions, goals, means, ends, and methods). He attempts to provide a philosophical understanding that would "lead to new programs of learning for the adult learner, adult educators, and the subject matter of adult education, and to a new paradigm of research, new research programs, and the subsequent emergence of new problems" (2,3). Other analyses pertinent to adult education include a description of feeling, experience, and consciousness, all of which attempt to provide an understanding of the person that should underlie all of adult education.

Stanage's analysis of adult education leads to this provisional definition: "adult education is the enactment of, and the systematic investigation of the phenomena constituting the adult education of persons: "feeling, experience, and consciousness, specifically of persons' free and deliberate motives for actions" (37). This knowledge of persons provides us with keen insight into the action of persons, in both private and public spheres.

Stanage's project is a challenging one which has been taken up by a number of doctoral students who have extended this form of analysis into various areas of human consciousness. For Stanage, this approach to adult education constitutes

> a way through to the theory and practices of adult education conceived as the most rigorous of human sciences. These have as their special subject-matter systematic investigations of the performative enactments of, and the systematic investigation of, the essential structures of the phenomena constituting adult education of *person.* These phenomena most specifically are of the deliberative and liberative actions of consciousing and responsible persons whereby they become transformed and empowered with vital motive for living. (304)

Others have contributed to the expanding understanding of phenomenology of adult education. Spiegelberg (1975), for instance, distinguishes among six forms or phases of phenomenology: descriptive, essential or eidetic, phenomenology of appearances, constitutive, reductive and hermeneutic. Returning to the philosophical basis of phenomenology, Spiegelberg observes that each of these unique forms is helpful in understanding elements of the social sciences. One, however, is particularly elucidating. Constitutive phenomenology is concerned with the ways in which experience becomes constituted or established in consciousness. This form of phenomenology is especially relevant in the closer examination of the historical or sociocultural phenomena, such as adult education.

Ihde (1977) and Stewart and Mickunas (1974) also suggest that the philosophical foundations of phenomenology offer new and challenging ways to view how we come to learn about, understand, and function in the world around us. Finally, van Manen (1990) recommend the phenomenological method when one wishes to understand the characteristic and essential themes of a socially significant phenomenon such as adult education.

Adult Education As Perspective Transformation

In the past two decades extensive attention has been given by adult educators to transformational learning and perspective transformation. Prominent in this area has been the work of Jack Mezirow (1991) and Mezirow and Associates (1990, 2000). Though what Mezirow and others have proposed is not a full philosophy of adult education but rather an adult learning theory, some attention to the humanistic nature of this theory is relevant in a book on the philosophy of adult education.

This theory of adult learning has its roots in cognitive psychology, psychotherapy, and critical social theory, especially that of the German philosopher, Jurgen Habermas. Although Mesirow has incorporated ideas from a wide variety of sources, a case can be made that humanistic psychology and philosophical humanism are at the basis of the theory.

According to Mezirow (1991) and Mezirow et al. (2000), we enter adulthood with a store of meanings, beliefs, and values which are the result of socialization. In adulthood we find many of these inadequate for making meaning out of human experience. In adulthood we are involved in personal meaning making, reinterpreting earlier values, beliefs, and meanings. The process of learning is precisely

the construing and appropriating of new meanings to our experiences. Adult learning involves an interpretative process in which we
make decisions "that may result in confirmation, rejection, extension, or formulation of a belief or meaning scheme or in finding that
belief or scheme presents a problem that requires further examination" (1991, 35). Learning also entails assessing reasons and justifi-
cations for our meaning schemes.

Mezirow does draw some implications for a philosophy of adult
education from his theory of adult learning. The goals of adult education "include helping learners to be self-guided, self-reflective, and
rational and helping them to establish communities of discourse in
which these qualities are honored and fostered" (1991, 224). Other
scholars have attempted to research ways in which transformational
learning can be promoted in the classroom and have dealt with the
ethical implications of attempting to bring adults to transformational
learning (Baumgartner, 2001).

Mezirow's theory of transformational learning has been criticized by a number of scholars for a lack of social critique that would
identify factors that impede learning, for focusing disproportionately
on personal learning, and for not assigning a role to social action for
transformational learning and emancipatory adult education (Clark
and Wilson, 1991; Collard and Law, 1989; Hart, 1990). Mezirow attempts to respond to these criticisms by relating the theory to adult
education for social action. Unfortunately, the theoretical bases for
the theory do not include an adequate analysis of social structures
and functions to buttress a more socially and politically oriented
adult education.

Adult Education As Transaction

Stephen Brookfield in a number of writings has argued for a
philosophy of practice in adult education which, while grounded in
humanistic principles, also draws on other philosophical traditions
such as critical theory and conceptual analysis. His concept of adult
education describes education as "a transactional drama in which
the personalities, philosophies, and priorities of the chief players
(participants and facilitators) interact continuously to influence the
nature, direction, and form of the subsequent learning" (1986, viii).

To the widely accepted humanistic principles of a respect for
participants in the teaching-learning transaction, a commitment to
collaboration in program planning, and a recognition of the importance of the educational value of life experiences, he adds the di-

mension of a critical appraisal of alternative values, attitudes, and behaviors.

In presenting his principles for a philosophy of practice, Brookfield stresses the humanistic principles of developing a sense of personal control and autonomy to be realized "in personal relationships, in sociopolitical behavior, and in intellectual judgments" (1986, 291). For Brookfield, nothing is more important for advancing the individuals' personal control and autonomy than the capacity to think critically, included in which is the recognition that all knowledge and value systems are culturally constructed (1986, 293; 1987).

In his earlier works Brookfield remained uneasily within the humanistic traditions. He espoused a philosophy of adult education that emphasized the principle of critical reflection on practice, derived from the work of John Dewey and Paulo Freire. Brookfield's emphasis on the processes of adult education, while staying clear of any distinctive social and political analysis in his earlier work, separated his work from that of the critical theorists and radical educators for whom such analysis is central to the task of adult education. In his most recent writings, to be treated in the chapter on Radical Adult Education, he moves beyond the humanistic orientation and advocates a more politically oriented philosophy of adult education.

Adult Education and the Paradoxes of Adult Learning

While he draws on many philosophical and sociological sources for his analysis, Peter Jarvis in *Paradoxes of Learning: On Becoming an Individual in Society* (1992) considers this work as fundamentally humanistic. Influenced by existentialism and critical social theorists such as Habermas, Jarvis explores various paradoxes in human learning: freedom and constraint, certainty and uncertainty, truth and falsehood, joy and sorrow. The social self develops through human learning acquired through paradoxical life and learning in society. The language and culture that we learn both shape our values and free us to shape our own values. From nonreflective learning we move to highly reflective learning which we are able to communicate to others through conscious actions since the purpose of most learning is action in the world. Although learning is shaped by our conscious interests, people have the capacity to "reflect back on their society, transcend their social environment, and demonstrate their individuality" (97).

Jarvis develops a more explicit educational philosophy when he discusses how persons grow through lifelong learning. Personal growth takes place through social interaction as described by Gabriel Marcel and Martin Buber who both noted that it is only in an open relationship with other people that reflective learning and authenticity can be fostered. Jarvis presents as a paradox of learning the contrast between the ideology which states that people are free and autonomous, and the fact that most learning is other-directed and other-controlled. He writes: "Self-directed learning is an ideological construct that mirrors much of the current thinking about an open society—but it has become fashionable in a society in which a great deal of public and private space is controlled by others" (142).

In such a situation, humanistic adult education often becomes impossible. Societal constraints also limit the capacity of individuals to achieve meaning and truth in their lives. This control operates in a special way in the world of work and the world of politics. Notwithstanding these constraints, Jarvis holds out the hope for meaningful change and even wisdom in one's life, presumably in the more private spheres of human experience.

While Jarvis's book focuses primarily on learning, it also presents some elements of a philosophy of education. Like the philosophers Rousseau and John Stuart Mill, Jarvis raises the ethical issue at the very heart of education: by what right does one impose ideas on others? He believes that educators should frequently raise the question of in whose interests they are teaching. Jarvis concludes as he began on a humanistic note: "Teaching and reflective learning and human growth and development are all facilitated in the process of genuine human interaction. Teaching is a humanistic enterprise, and only in human relationships is it possible to establish the best conditions for human growth" (245).

An Assessment of Humanistic Adult Education

Principles from humanistic philosophy and psychology have permeated the field of adult education. While Friere's radical pedagogy perhaps vies with Knowles's andragogy for theoretical popularity, educational practices grounded in humanistic philosophy far exceed the number of radical programs in the United States. When one adds to Knowles's humanistic theory of andragogy the philosophical efforts of McKenzie, Stanage, Mezirow, and Jarvis, one grasps the strong hold that the humanistic approach has on the philosophy of adult education.

One of the reasons for the popularity of humanistic adult education is its compatibility with democratic values. Education for maintaining a democratic political system becomes translated under this approach to education for the development of better individuals who will then promote a better life for all humanity. The humanistic emphasis upon the individual person as the center of the educational process reflects democracy's spirit of individualism. The humanistic approach also promotes cooperation and communication among individuals as a vehicle for interpersonal growth; cooperation is a necessity for making democracy work.

A second reason for humanistic education's hold in adult education is that unlike other levels of education, nearly all of it is voluntary. Educational activities must meet the needs of adult learners in order to survive. Practical considerations thus necessitate an emphasis upon individual needs and interests.

Indirectly, at least, humanistic adult education takes into account adult development. Humanists want to assist individuals to grow and develop toward self-actualization and toward becoming fully functioning persons. The notion of growth, development, and change is integral to much of the psychological literature on adult development. Adults are no longer viewed as finished products at the age of sixteen, eighteen, or twenty-one. Rather, adulthood is a period of change, psychologically, socially, and physiologically. Adult educators have begun to respond with activities designed to take into account adult development. As was noted earlier, one of the assumptions underlying andragogy related to meeting the needs of adults at the moment. And many of these needs are the direct outgrowth of the developmental tasks salient to the various changing stages of adulthood.

Assessing the impact of the humanistic approach on adult education is not an easy task, partly because its emphasis is less in programs than in psychological growth. That is, humanistic education is a stance or philosophical orientation toward the place of human beings in the scheme of things. Many adult educators have adopted its spirit in their approach to adult learners. The valuing of individuals, the commitment to educating the whole person—these are not readily measurable. Nevertheless, at least two programmatic components of humanistic education can be identified as important additions to adult education: (1) human development or human potential seminars, as found in the training programs of many businesses and industries, and which have found a wide audience in popular writings such as Bellah et al.'s *Habits of the Heart—Individualism and Commitment in American Life* (1985), and (2) groups and cooperative activities in settings as diverse as libraries, hospitals, factories, and schools. Self-help groups and twelve-step programs that focus on an individual's ability to overcome addiction are specific examples of this programmatic thrust.

Thus modern adult education programs in the United States testify to the impact humanistic philosophy and psychology have had on educational theory and practice. The basic principles of humanism with their primary focus upon the development of the person corresponds closely to the social and cultural values of contemporary America. Adult education programs that center on the needs and interests of the learners are indebted to a philosophy dedicated to the development of human beings .

// p.146 is blank

(STOP 10)

CHAPTER VI

RADICAL AND CRITICAL ADULT EDUCATION

Since the publication of this book in 1980, a number of factors have impacted our original conception of radical adult education. The term *radical,* while it reflects the notion of a philosophy that is concerned with challenging the status quo, has not seemed quite broad or powerful enough to capture the liberating, empowering, and transformative aspects that proponents of this orientation espouse. Neither does the term convey the strong critique of taken-for-granted assumptions and power relationships needed in order for social change to occur. The literature on radical adult education has expanded to include in addition to the various forms of Marxist analysis, two other orientations—those of critical theory and feminist theory. We have thus added "critical" to the chapter title to reflect more recent thinking stemming from the radical tradition.

This chapter will examine the radical tradition in adult education from a historical perspective. Special attention will then be given to the work of Paulo Freire, whose ideas have been influential in radical adult education throughout the world. Then the chapter will treat the influence of critical social theory in adult education as well as various forms of feminist pedagogy. Finally there will be an assessment of radical and critical adult education.

Historical Roots of Radical Adult Education

Radical educational thought stands outside the mainstream of educational philosophy. Most educational philosophies accept the given societal values and attempt to propound educational philosophies within these value structures. While progressives and humanists

attempt to utilize education to reform society, it is only the radical
critics that propose profound changes in society.

Radical educational thought flows from at least three sources.
The anarchist tradition developed in the eighteenth century and
continuing in the nintheenth and twentieth centuries has consistently opposed public education as destructive of individual autonomy.
The Marxist tradition has criticized education, especially schooling,
as a form of alienation in the modem industrial world. It sees the
overcoming of alienation as the first step in radical change. The
third tradition is represented by the Freudian Left and includes such
people as Wilhelm Reich and A. S. Neill. This tradition places its
main emphasis on changing personality traits, family structures,
and child-rearing practices as the first step in radical education. More
recently, critical social theory originating with the Frankfort School,
and radical feminism have influenced adult educators.

Though the main concern of radicals in all these traditions has
been with public schooling, many of their criticisms and proposals
are applicable to adult education. The ever-increasing institutionalization of adult education is a target for anarchist educators. Many
radical adult educators have drawn on various forms of Marxist criticism. Also, adult educators need to consider the proposals of the
radical Freudians with regard to family structures and the freedom
of the individual from repressive influences in society.

The Anarchist Tradition. The anarchist tradition in education
has been examined by Spring (1973, 1975). As a social and political
philosophy, anarchism has raised fundamental questions about the
role and nature of authority in society, and since the eighteenth
century it has questioned the very existence of state systems of
schooling and the possibility of nonauthoritarian forms of education. Educators influenced by this tradition include Paul Goodman,
Ivan Illich, and John Ohliger.

Anarchism opposes national systems of education because of its
conviction that education in the hands of the state serves the political interests of those in control. The central concern of this tradition is to preserve personal autonomy as much as possible. Francisco Ferrer, a Spanish anarchist, criticized educational systems
for conditioning students for obedience and docility (1913). An
educational system, in his view, expounded political dogmas and
attempted to shape individuals into useful citizens by removing personal autonomy and setting limits to the power of individuals. Max
Stirner (1967) contended that knowledge should not be taught because the process of absorbing knowledge turns the individual into a
learner rather than a creative person. The heart of education ac-

cording to the anarchist, should be the development of individuals able to choose their own goals and purposes free of dogmas and prejudices. The tradition also maintains that it is impossible to do this in government-sponsored educational systems.

One of the best-known proponents of radical educational philosophy was Leo Tolstoy (1967), the Russian Christian anarchist. Tolstoy made a distinction between culture and education. Culture represented the unconscious and nondeliberate transmission of knowledge and values that shaped the individual; education was the conscious and deliberate shaping of individual character and implied some form of objectionable compulsion. Tolstoy's concept of noncompulsory education was one without a planned program, where teachers taught what they wished and their courses were regulated by the demands of the students.

Certain ideas from the anarchist tradition surfaced in the educational reform movements in the 1960s and early 1970s. The emphasis on freedom and autonomy of the learner, the development of free schools, opposition to compulsory education, and the deschooling movement were, to varying degrees, inspired by anarchist principles of freedom and opposition to state control of education. As will be discussed later in this chapter, Ivan Illich's proposals for education in a convivial society and John Ohliger's opposition to compulsory adult education have connections with this anarchist tradition.

Marxist-Socialist Tradition. While the anarchist attempts to promote personal freedom and autonomy by removing education from state control, the Marxist-socialist tradition in education attempts to produce the free and autonomous person through a revolutionary change from a capitalistic political economy to a socialist form of government and economy. Marx himself did not give education an important role in the socialist revolution, for he considered it too closely tied to the 'interests of the dominant class. But such radical educators as George Counts, Theodore Brameld, and Paulo Freire have utilized Marxist ideas such as false consciousness, alienation, class struggle, and political revolution to develop a radical philosophy of education.

The first American educator who advocated a radical approach to education inspired by Marxist principles was George Counts, Professor of Education at Columbia University. In 1932, in the midst of the Depression, Counts challenged American educators to reach for political power and to lead the nation to socialism. In a famous speech before the Progressive Education Association he gave a Marxist analysis of the causes of the Depression and the social ills of the country and proposed using the schools as a means to cure these ills. To achieve these goals he urged that it was necessary to indoctrinate students about the evils of capitalism and the social values upon which it rests. For the next few years Counts's ideas were debated in journals and at conferences by outstanding American educators including John Dewey, Merle Curti, Sidney Hook, and Eduard Lindeman (Bowers 1969).

Although a number of American educators accepted Counts's analysis of the situation, they did not share his optimism that education could be an important force in bringing about the socialist society. To most educators, Counts' advocacy of indoctrination was a contradiction to the essential freedom that they desired in the educational process. Most educators shared the viewpoint of journalist Agnes de Lima (1932):

> . . . to expect teachers to lead us out of our morass is fantastic indeed. . . . A class long trained to social docility and economically protected by life tenure of office-on good behavior-is unlikely to challenge unduly the status quo. (p. 317)

An American educator who consistently maintained the Marxist-socialist position in educational philosophy was Theodore Brameld, one time professor at Boston University. In a number of works Brameld developed a reconstructionist philosophy of education. Throughout the years Brameld remained confident that education could make a significant contribution to bring about a socialist society, though he rejected the methods of indoctrination espoused by Counts. Brameld also separated himself from the progressive position on the role of the teacher for he advocated a more committed position on the part of the teacher (Brameld 1956).

In the 1960s and 1970s a number of educators, historians and social critics analyzed the American educational system according to Marxist and socialist principles. Michael Katz (1968) showed how the various educational reform movements in the history of this country failed to bring about the necessary radical changes. Educational reform according to his analysis is an attempt to avoid radical change by imposing moderate changes in structures or methods of teaching. Samuel Bowles and Herbert Gintis (1975) presented a Marxist analysis of the relationships between the school system and the capitalist society that it serves. The social criticism of Jonathan Kozol (1975) echoed a number of Marxist themes: class struggle, alienation, and revolutionary praxis. Kozol considered himself at that time a disciple of the Christian Marxist Paulo Freire.

The adult educator whose ideas are greatly formed by the Marxist tradition of radical criticism is Freire. As will be seen later in this chapter, Freire began ideologically as a Christian social democrat, and in later writings he combined this with the fundamental principles of Marxist social philosophy. To this philosophy of Marxism, Freire added a revolutionary pedagogy and philosophy of education. A number of contemporary British writers have also drawn on the Marxist analysis of society and education.

One form of Marxism that has influenced educational theory in the past three decades is the critical social theory of the Frankfurt School of Social Research. This school includes sociological work of Theodor Adorno, Hans-Georg Gadamer, Max Horkeimer, Herbert Marcuse, Erich Fromm and Jurgen Habermas. These scholars have engaged in a sustained criticism of society, especially capitalist society, since the years after the First World War. Critical social theory combines Marxism with elements of phenomenology, psychoanalysis and symbolic communication. Some common themes among critical theorists include a dialectical view of social reality in which human subjectivity is deeply involved, a rejection of a deterministic view of society, a unified view of reality that avoids a dualistic perspective, an emphasis on human liberation not only in economic but also in cultural terms, a rejection of the economic determinism of Marx, and an analysis of all forms of domination, hegemony, and cultural imperialism. A number of educators, including adult educators, have utilized these concepts to offer a sustained criticism of education in an industrialized nation.

The Freudian Left. One of the basic problems of the Marxist-socialist approach to educational change is its assumption that once people become aware of what they view as evil social structures, they will be able to bring about the necessary changes. The Freudian Left addresses itself to the problems inherent in this assumption. It points out that many persons are prevented from acting in their own self interests because of a structure of authoritarianism that is imposed from the earliest stages of child development. The solutions of the Freudian Left lie in sexual freedom, changes in family organization, and libertarian methods of childrearing and education.

The Freudian Left, represented especially by Wilhelm Reich, is critical of Freud for his conservative social philosophy. Reich felt that the result of Freudian psychoanalysis was to persuade people

to accept the given societal structures even if these were oppressive. Changes were to be made in individual consciousness and not
in societal structures and values. Reich's interest in Marxist social
thought led him to reject this position. He wanted psychology to be
concerned with changing political and social structures. Reich also
found a weakness in Marxist social analysis which he attempted to
remedy. Marx did not adequately explain why exploited workers failed
to strike out against their exploiters. For Reich the reason was psychological: a character structure of repression and authoritarianism
prevented this necessary reaction, even though individuals were
aware of their oppression. Character structures would have to be
changed through different forms of childrearing and a different type
of education. Reich analyzed the working class acceptance of fas-
cism in Europe according to these principles.

Though he had arrived at his philosophy of freedom before he
met Reich, A. S. Neill (1960), the founder of the famous British free
school Summerhill, identified a kindred spirit when he came to know
Reich. Neill saw the source of the world's problems in the repressions of children's emotional drives. He permitted no religious or
moral education in his school, where students were encouraged to
have their own sexual lives. They were free to attend class or not.
The students ran the school. For Neill, no person was good enough
to give another his or her own ideals. Believing that freedom alone
was the cure for the problem child, Neil advocated the free family in
which children were released from the internalized constraints that
come from moral discipline.

The ideas of the Freudian Left are not directly influential ideas
in adult education today; yet it is important for these ideas to be
examined because they raise important questions for the philosophical position of the radical adult educator. Radical educators at times
are rather optimistic in presuming the close connection between
knowing and acting. An analysis of psychological factors can shed
some light upon people's failure to act in what appears to be their
best interests. Reich and Neill's analyses offer, however, one possible explanation for explaining such failures to act, their lack of
freedom. It should be noted that the ideas of the Freudian Left,
however, have been assimilated into critical social theory, which is
largely a wedding of Marxist and Leftist Freudian thought.

This brief description of the radical tradition in education does
not do justice to the richness and diversity of ideas that radicals
have offered in the past three centuries. It does, however, present
the necessary intellectual background for understanding present day

radical educational thought/This dissenting tradition has been strongest in time of social and political unrest, as in the recession and the
1960s. In times of crisis, explanations are called for and new visions
are needed. The radicals are strong in both criticism and vision. In
making its criticisms and presenting its visions the radical tradition
questions the basic values, structures, and practices of society. The
radical theorists touched every area of societal life: family, schooling, work, religion, economic and political systems. While relatively
few educators actually practice out of the radical tradition, none can
afford to ignore the questions that it raises for contemporary society
and education.

Paulo Freire's Theory of Radical Conscientization

The most prominent philosopher of adult education in the radical tradition is the Brazilian educator, Paulo Freire. An exposition
and evaluation of his philosophy of education provides the example
of an educator who advocates a revolutionary pedagogy for both
developing and industrialized countries. The treatment of this revolutionary pedagogy includes the historical context of Freire's philosophy, an exposition and evaluation of his philosophy of adult
education, the educational practice of Freire's literacy program, and
a discussion of the relevance of this philosophy and practice for contemporary adult educational efforts. Extensive attention is given to
Freire because of his influential adult education theory, his valuable
method of adult education, and the wide influence he has had on
adult educators throughout the world.

An analysis of Freire's writings reveals an interesting philosophical journey. In his earliest works he was strongly influenced by a
Christian personalism that emphasized the individual in the face of
a growing technological and scientific culture. His works also exhibit many existentialist themes: freedom, intersubjectivity, authenticity, and dialogue. However, *Pedagogy of the Oppressed* (1970b)
marks a turning point in his thought. To previous ideas he assimilated phenomenology, an examination of consciousness and its various states, and Marxist thought. His writing after this time became
more radical, analytical and dialectical. A revolutionary rhetoric characterized writings from this period as he moved from the advocacy
of social democracy to a plea for the Marxist socialist revolution in
oppressed countries. In later writings Freire clarified issues in his
thought and engaged in dialogues with prominent educators
throughout the world.

Freire's Basic Philosophical Principles

Freire theory of pedagogy cannot be understood apart from his philosophical principles. He claims that his

> pedagogy cannot do without a vision of man and of the world. It formulates a scientific humanist conception that finds its expression in a dialogical praxis in which the teachers and learners together, in the act of analyzing a dehumanizing reality, denounce it while announcing its transformation in the name of the liberation of man. (1970b, 4)

Many important elements in Freire's general and educational philosophy are found in these words: a vision of humans and their world, dialogic praxis, a teacher-learner relationship, social analysis, human liberation, and the Marxist concept of denouncing and announcing worldviews and consciousness.

Freire's philosophy begins with a *philosophy or vision of the human being*. Freire contrasts at some length in his writings the consciousness and the action of humans with the consciousness and action of animals. Since humans are not immersed in reality in some determined manner, they know that they know and know that they are able to change their situation and environments. Because persons can do these things, they are subjects rather than objects. For Freire, humans can lift themselves to a higher level of consciousness and become subjects to the extent of their intervention in society, their reflection on this intervention, and their commitment to this engagement in society.

Humans differ from animals also in their capacity to create both culture and history. In the context in which Freire worked it was important for him to make learners cognizant of their ability to change the material and social conditions of their lives. Existential thought provided Freire with the important distinction between merely existing and really living. From Marxist/existentialist thought Freire adopted the concept of the human being as unfinished and always in the process of becoming. Marxist thought also provided the critical concept of human existence as the task of praxis since humans give meaning to history and culture, indeed create history and culture, by combining reflective activity with actions.

Freire's vision of the human being is powerful in its optimism. Few philosophers have presented as forceful an image in modern times//True humanization takes place in the world only when each person becomes conscious of the social forces working upon him or her, reflects upon these forces, and becomes capable of transforming the world. To be human is to be an actor in the world and to seek to guide one's own destiny. To be free, to be an actor in the world, means knowing one's identity and realizing how one has been shaped in one's social world and environment.

For Freire the opposite of humanization is dehumanization or oppression. The condition of oppression is what Freire calls the culture of silence. The culture of silence can come from either ignorance or education. Freire judged that Brazilian peasants were in a culture of silence because they were kept in ignorance of the true conditions of their poverty. For Freire assimilating the peasants into the social system that produces poverty was a form of oppressive education.

In discussing Freire's concept of humanization and oppression, we have moved from Freire's philosophy of human nature to his *philosophy and vision of the world*. Freire's view of social reality is decidedly Marxist. A dialectical historical process shapes social reality. Since humans are part of this process, they can bring about significant changes in the world by the exercise of praxis, action with reflection. In their relationship to the world, humans recognize it as a place filled with problems or contradictions. The human task is to break through these problems and to act to change the social reality in which one lives. Freire's analysis of the Third World concluded that it was characterized by social, political, and economic oppression. For Freire, these ideas and values are in conflict or contradiction with freedom, responsibility, and true humanization. Thus the various forms of oppression constitute the concrete problems or contradictions that are the task of his revolutionary pedagogy.

A third area in Freire's basic philosophical position is his Marxist and phenomenological *theory of human knowing or consciousness* in which thinking and knowing are dependent upon history and culture. The social reality in which we live shapes our ideas and our thinking. Coming to know for Freire is the process through which individuals become aware of objective reality and of their own knowledge of this reality. He contends that true knowledge of reality, which he terms "conscientization," penetrates to what reality really is because it is connected with praxis or reflective activity. Freire is true to the phenomenological position in attempting to avoid both materialism and idealism:

In reality consciousness is not just a copy of the Real, nor is the Real only a capricious construction of consciousness. It is only by way of an understanding of the dialectical unity, in which we find solidarity between subjectivity and objectivity, that we can get away from the subjectivist error as well as the mechanical error. And then we must take into account the role of consciousness or of the "conscious being" in the transformation of reality. (1972, 5)

Freire's discussion of his theory of knowledge is not just an exercise in epistemology, for it has for him political and educational implications. While the objectivist or materialist error leads to treating persons as things or objects, the subjectivist or idealist error leads to the assumption that the future will change when individuals change their consciousness. What both of these errors miss, according to Freire, is the transforming role of human reflection and action.

The Marxist influence on Freire's theory of conscientization is most evident in his demonstration of the relationships between levels of individual consciousness and levels of development and social organization. Individual liberation and societal liberation are closely tied in his theory. Freire (1973) employs an analogy from grammar to describe states of human and social consciousness. The lowest level of consciousness is *intransitive consciousness*, found in the culture of silence of peasant societies. At this level, where individuals are preoccupied with meeting their most elementary needs, they are characterized by the near absence of historical consciousness. Immersed in a one-dimensional oppressive present, peasants cannot comprehend the forces that have shaped their lives. Individuals at this level ascribe their plight to their own faults or to supernatural causes. Societies in which this consciousness is present are closed and oppressive.

Semi-intransitivity or magical consciousness is the second level of consciousness, one that is prevalent in the emerging societies of the Third World. Self-depreciation is a common characteristic of this consciousness, for individuals have internalized the negative images that the dominant culture ascribes to them. This consciousness is also marked by excessive emotional dependency. To be is to be under someone, to depend on him or her. This form of consciousness often expresses itself in defensive and therapeutic magic.

Freire calls his third level of consciousness *naive-transitiveness*. It is transitive because while people begin to experience reality as a problem they still have not fully emerged from the culture of silence. Although such persons begin to apply pressure and criticism to the dominant groups in society, nevertheless, their consciousness remains oppressed and susceptible to populist manipulation by power elites by force, propaganda, slogans, or dehumanizing utilization of technology. The advantage of this level of consciousness is that individuals begin to sense that they have some control over their lives. The danger is that they can still be pacified by receiving certain political and economic privileges.

The highest level of consciousness for Freire is *critical consciousness*, achieved through the process of conscientization. This level is marked by depth in the interpretation of problems, self-confidence in discussions, receptiveness, and refusal to shirk responsibility. The quality of discourse is dialogical since persons at this level can scrutinize their own thoughts and recognize proper causal and circumstantial correlations. Conscientization for Freire entails a radical denunciation of dehumanizing structures, accompanied by an announcement of a new reality to be created. It entails a rigorous and rational critique of the ideology that supports these structures and is brought about not through intellectual efforts alone but through praxis, the authentic union of action and reflection.

Conscientization for Freire is a social activity in which individuals communicate through dialogue with others about how they experience reality. For Freire (1970c)

> to know, which is always a process, implies a dialogical situation. There is not, strictly speaking, "I think," but "we think." It is not "I think" which constitutes "we think," but on the contrary, it is "we think" that makes it possible for me to think. (1)

This concept of knowing or conscientization has implications for Freire's theory of pedagogy where dialogue and social activity are essential to the learning process.

The final major area of Freire's general philosophy is his *theory of values*. His treatment of values makes explicit themes that are already implicit in the other areas of Freire's general philosophy. The highest human goal is humanization to be achieved through a process of liberation. This is a social goal and thus to be achieved in cooperation with others. Authentic human liberation entails the permanent transformation of social structures of a given society. Freire judges that in many situations only revolutionary political action can bring about authentic liberation..

The means of achieving personal and social liberation for Freire are dialogue and praxis//The role of dialogue in politics, social change, and education is expounded again and again in his writings. Dialogue demands the attitudes of trust, faith, humility, willingness to risk, and love. The authentic praxis that Freire advocates implies a commitment to Utopia. By this Freire seems to mean an orientation to change and a commitment to the future that demands a rigorous investigation of the ideological myths that sustain existing ideologies and social structures. He puts great faith in science as a force in demythologizing religious, political, and economic myths, but does not greatly develop how science accomplishes this.

In some writings Freire (1985) put emphasis on the value of religion as a force in human liberation from oppressive social structures. As a believing and committed Christian, he expounded a view of God that attempted to refute Marxist criticism of religion as a reactionary and oppressive force in society. He placed himself in the prophetic religious tradition that denounces evil social structures and calls believers to work for change in human society. In Latin America where Freire's ideas took root, left wing Catholics reached ideological agreements with Marxists on many areas relating to social and political action. Freire identified himself with a Latin American theology of liberation that attempts to emphasize the prophetic and activist elements in the Christian tradition (Elias 1994).

Some Criticisms of Freire's Philosophy. Freire's philosophy of the human being, though idealist and utopian, has certain weaknesses. In his earlier writings, Freire rarely gets beyond generalities or abstractions in developing his philosophy of the human being. His view of the human does not adequately present the dark side of humanity, one of deepest weaknesses of the Marxist and utopian vision.

Though Freire's theory of conscientization is impressive, it still suffers from a number of weaknesses. Freire has valiantly attempted to avoid the idealist position, but it appears that he does not succeed. His theory of conscientization depends on some sort of transcendent view of reality through which individuals come to see what is real and authentic. It all comes down to the dominant classes with their distorted view of reality and conscientized individuals with their view of the reality that really is.

Freire's idealist view of knowledge is also apparent where the connection between thought and action becomes blurred. Freire seems to assume that people involved in the circles of culture can fashion a new reality that will replace the old reality that they have come to denounce. He at times seems to assume that persons' knowledge of their true interests guarantees participation in activity to achieve these interests. There is also the real possibility that people involved in conscientization efforts might even become more entrenched in their thinking once they realize the full impact of oppression in their lives.

Freire's Educational Principles

Freire is a radical critic of traditional education. For Freire, traditional education equals banking education in which students receive, file, and store deposits. Knowledge in this view is seen as a gift bestowed on students by the teacher. This type of education, according to Freire, offends the freedom and autonomy of students and domesticates them since it emphasizes the transfer of existing knowledge to passive objects who must memorize and repeat this knowledge. For Freire this type of education is a form of violence, for in imposing curricula, ideas, and values, it submerges the consciousness of the students and produces an alienated consciousness since students are not actually involved in a real act of knowing, but are rather given a ready-made view of social reality. Furthermore in banking education learners become objects of the educational process, worked upon by teachers to achieve goals not of their own choosing. The aim of this education in Freire's view is not to understand the self but to change the individual according to alien goals.

In place of the traditional banking form of education, Freire offers a *libertarian, dialogic, and problem-posing education.* Cultural action for freedom is the expression that Freire uses to designate the educational process in which a group of persons, through dialogue, come to realize the concrete oppressive situation in which they live, the reasons for this situation, and possible solutions to their problems. In order for their action to be authentic, participants must be free to create a curriculum along with a teacher. Freire's problem posing education is thus based upon respect, communication, and solidarity.

Freire's dialogic education is problem posing in that it begins with an investigation of the cultural situation of the learners. This cultural situation provides the curriculum of problems that are to be discussed in the educational process. As the result of dialogue on these problems, teachers and learners alike arrive at a decision to become involved in concrete actions to solve these problems. The investigation of the culture of the learners includes discovering how their history and culture are conditioned by ideas, beliefs, myths, art, science, manners, tastes, and political preferences.

Though Freire emphasizes the importance of dialogue and equality between teacher and learners, he also gives a positive role to the *teacher* in the educational process. Notwithstanding this role, Freire insists that teachers must also be students and that students can also be teachers. The teacher can present material for consideration so long as he or she is open to clarifications and modifications. Teachers can suggest but not determine and impose the themes that serve to organize the content of the dialogues. The Freire method also utilizes expert knowledge from various social science disciplines in various stages of the educational process. Although Freire is thus not opposed to the direct presentation of views by teachers and experts, he is very concerned that this not be done in a purely didactic manner and that the heart of the curricular process begins and continues along lines of the problems that learners raise in their own situation.

For Freire authentic education is unquestionably *political action*. For him there is no such thing as neutral education. Education is either for domestication or for liberation. However, any theory of education that strongly advocates social and political purposes opens itself to the charge of indoctrination and manipulation. The situation in which Freire worked in Brazil and Chile made him sensitive to these charges, at least to the degree of avoiding conflict with conservatives. Freire answered charges of indoctrination by contending that his goal was to get people to learn by having them challenge the concrete reality of their lives as presented in their own words and in pictorial codifications of these words. He argues that in dialogic education a view of social reality was not imposed on participants, but by discussing a problematic situation participants were led to see the conditions of oppression under which they live. Through discussion they also begin to see that the present situation is not determined but can be changed.

Freire's educational philosophy is not only political but it is also a revolutionary pedagogy. Freire considered his main contribution to a theory of revolution his emphasis on the dialogical nature of revolutionary action, according to which leaders should be in constant dialogue with the people at all points of the revolution. He wrote *Pedagogy* (1970b) to defend the eminently pedagogical nature of the revolutionary action. He contended that

> critical and liberating dialogue, which presupposes action, must be carried on with the oppressed at whatever stage of their struggle for liberation. The content of that dialogue can and should vary in accordance with historical situations and the level at which they can perceive reality. (52)

Though Freire advocates dialogic education as part of revolutionary action, he is realistic enough to make a number of exceptions. Freire has great difficulty making his hero, Che Guevara, an advocate of dialogical revolutionary action. He quotes the revolutionary leader's words:

> Mistrust: at the beginning, do not trust your own shadow, never trust friendly peasants, informers, guides, or contact men. Do not trust anything or anybody until a zone is completely liberated. (1970b, 169)

Freire also denied the revolutionaries' need to dialogue with the former oppressors. He agreed with Guevara's admonition to punish the deserter from the revolutionary group for reasons of cohesion and discipline of the group. He also agreed with the guerrilla leader in his nontolerance of those who were not ready to accept the conclusion that the revolution is essential. Freire's effort to maintain the essentially dialogical and educational aspect of revolutionary action may have been compromised in light of these notable exceptions.

Theory and Practice in Radical Adult Education: Paulo Freire's Method

Freire developed his educational method or practice for the purpose of teaching literacy. In later writings he extended the use of this method to post-literacy or political education. The best description of this method is found in *Education for Critical Consciousness* (1973), a work that Freire wrote while in prison during the early years of his exile.

Literacy Campaign. Freire's literacy campaign began with *Stage One, the Study of the Context.* An interdisciplinary team studied the context in which the people live in order to determine the common vocabulary and the problems that confront people in that area. A maximum amount of participation by the people was sought at this level. People's thinking, aspirations, and problems were discussed through informal conversations. The team faithfully recorded the words and the language of the people. Since Freire's method was deeply contextual, he developed different lists of words and problems for rural and urban areas; and, after his move to Chile, he had to develop new lists of words. Freire decided to elicit words from the people themselves because he was against the practice of supplying primers that utilized common words. Freire contends that words should come from the people and not be imposed on them though the use of primers.

Stage II was The Selection of Words from the Discovered Vocabulary. From the words investigated, the team chose words that were most charged with existential and relevant meaning. Freire was interested not only in the typical expressions of the people but also in words that had major emotional content for them. He called these words *generative* because of their power to generate other words. Freire had various criteria for his choice of generative words for his literacy training. The first criterion is the capacity of the words to include the basic sounds of the Portuguese or Spanish language. The words of these languages are based on syllables with little variation in vocalic sounds and with a minimum of combinations of syllables. Freire discovered that sixteen to twenty words sufficed to cover all the sounds of the language.

The second criterion for the choice of generative words is that the vocabulary, when organized, would enable participant to move from simple letters and sounds to more complex ones. Freire in this way ensured success for the method by providing a sense of accomplishment at the earlier stages of the training. With the basic words as a point of departure, participants could discover syllables, letters, and specific difficulties with syllables in their own idiom. The words chosen, if truly generative, should thus serve as starting points for the discovery of new words.

The third and most important criterion for a word to be chosen as a generative word is its capacity to confront the social, cultural, and political reality in which people live. For Freire the words have to suggest and mean something important for participants; they must provide both mental and emotional stimulation. For example, some of the words chosen for use in the state of Rio de Janeiro were: *favela*-slum; *terreno*-plot of land; *trabaho*-work; *salario*-salary; *governo*-govemment; *manqué*-swamp (also the zone of prostitution in Rio); and *riquezza*-wealth. Such words provoked discussions on pressing problems in the lives of the people: poverty, property rights, and distribution, the meaning and value of work, just wages, the power of government over their lives, the evils of prostitution on a personal and social level, and inequities in the distribution of wealth.

Stage III was The Actual Process of Literary Training. In Brazil this included a *motivation session* in which the learners analyzed the concept of culture. (In Chile Freire incorporated these sessions into the literacy training itself for he found that the Chileans were less interested in this type of discussion.) In these sessions the group coordinator showed pictures without words. The purpose of doing this was to provoke among the participants some sort of debate and discussion about the notions of human nature, world, nature, the distinction between nature and culture, differences between humans and animals, human culture, and patterns of human behavior. A further purpose was the development of group consciousness where illiterates would actually view themselves as engaged in the process of learning and reflecting. The process of conscientization began with these sessions.

The team then proceeded to the *development of teaching material for each situation to be analyzed.* These were of two types: a set of cards or slides that showed the breaking down of words into their syllables and a set of cards that depict situations related to the words and designed to evoke certain images in participants. These pictures were designed to stimulate thinking about the situations that the words imply. Freire referred to this process of developing images of concrete realities as codification. Through various pictures, situations from the lives of the people, such as poverty, were codified or presented in pictorial form.

Freire gave certain guidelines for these codifications. They must be neither too clear nor too vague. If they were too clear, there would be the danger of imposing particular views on participants. If they were too vague, they would serve not as stimulations for thought but as puzzles or enigmas to be solved. This creative use of images or codifications was a distinctive aspect of Freire's method. The codifications were not just aids in the teaching process; they were at the heart of the educational process because they initiated and stimulated the process of critical thinking.

The actual *literacy training,* or what Freire called *decodification,* included sessions built around words and pictures. For example, the word *favela*-slum-was printed with a picture of a slum in the background. The participants then broke down the codified whole, both word and picture. They also discussed the existential situation of the slum and the relationship between the word *favela* and the reality it signifies. Then a slide was projected with only the word *favela,* which as a generative word is now separated into its syllables: *fa-ve-la.* The family of the first syllable was shown: *fa, fe, fi, fo, fu.* This was repeated with the remaining syllables. The participants were then encouraged to create other words using these syllables and their families. When the second generative word was shown, the learners created other words using syllables from both words. From knowing five or six words, participants began to write brief notes. At the same time they continued to discuss and analyze critically the real context represented in the codifications.

When Freire was still director of the National Literacy Program in Brazil, he planned a post-literacy campaign for those who had already passed through the first stage of literacy training. He was never able to institute this program because of the military coup in 1964. Freire utilized this part of his method in Chile. *Pedagogy of the Oppressed* (1970b) is a further development of this post-literacy phase.

Paulo Freire and Adult Education

The educational philosophy and method of Paulo Freire arose in concrete historical circumstances as a method and then a philosophy to bring oppressed people to both literacy and political consciousness. It was an attempt to democratize the culture of Brazil and later of Chile. The method presents both a theory and a method for cultural and political change. People in many countries of the world have adapted this method to literacy education with or without its political purposes.

Illiteracy is a problem that is not restricted to the countries of the Third World. Adults in many countries do not learn to read and write. The use of Freire's method in literacy education has added some new dimensions. Literacy education begins with the words, language, and idioms of the students. Literacy education is closely connected with the cultural and political life of the students. Since illiterates in most countries belong predominantly to the lower classes, the cultural and political dimensions of Freire's literacy education are applicable to them.

Freire calls his educational theory and method a "pedagogy of the oppressed." Educators have found his method relevant in other situations where actual oppression exists. Shaull (1970), in his foreword to the English edition of *Pedagogy of the Oppressed,* commented that

> if we take a closer look, we may discover that Freire's methodology, as well as his educational philosophy are as important for us as for the dispossessed in Latin America. Their struggle to become free subjects and to participate in the transformation of their society is similar, in many ways, to the struggle not only of blacks and Mexican-Americans but also of middle class people in this country. The sharpness

and intensity of that struggle in the developing world may well provide us with new insights, new models, and new hope as we face our own situation. (10)

Freire's philosophy and methodology has relevance for any group that is concerned with such issues as oppression, liberation, consciousness raising, and community political and social action. Freire's Institute in Geneva, for example, attempted to apply the principles of conscientization to the women's liberation movement in two booklets, *Liberation of Women: To Change the World and Re-Invent Life* (1974), and *Toward a Woman's World* (1975). It is notable that bell hooks (1994), an African American educator and a radical feminist, drew inspiration from Freire's writings.

Besides its relevance for literacy education and the education of the oppressed in our society, the real relevance of Freire's philosophy and methodology lies in its questioning of two basic educational assumptions. The first of these is the presumed neutrality of education. In Western educational thought education is often regarded as the public transmission of neutral bits of information about the world. What is taught is viewed as devoid of any ideological content. In Freire's analysis of the relationship between education and culture, it is culture that produces education and uses it for its own self-perpetuation because the assumptions of the culture are contained in the educational process. Education is clearly non-neutral and value laden. An example of this non-neutrality is our "discovery" of the treatment of blacks, women, and Native Americans in the history of the United States, groups that were generally excluded from historical accounts in order to promote a particular view of the past.

The second assumption against which Freire struggled was the relative status of teacher and student and the psychological effects that existing methods have on students. His criticism of traditional education as banking education was an attempt to deal with this problem. Knowledge for Freire is power, something political. In getting a person to know or learn what the teacher wants him or her to learn, the teacher exercises power and control over the student. Education and other forms of socialization have been used to indoctrinate groups of people into specific attitudes and behavior: women to accept an inferior role; the poor to blame themselves for their poverty; the unemployed to see themselves as deficient; groups of people to accept arbitrary religious authorities; and masses of people to accept the need to produce and consume. When education is thus domesticating, people are prevented from thinking their own thoughts, arriving at their own decisions, having the consciousness that change is possible.

It was Freire's contention that education can be for liberation only if equality were established between teachers and students. The lives, experiences, insights, questions, and problems of students must form the center of the educational process. Freire did not call for a reversal of roles between teachers and students but rather advocated teachers and students together initiating and sustaining the process of dialogue on issues that are real in the lives of both. Education in this sense is liberating not only in the sense of consciousness raising but also because of its connection with action; knowing, for Freire, is inseparable from deciding to do something because of knowledge. To preserve, to change, to destroy, to fully experience are possible actions one might take as a result of knowing something.

Paulo Freire was probably the most known and influential adult educator in the second half of the twentith century. His influence has been worldwide. Those desiring a clearer explanation of Freire's actual literacy process will find his *Pedagogy in Process* (1977) a satisfactory introduction. A valuable collection of his political and religious writings is found in *The Politics of Education* (1985). Many of his recent ideas are found in books that reproduce conversations with scholars and practitioners (Freire & Faundez 1989; Freire & Macedo 1987; Shor & Freire 1987). Useful studies on Freire include McClaren (1993; 1994) and Elias (1994).

The Deschooling Movement and Adult Education: Illich and Ohliger

The late 1960s and early 1970s saw the emergence of a radical approach to educational reform, based to a degree on anarchist principles. The intellectual leader of this movement was Ivan Illich, the founder of the Center for Intercultural Documentation (CIDOC), in Cuernavaca, Mexico. In numerous articles and books Illich proposed the elimination of schools from society as the necessary condition for freeing people from their addiction to manipulative and oppressive institutions. Illich's criticism and rejection of schooling was based not so much on its failures as on its central position in maintaining over-industrialized and over-consumerized society. Illich's ideas were extended into the field of adult education by John Ohliger, a professor of adult education and founder of Basic Choices, a Midwest Center for Clarifying Political and Social Options.

 (STOP 11)

R p-167

Though Illich was foremost a radical social critic, his philosophical views on education and learning were at the heart of his thinking in the 1970s. The type of learning that Illich espoused was one that promoted human freedom, equality, and close personal relationships. True learning is learning in which a person freely consents to participate. For Illich no one has the right to interfere in the learning of others without their consent. He contended, in addition, that most learning is not the result of teaching, but rather is gathered incidentally as one participates in life. The learning that persons cannot gather incidentally from life and things, they can easily appropriate from a skill master, a peer, or books, and other learning instruments.

For Illich, then, the fundamental aspect of learning was that it is freely chosen learning from life, both from things and from persons. Compulsory learning is always harmful for the individual and for society. Illich made rather extensive claims for the freedom to learn which he espoused. For him freedom to learn would result in immeasurable re-creation among people who share an issue that for them is socially important. Free learning would enable people to be spontaneous, independent, and interrelated (1970, 52): This type of learning would increase persons' poetic ability, their power to endow the world with personal meaning, and their creative energies (1973, 60 ff).

Illich did not fail to propose alternative arrangements for the convivial society that he envisioned. He advocated the establishment of four classes of learning networks. The first network would provide access to educational objects such as books, radios, microscopes and television. A second network would be a *skill exchange* wherein students who wish to master a skill could contact a master who would demonstrate it for the learner. The third network was *peer matching* on the basis of common interests, to be accomplished through computers. The fourth and final network was a *system of independent educators* who would pursue jointly determined, but difficult, tasks. It is interesting to note that these networks have become a reality in today's world of education, though they have not replaced educational institutions.

Illich's purpose in proposing these networks was to present educational alternatives. He contended that these networks would avoid institutionalizing the value of learning and at the same time would make learning both free and incidental. Though Illich's description of his networks shows imagination and boldness, there also appears to be a certain simplicity in his expectations for them. He made the education of all persons sound rather simple when he described it in terms of access to things and people. Illich was no doubt right in arguing for a breakdown of the excessive bureaucratization of education. But his concrete proposals were mere skeletons with a minimum of muscle.

Illich proposals were widely debated in the 1970s. The criticism of Jonathon Kozol is significant for in many ways he was sympathetic to Illich's ideas and visited Illich's center in Cuernavaca on a number of occasions. Kozol (1972) confessed that on returning to the Boston ghetto, he was less impressed with Illich's views. He wrote that

> it is a luxury at 2,000 miles distance to consider an educational experience that does not involve credentials or curriculum, or long-term sequential learning. In immediate terms, in cities such as Boston and New York, it is unwise and perhaps destructive to do so. Instead, we must face up to the hard truth that these credentials and measured areas of expertise and certified ability constitute the irreducible framework of our labor and struggle. (33)

Kozol's main point is that millions of people in the cities of the United States are without the survival skills that Illich contended could be picked up incidentally. Kozol learned from experience that both adults and children in our society desperately needed these survival skills.

Twenty-six years after Kozol's critique, Collins (1998) "reappraises" the contribution Illich made and points out how his views can be instructive to educators today:

> The major insights of Illich's project . . . remain relevantly provocative for a critical theory and practice of education. . . . Illich highlights the ways in which our institutions and conventional approaches to education and the provision of social services are failing ordinary men and women. His critique of the schools extends to society as a whole. From this viewpoint all of society is a vast school. (28)

"A voice crying in the wilderness" might be the best way to describe the efforts of professor John Ohliger to apply the ideas of Freire and Illich to adult education in the United States. In numerous articles and talks, Ohliger alleged that more and more adult education institutions define people as inadequate, insufficient, lacking, and incomplete. Over many years he kept a careful watch over the number of courses that adults were required to take by law, regulation, or pressure. His enumeration of the groups involved in compulsory adult education is extensive:

> traffic offenders and judges; parents of delinquents and public school teachers; illiterates on welfare; nurses; pharmacists; physicians; optometrists; nursing home administrators; firemen; policemen, dentists, psychiatrists; dieticians; podiatrists; preachers; veterinarians; many municipal, state provincial, and federal civil servants; employees of all types pressured into taking courses, classes, joining sensitivity training or organizational development groups; and of course the military, where most, if not all adult education is compulsory. (1974, 21)

The institutionalization of adult education was the chief target of Ohliger's criticism. Compulsory adult education had become pervasive in the health professions. Adult education had become more embedded into the structure of the schooling establishment. Adult degrees, external degrees, and open learning for adults are ways that the educational establishment has developed for making education a commodity for thousands of adults. Ohliger viewed the UNESCO book *Learning To Be* as dangerous in preferring official knowledge or learning over the personal or experiential learning that a person gains incidentally through mere living. Ohliger closely echoed Illlich when he asked,

> As we seem to be moving toward a society in which adults are told more and more that they must consume official knowledge in lifelong learning, is it any wonder that we say that adult education is becoming an oppressive force that is taking over people's lives? (9)

In his proposals for the practice of adult education, Ohliger showed his indebtedness to both Freire and Illich. He briefly described three types of adult education that educators have to choose from. The first form takes place within institutions of adult education. Here the task is to loosen and resist the economic and bureaucratic controls that stifle educators. A second form of adult education takes place outside the establishment, or at its fringes. Here Freire's approach can be helpful in working with individuals and groups that are moving toward awareness of political and economic oppression. The third path is cultural, and it involves

> living/learning as individuals, in small groups, or new communities as examples of, or as seeds for, a future society in which what is now called less will be recognized as more. Here is where the ideas of Ivan Illich's American colleague Everett Reimer, would be worthwhile for adult educators. (1974, 101)

In linking Ohliger's radical ideas to the more recent critical social perspective, Collins (1998) points out that by Ohliger's "asking whether lifelong education is really about lifelong schooling from cradle to grave, . . . a moral and a political dimension" was brought to the discourse around lifelong learning:

> From a critical, rather than a merely taken-for-granted perspective, this discourse gains relevance to the extent that it acknowledges the prevailing inequalities in the distribution of knowledge, the relationship of knowledge acquisition to power, and the innate capacities of ordinary men and women to determine their own education and that of their children. (137)

The ideas of Illich and Ohliger, though intriguing, have not found many adherents among adult educators. The reason for this will become clearer in the overall evaluation of the impact of radical adult education on this field in this country.

Radical Adult Education from a Marxist Perspective

Radical adult education remains a strong force in Great Britain. A valuable presentation of this orientation is found in Jane Thompson's (1980) edited collection. Working from a basically Marxist orientation and influenced by the new sociology of education, Thompson argues for a form of adult education committed to a radical reorganization of society. The intellectual resources of the contributors in this collection include Marx; Antonio Gramsci, the Italian Marxist; Pierre Bourdieu, the French sociologist; Basil Bernstein, a British sociologist; and Paulo Freire.

The contributors to this collection are critical of approaches to adult education which they term liberal progressive and which are associated with R. S. Peters, Paul Hirst, Richard Dearden, K. H. Lawson, and R. W. K. Patterson, all influential British philosophers of education. This tradition is critiqued for restricting education to purely educational matters and not providing it with a social and political purpose. Liberal progressive education includes liberal adult education which is viewed by the radical educators as of some value but ultimately irrelevant to the lives of many adults in Britain and immaterial to progressive ventures such as education for the disadvantaged, arts workshops, community development, and workers' education. The authors raise questions about adult education in Britain with regard to the allocation of resources, its institutional forms, the content, and the processes, as well as the nature of relationships between teachers and students.

Sallie Westwood (1980) proposes "that adult education be reconceptualized as a cultural field in which the cultural competence of the working class is as valid as that of the middle class" (44). This can be done, she argues, by analyzing the role of adult education in relation to advanced capitalism in order to offset the middle-class bias of the field. Nel Keddie (1980) contends that adult education's claim to distinctiveness is based on the ideology of individualism which it shares with initial education. This ideology results from an undue reliance on behaviorist and psychological analyses of teaching and learning. Keddie calls for a critical examination of current adult education practices while asserting that the main problems in the field are not with the adults who do not come, but with the nature of the adult education which is offered. She concludes her insightful essay:

> The issue is not whether individuals have needs nor whether they should be met but how those needs are socially and politically constituted and understood, how they are articulated and whose voice is heard. Adult education responds to the collective voice of individualism, but it has in a large measure failed to identify or to identify with the needs of those who reject the premises on which individualism is based. (64)

In addition to Thompson's and Westwood's books, Inkster's (1985) *The Steam Intellect Societies* also draws on Marxist thought. This book is an edited volume about the Industrial Revolution and the resultant educational innovations designed to bring knowledge in science and technology to the average working person. In particular it is a history of mechanics institutes which first appeared in Britain in the 1820s and spread with industrialization to other parts of the world. Chapter authors situate the mechanics institutes within technical training and adult education. The impact of industrialization, or the "steam intellect," in terms of culture and class is discussed in chapters such as "Mechanics Institute and Working Class Culture: Exhibition Movements, 1830-1840s," "Polarised Culture and Steam Intellect: A Case Study of Liverpool and its Region, Circa 1820-1850s," and "Mechanics Institute and the State."

Youngman's *Adult Education and Socialist Pedagogy* (1986) attempts to advance a socialist, Marxist framework for guiding adult education practice worldwide. In more explicit terms than Inskster, Youngman states that capitalism presents obstacles to social justice and educational equality. In addition to chapters on the economic and political context of adult education and on Marxist theory and its relevance to adult learning, Youngman devotes a chapter each to a critique of traditional learning theories and to Freire's pedagogy. He considers, but ultimately rejects Freire's pedagogy as a basis for restructuring adult education. Freire's philosophy and pedagogy, Youngman feels, is too eclectic to be useful, for "if a capitalist corporation and a socialist teacher can both refer to the same source of ideas, then obviously that source is deeply equivocal" (1986, 190). What Youngman proposes instead is a socialist pedagogy that has the dual aims of challenging "the ideology and culture of capitalism," and developing "the general knowledge and technical expertise necessary to reorganise production and society in a fully democratic way" (1986, 197). To this end he offers nine philosophical principles of a Marxist approach, and six pedagogical principles derived from a Marxist theoretical framework. Youngman's thoughtful critique and clear writing style result in this book being a substantive contribution to the literature representative of a radical Marxist perspective.

In 2000, Youngman published *The Political Economy of Adult Education and Development*. In this book he critiques the theoretical framework of his earlier work as "unevenly developed, partly because the book's focus was on pedagogical practices rather than structural analysis" (42). Using a Marxist political economy approach, Youngman analyzes the main competing theories of development including modernization, dependency, neoliberal, and people-centered or populist approaches which include feminism, environmentalism, and ethnoculturalism. It is his contention that different development theories and strategies impact the work of adult educators in

developing countries. Using a Marxist political economy lens, in separate chapters Youngman analyzes the relationship between imperialism, aid and adult education, social inequality and adult education, and finally, the state, civil society, and adult education. The
"fundamental" question that he addresses is "what kind of adult education for what kind of development?" (246).

In another recent contribution to this perspective in adult education, Holst (2002) argues for a reassessment of the Marxist tradition and its value to adult education. He explores the linkages between social movements, civil society and radical adult education.
With the rise of new social movements, which "do not directly operate in the realm of the economy, nor do they try to overthrow the
state," theoreticians have had to "[rejuvenate] the concept of civil
society to understand the place of new social movements in society"
(16). Holst weaves an analysis of civil society, class struggle, social
movements (old and new), and capitalism with adult education scholars' understanding of Freire, Hegel, Gramsci, and Marx. Holst is
concerned that new social movements championing feminist,
antiracist, sexual and environmental issues might lose sight of the
working-class struggle against capitalism and the state apparatus.

The Italian Marxist and founding member of the Italian Com-
munist Party Antonio Gramsci has also had influence in radical adult
education, especially in England and Europe. Gramsci was fundamentally a journalist who saw the value of education in bringing
about social and political change. He adopted the slogan "Educate
yourselves because we will need all our intelligence. Rouse yourselves because we will need all your enthusiasm. Organize yourselves because we will need all your strength." (Gramsci 1995, 122)
Gramsci's valuable ideas are found in his prison notebooks and letters to friends. These writings are fragmentary and thus open to
many interpretations.

In his analysis of education, Gramsci made extensive use of the
term hegemony, the condition in which society's ideas, structures,
and actions are dominated by a single class. Although ordinary people
view social conditions as preordained, in fact they are constructed
and controlled by powerful elites. Schools and other educational institutions reinforce the hegemony of dominant classes. Like Freire,
Gramsci also believed that education has the power to challenge
this hegemony.

Freire's concept of conscientization is an echo of Gramsci's view
of education, which Freire cites in his work. For him subordinated
groups must discover themselves by looking critically at their cul-

ture. One can take action only after people become fully aware of their situation. Like Freire, Gramsci used discussion groups to promote educational dialogue. His goal was to develop a group of organic intellectuals of the working class. He describes his educational methods as "the detailed work of discussing and investigating problems, work in which everybody contributes, in which everybody is master and disciple." (Gramsci, 1971, 75). The close connection between Gramsci and Freire has been skillfully explored by Peter Mayo (1999) and John Holst (2002). Similarities also exist between Gramsci's theory and the transformative learning of Mezirow and critical thinking of Brookfield.

Critical Social Theory and Adult Education

The main architect of critical theory who has influenced adult educators is Jurgen Habermas, a German philosopher. Habermas sought to move beyond a Marxist social analysis and in so doing split with the famous "Frankfort School" of social theorists (Welton 1993a; 1993b; 1995). As noted in the section on Humanistic Adult Education, Mezirow's theory of perspective transformation was originally influenced by Habermas's notions of technical, practical, and emancipatory forms of knowledge. Other adult educators writing from a critical theory perspective and influenced by Habermas include Griffin, Collins, Welton, Finger, and Wilson.

A sustained attempt to apply critical sociology to adult education can be found in Colin Griffin's *Curriculum Theory in Adult and Life-long Learning* (1983). Although working in the field of curriculum theory, Griffin's work can easily be identified with the work of philosophers of adult education. Griffin explains how critical sociology rejects the mechanistic and technical approaches to adult education by focusing on issues of knowledge as ideology, cultural reproduction, and the power of social control as these relate specifically to education. Griffin argues against approaches to define adult education in terms of adult characteristics, needs, design, strategies, and structures (as in andragogy). An adequate theory of adult education would look rather at the issues raised in philosophy, sociology, and politics. As aims for adult education, Griffin proposes not the concepts of needs, access, and provision, but an ideology of autonomy, individuality, and equality. Adult educators need to focus, he asserts, less on technique, methodology, and administration, and more on philosophical and political ideas that lie at the heart of the enterprise. Underlying these suggestions is Griffin's concrete proposal to adopt the ideas of Gelpi (1979) who has dealt with the social construction of knowledge in relation to production as the most fruitful basis of a curriculum theory for adult and lifelong learning.

In a later work, *Adult Education As Social Policy,* Griffin (1987) argues that policies of adult education are in some sense social, and hence subject to the influence of ideology and cultural reproduction. He suggests that a better way to understand adult education is through the critical analysis of the political, economic, and social aspects of its structure. Griffin acknowledges that the "analysis of any kind of educational policy will of necessity be a complicated exercise" (133), given the lack of standards and prescriptive nature of adult education.

Michael Collins (1991, 1998) has offered a similar argument against forms of adult education based purely on psychology and technical rationality. Like Griffin, he decries the concentration of adult educators on technique and method at the expense of broader social and political analyses. He sees the field of adult education as controlled by the ideology of technique. Collins softens his critique of the ideology of technique when he comes to discuss the elements of adult education programming by making it clear that he does not propose abandoning technique and concern for personal development but rather its authoritative deployment.

Collins takes the vantage point of the critical social theorists Habermas, Marcuse, Adorno, Bourdieu, and Horkheimer. It is his judgment that Habermas's fresh approach to dialogue as communicative action and praxis as a dialectical process adds an important element to Freirean theory. He is also informed in his analyses by the concepts of Foucault and Gramsci on power, knowledge, and hegemony

Collins's own theory of adult education, which is based on social learning theory, is "directed at social structures and practices that enhance or obstruct the potential for autonomous learning" (1991, xii). In his view, this theory should inform both research and practice in the field of adult education. According to Collins, this approach holds potential for enhancing the vocation, mission, and competence of adult educators. Rather than relying on behaviorist philosophy, adult educators should focus on caring relationships in pedagogical settings. One sees here the combination of critical theory, phenomenological analysis, and humanistic concern.

In addition to critical social theory, Collins finds Freire's work on adult education and community development particularly helpful in program planning. He stresses the importance of attending to values in the evaluation process, and critiques the emphasis on the professionalization of the field at the expense of social action.

Collins points out that many adult educators who have used the work of critical theory have reduced their insights to psychology and have not adequately probed its ethical and political implications for a transforming pedagogy. He calls for political involvement in addition to theoretical work, teaching, and analysis. Educators should be involved in movements for social change. He also cautions against some of the negativism and pessimism among social theorists. "What is required" of adult educators today is "a rearguard action in defense of past gains. A critical pedagogy that has any relevance" must "give reasons . . . why human emancipation should be the primary goal of education" (1998, p. 77). Collins presents an eloquent summary of this thought:

> A critical practice of adult education provides a context where shared commitments towards a socially more free, just, and rational society will coalesce. If these shared concerns are to drive a transformative pedagogy, though, conventional notions of professionalization will have to be set aside in favour of a vocation that seeks to work directly with the kind of popular constituencies identified in previous chapters and create opportunities for alternative democratic discourses within formal agencies. Ultimately, a vocation to adult education seeks to realize, as critical practice, a just state of affairs where education is determined through the practical interests of free men and women. (1991, 119-120)

Although there are many in the field of adult education intrigued with the precepts and implications of critical theory, several are emerging who suggest a new role for critical theory. Matthias Finger, for instance, opened an examination of new social movements (NSMS) as indicative of a "transition from the old social and political movements to new ones . . . heralding a new conception of adult education" (1989, 15). He suggests that a truly critical perspective places the individual as the central focus with the role of adult education being the fostering of such cultural transformation and self-actualization of the person. Welton (1993b) furthers this dialogue by observing that the new social movements are precursors to a new historic movement and a "concept of social justice attuned to the particular predicament of the marginalized and underprivileged" (161). Welton concludes, "From a critical educational perspective, the full developmental potential of nature and human beings cannot unfold if the present values and institutional arrangements persist" (163). Finally, Wilson (1993) echoes Collins's concern for the detrimental emphasis on professionalization of adult education. Wilson's argument centers on the issue underlying the predominant concern for professionalization, namely that of control of the discipline itself. He critically suggests that our "social movement heritage met its demise . . . with the emergence of the professionalization movement," an unfortunate direction in light of our goal of "understanding and acting effectively in our educational world" (14). In other writings Wilson challenges the uncritical adoption of a "positivist ideology" underlying professionalization of the field. (Wilson and Hayes, 2000a, p. 12). Wilson and Hayes (2000b) make the case that professional practice in adult education is

> more than an acquired repertoire of instrumental problem solutions, the focus of traditional scientific knowledge construction and professional training. . . . Informed professional action also depends significantly on how practitioners rely upon their assumptions, values, and experiences to "see" and thus shape their daily work. (17)

In a number of articles Stephen Brookfield has made the case for critical theory as a basis for a theory of adult learning and education. At the heart of his project is his desire to place ideology critique at the center of adult learning. He poses the question: "How is it that adults learn to detect, critique, and then challenge ideological manipulation?" (2001, 13) Reviewing the work of Marx, Marxists and especially critical theorists of the Frankfort School of Social Research, Brookfield comes to the conclusion that "a critical theory of adult learning should have at its core an understanding of how adults learn to recognize the predominance of ideology in their everyday thoughts and actions and in the institutions of civil society" (20-21). Brookfield recognizes that he is advocating a theory of social and political learning that would challenge ideology, recognize hegemony, and unmask power.

Brookfield is aware that though many adult education theorists have proposed critical theory as a theory of adult learning and education, the field is still resistant to this form of radical adult education. To counter this, he has proposed the more moderate and accessible theories of Erich Fromm (Brookfield, 2002). He believes that Fromm's humanism softens the radical thrust but still retains a penetrating criticism of capitalist society, Brookfield has pinpointed the problem that all political educators face, especially radicals: "How to respect the agendas adults bring to a democratic negotiation of curriculum while contradictorily challenging these agendas by offering (and sometimes insisting on) radically different politically contentious options for study" (106). Finally, Brookfield (2003, 154-169) attempts the difficult task of bringing critical theory to bear on the troubling issue of race. Others have made a strong case for employing critical race theory in examining "endemic and systemic" racism in adult education theory and practice (Ianinska, Wright, and Rocco, 2003, 175).

Feminist Theory in Adult Education

Feminist theory is a comprehensive philosophical perspective that seeks to explain the nature of unequal power relations based on gender, race, and class. There is no one model of feminist theory; rather there are "theories" as in liberal, Marxist, socialist, radical, and postmodern feminist theory. At the core of these "theories" is a body of interrelated principles that tries to explain women's oppression. The feminist perspective in adult education, known generally as feminist pedagogy, has its roots in the radical philosophy of education, as well as critical theory and humanistic psychology. An underlying assumption of feminist theory and feminist pedagogy is that unequal power relations exist that foster the oppression of women. Feminist pedagogy attempts to examine the oppression of women through the context of education. It can be said that all of feminist pedagogy is emancipatory in focus and is concerned with the empowerment of women (Hayes, 1989; Maher, 1987; Tisdell, 1993a, 1998). However, Tisdell (1993b) points out that although feminist pedagogy is emancipatory in focus, not all feminist pedagogy literature deals with the nature of structured power relations or women's collective experience of oppression.

A helpful way to examine feminist pedagogy in adult education is through Maher's (1987) analysis. Maher sees feminist pedagogy as falling into two categories: the liberation models and the gender models. The liberatory models approach education from the perspective of neo-Marxist educational theorists and critical theory. Concerned with the structured nature of power relations and systems of oppression based on gender, race, and class that are reinforced through education, critical or liberation models of feminist pedagogy addresses structured power relations both in the classroom and outside the classroom in the academy and society. They attempt to recover women's voices, experiences, and viewpoints and use these as a means for self-discovery and resistance. Although heavily influenced by the work of Paulo Freire and neo-Marxist educational theorists, liberatory feminist pedagogy is critical of Freire and Marxist educators because of their lack of attention to oppressions based on gender and race, or the interlocking systems of oppression involving gender, race, and class.

A feminist adult educator writing from this perspective is Hart. In *Working and Educating for Life: Feminist and International Perspectives on Adult Education*, Hart (1992) examines and critiques the nature of work and of worker education in a patriarchal market economy and the underlying assumptions, attitudes, and themes of work and worker education as it is presented in much of the adult education literature. She takes issue with the valuing of commodity production over subsistence production because it is subsistence production that sustains life. Gender and race/ethnicity relations are at the center of Hart's analysis since it is mainly women, people of color, and peasants, both men and women, who do the subsistence work throughout the world. Hart offers a view of the possibilities of what work and worker education might look like if work were primarily conceived of as activity that supports human life rather than being conceived of as primarily activity that leads to profit. Hart uses mothering as an example and a metaphor for life affirming work because mothering and other subsistence work are based on connections and relationships absolutely essential to our survival. She calls for the development of principles and premises of an education "which is similarly productive in the life giving, life-enhancing sense as production for life . . . an education for life must deliberately reestablish the original connection between human work or production and the preservation and improvement of life" (213).

Another adult educator writing from the liberatory feminist perspective is Blundell (1992) who offers a critique of the curriculum of adult education based on a feminist analysis. According to Blundell, although women constitute a majority of both teachers and students in adult education, no detailed research has focused on gender issues in relation to the curriculum. Her discussion is structured around the four major discourses within the social and political theory of feminism-liberal, radical, Marxist, and socialist feminism. She argues that adult education often successfully masks its patriarchal bias by not examining the role knowledge plays in legitimizing existing gender relations. Blundell calls for a feminist transformation of adult education curriculum that will "transcend the needs-meeting and ultimately reinforcing ideology into which adult education currently [is] locked" (214).

The gender models of feminist pedagogy are concerned with those aspects of female identity that come from women's socialization as nurturers. They focus on the individual rather than the structure of power relations in society. These models of feminist pedagogy are emancipatory in the personal psychological sense, but do not necessarily attempt to address the structure of power relations in the larger context of society. According to proponents of this perspective, women's concern for connection, relationships, and responsibility for others makes them more empathetic, sensitive, and more able to express emotions than men. Feminists within this perspective view knowledge as contextual and subjective rather than universal. They affirm a "connected" way of knowing that comes from women's socialization in the role of nurturers, and they critique masculine thought and the universality and objectivity of the scientific method.

Belenky, Clinchy, Goldberger, and Tarule's (1986) book, *Women Ways of Knowing: The Development of Self, Voice, and Mind,* articulates a gender model of feminist pedagogy that advocates a "connected" approach to education. This approach affirms women's experience, voices, and ways of knowing. According to Belenky et al., the nature of truth and reality and the origins of knowledge shape the way we see the world and ourselves as participants in it. "If a woman is to consider herself a real knower, she must find acceptance for her ideas in the public world" (220). In "connected" education, the teacher tries to create a learning environment in which the members can nurture each other's thoughts to maturity. The goal of connected education is to help women to develop their own authentic voices and to see themselves as independent thinkers and constructors of knowledge.

Also approaching adult education from a gender model, Hayes (1989) questions the effectiveness of traditional instructional practices in light of women's experiences and stresses the need for a feminist approach to teaching that encompasses teacher-learner collaboration, cooperative communication styles, and a holistic approach to learning and theory building. Hayes and Smith (1994) have analyzed the portrayal of women in the major journals in adult education and offer new educational strategies for research, teaching, and learning. They call for research on women and gender in adult education that uses women's experiences and perspectives as a focal point. This women-centered focus will allow adult education scholarship to strive for a more pluralistic understanding of women and men as learners and to move toward a broader understanding of gender as a socially and culturally defined system that shapes and is shaped by adult education.

Both the liberatory model and the gender model of feminist pedagogy have significant implications for adult education. Maher (1987) recommends a synthesis of the two models to create a model of feminist pedagogy that includes both the liberatory model's emphasis on power and the gender model's emphasis on the personal domain.

Taking up Maher's challenge to forge a synthesis of the liberatory and gender models, Tisdell (1998) proposes a poststructural feminist pedagogy that weds the psychological orientation of the gender model with the structural factors of the liberatory perspective. This model allows for learner differences while problematizing the power and authority of the teacher. She explains how examining connections between the individual and the intersecting systems of privilege and oppression might lead to change:

> As learners examine how social systems of privilege and oppression have affected their own identity, including their beliefs and values, the "discourse" is disrupted, thus shifting their identity, as well as increasing their capacity for agency. . . . One also begins to see that there are different "truths" and perhaps not one "Truth," and that social systems have allowed members of privileged groups to control what has counted as "knowledge" in determining the official curriculum through the politics of the knowledge production process. (1998, 146)

bell hooks (1994), an African American educator, has mined a number of traditions to develop an approach to education that can be termed radical feminist. hooks asserts that her "pedagogical practices have emerged from the mutually illuminating interplay of anticolonial, critical, and feminist pedagogies" (10). She expressed her indebtedness to Freire's liberatory education, all the while recognizing criticisms of Freire made by some feminists. She asserts that Freire's "writing gave me a way to place the politics of racism in the United States in a global context where I could see my fate linked with that of colonized black people everywhere struggling to decolonize, to transform society" (53). She boldly states that she preferred his work to that of many white bourgeois feminist thinkers since he clearly recognized the plight of the disenfranchised throughout the world.

hooks also associates herself with critical theory and the critical pedagogy. Her work contains a powerful critique of how "white supremacy, imperialism, sexism, and racism have distorted education so that it is no longer the practice of freedom" (29). She boldly advocates a revolutionary pedagogy of resistance to multiple societal oppressions.

Though hooks's context is primarily the education of young adults in college classrooms, her radical pedagogy has reverberated throughout educational circles. She speaks eloquently of the vocation of the educator:

> The learning process comes easiest to those of us who teach who also believe that there is an aspect of our vocation that is sacred. who believe that our work is not merely to share information but to share in the intellectual and spiritual growth of our students. To teach in such a manner that respects and cares for the souls of our students is essential if we are to provide the necessary conditions where learning can most deeply and intimately begin. (13)

Hers is a radically engaged pedagogy that draws not only on Freire but also on Thich Nhat Hanh's philosophy of engaged Buddhism, which emphasizes the role of the teacher as healer of mind, body, and spirit.

hooks is a strong advocate for a feminist approach to multicultural education. She recognizes that many educators often fail to teach from a standpoint that includes awareness of race, sex, and class oppression because of a fear of bringing emotions and passions into the classroom. Anticipating the critique of liberal education offered by Martha Nussbaum (1997) she advocates allowing powerful emotions to rise in educational settings. hooks's brand of multiculturalism wants to break down barriers that have shaped the way knowledge has been dealt with in educational settings. A sympathetic analysis of hooks's work is found in Florence (1998), who also applies her ideas to her Kenyan homeland.

Radical Adult Education: An Assessment

It should be an obvious fact that radical adult education has had a limited impact on the practice of adult education in this country.

This is equally true of the impact of other forms of radicalism in American culture. Radicalism has been a minor force in the American tradition. Its ideas have received a serious hearing from large numbers of people only in the 1930s and 1960s when, in the face of various crises, radicalism, together with other reform proposals, was discussed openly in books, articles, and journals of thought. Radical educational thought has had its strongest appeal in precisely these decades of crisis.

Brookfield (2002) has commented on the resistance of adult educators to radical thought even though it is prominently represented at conferences and in journals. He notes that in his conversations with adult education graduate students, teachers, and program developers, he finds that they have dismissed the critical or radical tradition as irrelevant to their practice. He attributes this phenomenon to the language of the radical tradition, which his students describe as "opaque, impenetrable, and intimidatingly unfamiliar" (97). Language may be a problem but there are other issues.

There are a number of particular reasons for the unreceptivity of adult educators to educational radicalism. Adult education in this country is conducted within institutions that are basically conservative of traditional values and societal structures: public schools, religious institutions, business and industry, governmental and military institutions. Though adult educators have often expressed criticisms and reservations about the values and structures of these institutions, they maintain strong commitments to the institutions within which they work. If they advocate measures of change, these are most often moderate.

Holst (2002) also points out that as adult education itself has become "an increasingly professionalized field within a capitalist economic system, its significant radical tradition is being forced to the margins" (5). The radical tradition is being replaced by human resource development (HRD) as the dominant focus. Further, radical activities are likely to take place in informal settings led by those who see themselves as activists, not educators. Furthermore, "when these activists engage in explicitly educational activities—study groups, speaking and lecturing, leafleting, and so forth—they often label it party or movement work without separating it out as specifically adult education" (5).

Any concern for change among adult educators usually focuses upon personal and individual change and not radical social or political change. In this characteristic adult educators differ little from other educators. It is the rare American professional who espouses

or proposes radical measures of social and political change for dealing with individual and personal needs/The popularity of a humanistic philosophy of education, such as that espoused by Carl Rogers,
is more consonant with the ideological outlook of the vast majority
of American professionals in the helping professions.

Though it is true that radical thought has not greatly influenced
the practice of adult education, there are a number of advantages in
a serious examination of this tradition, some of which have been
presented in this chapter. Radical thought is a good antidote to com-
placency. Radicals are strong on societal criticism and equally strong
on presenting alternative and utopian futures. Adult educators engaged in direct work with individuals for short-term purposes can
easily lose sight of societal ills and long-term visions. Connection
with the radical tradition can make adult educators more critical
and reflective in their work and also provide visions of alternative
or future possibilities.

In presenting a view of the nature of human beings and society,
radical adult education challenges the traditional view of the primary functions of education as transmitting the culture and maintaining its societal structures from generation to generation. Radicalism prefers not to transmit but to change the culture and its
structures, for it believes that these are, in the present situation,
destructive to human freedom and oppressive to human dignity.
There is enough truth in the radical's contention that education
must be the creator rather than the *creature* of the social order to
make adult educators question the basic thrusts of their efforts.

Though radical adult education has a number of contributions
to make to theorizing about the nature and functions of adult education, as a unifying philosophy it must be considered inadequate. Its
major weakness is its failure to take into account the pluralistic
nature of most cultures. American pluralism strongly militates
against the adoption of a monolithic-utopian educational philosophy,
such as is proposed by radical adult educational philosophy. Many
years ago Randall (1948) identified this pluralism in his definition of
the spirit of American philosophy:

> The roots of this pluralistic attitude lie deep in American
> experience. There is first the fact that American thinkers
> have always been able to enjoy a certain perspective on the
> various cultures of Europe. They have been bound to no
> single intellectual tradition. . . . Secondly, the fact that
> America is a continent and not a nation has long led to an

emphasis on regionalism, on the wide differences between the various sections of our country,//Thirdly, there is the deep-seated and traditional religious pluralism of American life. . . . Long accustomed to this diversity of faiths in the most important matters, Americans have found other diversities equally natural. Finally there is the historical pluralism fostered by the extraordinary changes in American life. (126)

//p. 186 is blank

(STOP 12)

CHAPTER VII

ANALYTIC PHILOSOPHY OF ADULT EDUCATION

Since the 1960s, a predominant force in educational philosophy in English-speaking countries has been the work of philosophers of education who have utilized the various methods of analytic philosophy. This approach to educational theory has tended to avoid systems building in philosophy in order to concentrate on the careful analysis of educational concepts, arguments, slogans, and policy statements. Analytic philosophers in education have attempted to construct a solid philosophical foundation through careful analysis and argumentation. The contributions of this approach have been substantial. Numerous books, articles, and journals have presented the results of this rigorous philosophical approach.

Though analytic philosophers of education have been writing for decades, it is only with the work of Paterson, Lawson, and Monette, that works of an analytic nature have appeared in this area. Of course, various forms of analysis are found in the current work of philosophers and scholars in adult education, e.g., Stephen Brookfield and Michael Collins. But they are not analytic philosophers as professional scholars.

Since analytic philosophy has become such a prevalent form of philosophy in education in the United States, Britain, and other English speaking countries, one might have expected that the field would have received more extensive analytic treatment. This approach to philosophy could provide for some the long awaited philosophical foundation that adult educators have contended that the field needs. Not all adult educators, however, are be pleased with this approach since even in its beginnings it has questioned some of the basic principles generally accepted by adult educators in this country. Recent philosophical writing in adult education has tended to draw more on existentialism, phenomenology, critical theory, feminist theory, and most recently postmodernism.

// The task of introducing the analytic approach to adult education is not an easy one. We will attempt to do this by first outlining the historical development of the various forms of analytic philosophy. Second, the basic procedures and techniques of this approach will be explained. Third, some of the key contributions of this approach to adult education will be examined and critiqued. Finally, an assessment will be made of the impact of this approach for the field of adult education.

Historical Background for Analytic Philosophy of Adult Education

In a certain sense, all philosophers are been engaged in the analysis of language. All of Plato's dialogues include the careful analysis of such concepts as virtue, justice, the good person, and the good society. In the *Meno,* for example, Plato poses the question: Can virtue be taught or is it something inherent in an individual? He attempts to answer the question by presenting a skillful dialogue on the meaning of virtue and of teaching. Socrates, Plato's teacher, had made use of skillful questioning to lead his disciples to a clearer understanding of the language they used. Aristotle, Plato's disciple, continued this analytic tradition in his analysis of such concepts as happiness, habits, voluntary and involuntary actions, truth, goodness, and beauty.

In medieval times the scholastic philosophers, Thomas Aquinas, Duns Scotus, Peter Abelard, and William of Ockham used careful analysis and argumentation to present both philosophical and religious views. One of the chief problems of medieval philosophy concerned the reference point of such universal or abstract terms as justice, goodness, and beauty. For some scholastics, abstract terms were mere words without objective reference points. For other medieval philosophers words had some basis in reality either in ideal forms or essences, or in concrete objects from which they were abstracted. In the later medieval period the language analysis of philosophers became so refined and hair-splitting, that scholasticism became a term of derision to critics of this form of philosophy.

Modern philosophers were also keen in their analysis of words and concepts. One finds in Descartes, Spinoza, Kant, and Hegel an attempt to arrive at a clarity of language and argument. Their philosophical treatises are replete with distinguishing the various shades of meaning that words and concepts have.

Although the clarification of concepts in philosophy has been present in the work of all previous philosophers, it is only in the past century that a distinctive analytic approach to language emerged. This philosophy differs from previous work of the past in abandoning metaphysical statements about the nature of the world, God, reality, human beings, and instead concentrates on the analysis of language as the exclusive function of philosophy. In its anti-metaphysical posture, this philosophy created a revolution in philosophy, the impact of which has been widely debated.

It is important at this point to note that the term analytic philosophy includes a number of different forms, only one of which, conceptual analysis, has become prominent in educational philosophy. Four forms of analytic philosophy have been identified by scholars: (1) Scientific Realism, (2) Logical Analysis or Logical Atomism, (3) Logical Positivism, and (4) Linguistic, Ordinary Language, or Conceptual Analysis (Weitz, 1966, 1). A brief description of each of these affords a helpful vantage point from which to view the work of conceptual analysis in education. All of these approaches accept the truth of Wittgenstein's claim that the task of philosophy is not to change the world but "to leave everything as it is." The task of these philosophers is to make the world clearer.

The beginnings of modern analytic philosophy took place in the development of Scientific Realism, found in the early writings of George Moore (1903) and Bertrand Russell (1912). This theory asserted that matter was not reducible to mind and that universal ideas were not reducible to particular ideas. Presented in opposition to the Idealism of Hegel and the English philosopher Bradley, this form of Idealism blurred the distinctions between matter and mind, universals and particulars.

Scientific Realism also had other tenets. On the nature of truth it contended that there was truth only when there was a correspondence between what was in the mind and what existed in reality. Belief was also viewed as a correspondence between a subjective state and an external situation. Furthermore, value was considered a real property of an object or situation, no less real than the material qualities of objects.

The position of Scientific Realism was not one that Moore and Russell maintained throughout their lives. Yet it was a position that forced both men to focus on the nature of language and the reality to which language corresponded. Moore later developed a Philosophy of Common Sense and Russell became more interested in science, mathematics, and in Logical Analysis as an approach to philosophy/While Moore accused philosophers of abusing language when they used it differently from common, ordinary language, Russell developed a more influential stand in philosophy in his procedure of Logical Analysis.

Russell's Logical Analysis is the second phase in the development of analytic philosophy. Other descriptions of this approach to philosophy include the analysis of denoting phrases, the clarification of unclear symbols, the method of dispensing with abstractions, and logical constructionism. For Russell, all of these denoted a set of techniques for the replacement of defective symbols or words (Weitz 1966, 4). Through logical analysis Russell attempted to give philosophy the exactness that mathematics and science had in his time. Thus to determine the meaning of a sentence, it had to be broken down into its molecular parts. Sentences in language are true if the parts refer to what actually exists. In this analytic approach, Russell reduced each problem into its parts, and then examined each part to pick out its essential features. He saw the task of philosophy not in arriving at great answers or in making grand syntheses, but in working out careful analyses. This approach was reductive in breaking down all propositions to their smallest components; it was also empirical, for each aspect had to correspond with some part of reality.

The basic ideas of Russell's Logical Analysis were accepted and extended in the early philosophical work of Ludwig Wittgenstein. In his *Tractatus Logico-Philosophicus* (1921), Wittgenstein discussed the nature and function of language, mathematics, scientific laws, and the relation between language and the world. As will be seen shortly, Wittgenstein repudiated much of this earlier view. Yet, this earlier work, which was rather close to Russell's position, has had a great influence in the history of analytic philosophy.

The basic themes of the *Tractatus* are clear, though the book is notoriously difficult in its details. Wittgenstein contended that philosophical problems are the result of misunderstandings in language and logic. He asserted that these difficulties could be solved or avoided by creating and using an ideal language. This new language must be exactly representative of the reality to which it points. Thus only statements have meaning that represents reality in some way.

According to the *Tractatus*, the purpose of logical analysis is to make every statement an adequate picture of the reality it represents. Analysis is thus the process of reducing statements to their atomic and constituent parts. The view of knowledge that is implied in this theory is that knowing is really a relationship between reality and language, not between the knower and the known.

The implications of this form of analytic philosophy are extensive. It rendered all statements meaningless that are not based on sensory knowledge or logic. Religious statements, traditional philosophical statements about the world, statements expressing appreciation, and values are all meaningless propositions in that they actually reveal nothing about the world in which we live. They may tell us something about the person making the statements, but they tell us nothing about the world or objective reality outside the mind of the speaker. The further implications of this philosophical viewpoint are found in Logical Positivism, the third form of philosophical analysis.

The third phase of language philosophy was Logical Positivism, a dominant form of philosophy from the 1920s to the beginning of the Second World War. Among the doctrines of this approach are

> the verifiability theory of meaning, the rejection of metaphysics, the emotive theory of moral judgment, the unity of science, the conception of language as a calculus, the conventionalistic interpretation of logic and mathematics, and the claim that legitimate philosophy consists solely of logical analysis. (Weitz, 1966, 8)

The principle of verification is the chief tenet of this approach to philosophy. According to this principle, propositions have meaning only if they can be empirically or logically verified. Logic, mathematics, and the sciences have meaning since their statements can be verified through empirical data or logic. All other assertions are considered meaningless.

The most influential proponent of Logical Positivism in the English-speaking world has been A. J. Ayer (1959). The task for philosophy, according to Ayer, is to classify language, distinguish true propositions from false ones, and explain the meaning and justification of statements. Using the verification principle, Ayer attempted to show that religious, evaluative, and metaphysical utterances are meaningless statements.

The position of the logical positivist has not prevailed in analytic philosophy. Especially after the Second World War, but beginning before it, the major propositions of Logical Positivism were rejected by such influential analysts as Wittgenstein in his *Philosophical Investigations* (1953), Gilbert Ryle in his *Concept of Mind* (1949), and John Wisdom in his *Other Minds* (1952). All three of these philoso-

p192

phers attacked the verification principle and ushered in the fourth stage of analytic philosophy called Conceptual Analysis, Ordinary Language Philosophy, or Linguistic Analysis. It is this fourth phase of analytic philosophy that has greatly influenced contemporary analytic philosophers of education.

One of the earliest proponents of conceptual analysis was John Wisdom, Professor of Philosophy at Cambridge University. In an essay "Philosophical Perplexity" (In Weitz, 1966), he attempted to provide a general account of the many puzzles and paradoxes of traditional philosophy. Wisdom proposed the notion that the task of philosophy was the resolution of puzzles and not the answering of problems. Wisdom thus reduced philosophical questions to language questions and philosophical answers to recommendations for proper language use.

Wisdom's work has a strong parallel in the writings of Gilbert Ryle. Ryle's book called *Concept of Mind* (1949) is a classic work in contemporary philosophy of conceptual analysis. In this work, Ryle argues that the mind can be reduced to the mental behaviors of the person. The mind is not an extra being, a "Ghost in the Machine," but a person's abilities, liabilities, and limitations. Ryle's work is basically an argument for metaphysical behaviorism. But what is of interest here is more his methodology, that of arriving at his basic theses through an analysis of the words and concepts used in ordinary language. Ryle (1967) has also contributed directly to education by his careful analysis of such concepts as teaching, training, and education.

Though Ryle, Wisdom, and others have made important contributions to conceptual analysis, it is the later work of Wittgenstein that was most influential in shaping language philosophy in the past two decades. In *Philosophical Investigations* (1953), Wittgenstein abandoned the narrowly framed verification principle for the position that the meaning of language is in its use. To understand a word is to be able to use it in accordance with custom and social practice. Thus there is no need to construct a new language, as the logical positivists attempted. Rather, attention should be directed to determining the correct usages that words had in ordinary language.

Language thus becomes something that can be used to suit one's purpose. Language in this view is a social phenomenon, a cooperative achievement. To determine what language means one looks not only to its reference in the real world, but also to what the person intended the language to mean or to do.

The role of the philosopher, according to the conceptual analysts, is not to construct explanations about reality but to eliminate language confusions/ Philosophy is a method of investigation that results in pure description. In this theory no language, no matter how abstract, metaphysical, or theological, is to be dismissed. The philosopher's task is to determine what the language means for the persons and groups who use it. Words have only the meaning that people give to them. Philosophy attempts to clarify these various usages of language. In this role, the language philosopher is more like the social scientist who attempts to maintain a value-neutral position about the references of the language that people utilize to express themselves.

Language, according to ordinary language philosophers, has many tasks and many levels; it may or may not be used to describe the world. The philosopher tries to find out on each occasion what is being intended by the language used, without the preconception that one type of language is basic and the others are reducible to it. This was the position of the logical positivists, who took the language of science and mathematics as normative for what language should be. In describing the uses of language to achieve many purposes, Wittgenstein employed the analogy of playing games. Both games and the use of language are governed by rules. To understand people's language, we must understand the rules by which they use language. Understanding some language games like poetry and technical writing may demand intensive training. To read the books of scientists, philosophers, statisticians, and poets, one must know and understand the rules of the language being used.

Wittgenstein has presented a list of some of the different things that people do with language:

> Give orders and obey them; describe the appearance of an object or give its measurement; construct an object from a description; report an event; form and test a hypothesis; present the result of an experiment in tables and diagrams; make up a story and read a story; playacting; sing catches; guess riddles; make jokes. . . . Ask, think, curse, greet, pray. (Wittgenstein, 1953, 23)

An examination of this list shows the complexity that is involved in determining how language functions. It is to this complexity that language philosophers have directed their attention.

Language philosophers have come in for their share of criticisms from philosophers of other orientations. Philosophers criticize analysts for proclaiming that their analyses are done in a neutral manner, that they are able to keep their own presuppositions and preferred theories out of their analyses. The critics contend that:

> Philosophers cannot set aside their values while they engage in analysis, and a better approach—from the perspective of critics—is to ferret out these values, confess them, and build one's case frankly on them. (Noddings, 1995, 42)

This summary of the more significant developments in twentieth-century language philosophy should provide a background for understanding the analytic approach to educational philosophy that is presented in this chapter. The next step is to examine the nature, purposes, methods, and limitations of linguistic or conceptual analysis.

Philosophy As Conceptual or Linguistic Analysis

As we have seen in the last section of this chapter, conceptual analysts view the task of philosophy differently from traditional philosophers. Traditional philosophy is concerned with developing a system of thought about all aspects of the world: God, human beings, nature, knowledge, values, and beauty. Scheffler (1960) has indicated how linguistic analysis differs from this approach:

> Philosophical analysis, in substantially its current forms, got under way interested fundamentally in the clarification of basic notions and modes of argument rather than in synthesizing available beliefs into some total outlook, in thoroughly appraising root ideas rather than in painting suggestive but vague portraits of the universe. (7]

Conceptual analysis then is concerned with the grounds for knowledge, beliefs, actions, and activities that make up human life. All areas of human activity can be subjected to this form of philosophical analysis.

Another way to make the distinction between conceptual analysis and traditional philosophy is to use the distinction that Frankena proposes. Frankena (1970) distinguishes between *analytic philosophy* with its emphasis on the analysis of concepts, arguments, slogans, and statements and *normative philosophy,* which makes normative or descriptive statements about the world, human beings, and human actions. Applied to education, the distinction is between

p 195

analyzing the concepts of education, teaching, or learning, and prescribing what education and schools should or should not do with
regard to aims, content, methods, and evaluation (Frankena, 1970).

Conceptual analysis achieves its goal of clarifying language
through the use of various techniques, tools, and methods. Conceptual analysts first of all employ the tools of logic that have been in
use in philosophy since the writings of Aristotle. These involve the
use of definitions, deductive and inductive reasoning, the uncovering of logical fallacies, and the establishment of criteria for determining the truth or falsity of statements. At first sight, many analytical books and articles appear to be exercises in logical reasoning.

In their work of analysis, however, contemporary analysts have
developed a number of methods that go beyond the conventional
logical tools of traditional philosophy. A consideration of a number of
these tools with some examples may give a better idea of how conceptual analysts proceed.

Analysts distinguish three types of questions: questions of fact,
questions of value, and questions of concept. A *question of fact* is:
How extensively has democracy spread over the entire world? A
question of value is: Is democracy a desirable form of government? A
question of concept is: Is democracy compatible with communism? It
is the final question, the question of concept, that the language philosopher is most concerned with, though the first two questions are
not ignored. To answer the first two questions one must first of all
arrive at an accepted concept of democracy to test its factual extent
or judge its value. (Green, 1971)

Questions of concept, for example, entail examining ways in
which such words as "democracy" and "communism" are used. Conceptual analysis involves making a cognitive map of the ways in
which the two concepts are used in order to see the similarities and
dissimilarities between the terms. Another way of phrasing a question of concept is to ask whether the one can exist without the other.
If the one can exist without the other, then the two concepts are
distinct. Questions of concept are answered not by merely giving
definitions of the terms but by examining the ways in which the
terms are used. We can adequately analyze concepts by contrasting
and comparing them to similar concepts. As will be seen later, a
proper analysis of adult education demands a comparable analysis of
adult training, adult learning, lifelong education, and other allied
concepts.

Conceptual analysts recognize that there are not usually right
answers when it comes to the analysis of concepts. For example, the

concept of education has a variety of meanings or usages in ordinary language. These usages are not totally arbitrary. The concept of education is more appropriately applied to persons than to animals or plants. We usually distinguish education from training and indoctrination. Thus, there are some usages of the term that are nearer to the heart of the concept than others. It is getting to the heart of the concept as it is ordinarily used that is one of the principal tasks of the conceptual analyst. The attempt to get at the heart of a concept has led to the charge that conceptual analysis is guilty of essentialism or claiming that words have meanings that transcend particular social contexts. Critics argue that the same word can have different meanings in different cultural contexts.

Besides isolating questions of concept and avoiding the search for *the* right meaning of a concept, conceptual analysts use a number of other techniques. Analysts look for *model cases* in which the concept is used in such a way that everyone would agree that this is a good use. We will see in a later section of this chapter that some adult educators present liberal adult education as a model case for adult education. They examined the key characteristics of liberal adult education and compare other forms with it. They also made the rather debatable point of advocating that the term education in adult education be restricted only to liberal adult education. This position will be examined later.

In addition to model cases, analysts examine concepts through the use of *contrary cases,* cases in which the term obviously cannot be appropriately used. Thus one cannot speak of a stone being educated. This indicates that some form of life or ability to change from within is needed for an educational process. Contrary cases have value in conceptual analysis especially in the preliminary stages when one is first setting out to form a cognitive map of usages of the concept.

As has been mentioned above, analysis of concepts is most often applied to a group of related or allied concepts. Various terms are analyzed in order to become clearer about their meanings: teaching, learning, training, conditioning, indoctrination, explanation, development, and personal relationships. Through the analysis of related concepts one comes closer to a better understanding of the concept one is considering, and those features of it that separate it from others. If we know the essential features of a concept, we will more likely use it in a proper manner and thus avoid conceptual and linguistic confusion.

Many concepts that we use in ordinary language are what analysts refer to as *borderline usages* or *cases.* These are also called odd

or queer cases because although the usage of the concept is legitimate, it is somewhat strained. A possible borderline use of education is in the concept of self-education. There is something strange
about speaking of someone educating himself or herself. Self-learn-
ing is less odd, for we readily accept that persons can learn on their
own. But the term education in its ordinary usage usually implies
some kind of encounter with another person. This is not present in
the case of self-education. The value of looking at odd or borderline
cases is to determine the missing element that makes the usage
odd. This gives us a better handle on the essential qualities of the
concept.

An important distinction that conceptual analysts make is between concepts that are *ambiguous* and those that are *vague*. A concept is ambiguous if it can bear more than one meaning. The cause
of the ambiguity may lie in the concept itself. The word trunk, for
example, is ambiguous for it can refer to baggage, a part of a tree, or
a part of an elephant. The context makes it clear what the meaning
of the concept is. Yet some concepts remain ambiguous even in a
context. If we were to say that Aristotle's teaching was terrible, we
could not know whether the reference was to the manner of teaching, or to the content of teaching. Thus the term is ambiguous even
in its context. (Green 1971, 33-38)

Ambiguity is one thing, but vagueness is another. Concepts are
vague if they refer to a quality that things have in different degrees.
Large and small are vague words; baldness is a vague word. How
large, small, or bald does a person have to be to possess this quality?
Rationality is also a quality that is vague because different people,
children, adolescents, and adults possess it in varying degrees. Adulthood or maturity is often a vague concept. It refers to qualities that
persons have in varying degrees and different criteria may be used
in defining it: chronological, legal, or psychological.

The distinction between ambiguity and vagueness of concepts is
an important one in conceptual analysis. It is the use of vague and
ambiguous concepts that produce much of the language confusion
that exists in talk about education and other areas. Analysts attempt to remove ambiguity and to make vague usages more precise. Adult education abounds with vague terms that call for more
precise analysis, which many theorists present: self-directed learning, andragogy, discovery learning, facilitation, transformative learning, etc.

From an examination of these various techniques that conceptual analysts use, it is appearent that they are searching for definitions or criteria by which concepts are correctly used. Analysts have

recognized, however, that the very concept of *definition* needs some clarification//Israel Scheffler has pointed out three meanings of the concept of definition (1960, chapter 1). At times a definition *is stipulative,* as when authors give a meaning to a term according to the way that they will use it. The stipulative definition is usually somewhat different from the common usage, or it is an attempt to choose one out of numerous possible meanings. A person may use the term culture as referring only to artistic achievements in a work, recognizing that in common usage the term has much broader usages.

A definition is *descriptive* when it proposes to describe what is being defined. Descriptive definitions answer the question What does the term generally mean in common usage? Dictionaries give some descriptive definitions, but they do not give all the possible meanings or usages that a concept may have, together with distinctions from allied concepts. In a later section of this chapter we will examine the concept of "needs" to discover the various descriptive usages of this term. Distinctions exist, for example, between real and felt needs, ascribed or prescribed needs. A full analysis of such a basic concept in adult education has been presented in the work of Monette (1977, 1979). Much of conceptual analysis is an attempt to arrive at the full range of descriptive usages of a concept in order to be sure about how the concept is being used in particular cases.

The third type of definition proposed by Scheffler is the *programmatic definition,* which tells overtly or implicitly what should be done rather than what is done. For example, when we say that education is the process for developing critical abilities in individuals, we are giving a programmatic rather than a descriptive definition of the concept. We are not telling what actually happens but are prescribing what should happen in an educational process. It is difficult in describing such value-laden concepts as education not to include prescriptive or programmatic elements in our definitions. Thus the definitions we usually use are often a combination of descriptive and programmatic elements. In an examination of proposed definitions of adult education we will notice that many such definitions have strong programmatic features, especially those definitions that want to restrict the term to mean liberal adult education.

In traditional philosophy it has usually been the case that discussion begins with a definition of terms. In analytic philosophy this process is reversed. The purpose of analysis is to arrive at definitions of concepts that can then be used in developing philosophical statements or policies. The quest for clarity need not begin with a consensus on definitions. Some general agreement is important at the beginning, but the lack of full agreement at the start is not necessary, and in fact may cut off fruitful discussion in philosophy.

Besides making our usage of definitions more precise, analysts have also given great attention to the *examination of metaphors* that are used in the field of education. Metaphors are used to help explain what we mean. The unknown is made clear by a comparison to the known. Various metaphors have been used to elucidate the meaning of education: growth, development, personal encounter, transmission, social reconstruction, and behavioral modification. Each theory of education examined in this book has a basic metaphor by which it attempts to describe the fundamental process of education, together with its objectives. Even the word analysis is a metaphor taken from the realm of chemistry. Each of these metaphors is helpful in explaining some aspect of what education is. Metaphors are constructive when they make clear something about the concept being discussed. Thus when Dewey referred to education as growth, he emphasized that in education there is necessarily involved a process of change and development, similar to biological evolution.

Analysts have been careful to point out the limitations involved in dealing with metaphors, similes, and analogies. All metaphors eventually break down because they cannot explain all aspects of the reality in question. Education as growth explains the development or change aspect involved in education, but it does not adequately lend itself to treating the human factors involved in educational processes. Human growth through education is not the orderly process that it is with the sphere of animals and plants. Though education might be compared to an artist forming a work of art out of some material, the analogy breaks down because it does not account for human responsiveness in the educational process. Education is certainly similar to shaping, but the analogy limps when we consider what power humans have in determining the directions in which they will be shaped.

Analysts such as Scheffler (1960) and Green (1971) have performed a useful task in showing both the value and limitations of educational metaphors such as growth, formation, and artistic creation. From this discussion, it is appearent that no single metaphor can form an adequate basis for describing such complex processes as education, teaching and learning, explaining and understanding. Educational metaphors aid in organizing thought and in developing theories, but they are not precise descriptions of the processes they attempt to illuminate. (STOP 13)

Metaphors are not the only aspect of educational language that have come under analytic scrutiny. Analysts have also directed their attention to the common use and misuse of *slogans* in education. Slogans in education include: We teach children, not subjects; No child left behind; Andragogy not pedagogy; No teaching without learning. Slogans function in educational discourse more as symbols and rallying cries of movements, ideas, and attitudes. Slogans are not to be pondered as serious educational theory because usually they are oversimplifications of the issues involved. But in some way the slogan capitalizes on a movement, provides it with a symbol, and gains adherents to it. B. Paul Komisar and James McClellan (1961) have examined the use of slogans in education and have pointed out how entire systems of thought may be based on slogans, or emotive statements. The practical meaning of the slogan Andragogy not Pedagogy may have been its power to mobilize the adult education movement in the 1970s (Elias, 1979).

What has been presented thus far in this chapter should give some idea of the nature and techniques used in conceptual analysis. What remains in this section is the problem of the *purpose* of this form of educational philosophy. Analysts do not usually analyze concepts just for the sake of analyzing them. Conceptual clarity is sought in areas where there is confusion and where this confusion has led to practical difficulties and differences of opinion and policy. Many concepts used in education and in other areas of human endeavor need clarification if there is to be any intelligent discussion of problems and issues. Talk about adult education and its objectives often has a certain confusion attached to it. Certain statements such as these are made: education should be adapted to the needs and interests of the learners; education should be learner centered. If these phrases are to be understood, there must be some clarity about the meaning of the terms and the way that these expressions are used.

As practiced by many analysts, conceptual analysis is purportedly a value free or neutral philosophical activity. Increasingly, however, those who do conceptual analysis have attempted to go beyond the analysis of concepts to make normative proposals about what education should be. Analysts such as R. S. Peters (1967a) and Jonas Soltis (1968) have emphasized that since educating involves questions of value in an important way, philosophers who are involved in it cannot escape the value questions. Peters and other British analysts such as Lawson and Paterson often move in their philosophical

writings into the area of normative philosophy in taking stands on
value questions in education. Still there are philosophers of education such as Susan Laird (1988) and Lynda Stone (1992) who criticize
the analytic tradition in education for its emphasis on rationality
and intellectual acts that are abstracted from genuine educational
interests and predicaments. They argue that our notion of rationality should include attention to emotional life.

Conceptual Analysis in Adult Education

Lawson (1975, 1982, 1998) and Paterson (1979) have done the
most extensive work in the conceptual analysis of adult education. A
number of articles by Maurice Monette utilized this philosophical
approach to some degree in elucidating the concept of needs in adult
education (1977, 1979). The purpose of this section is to review some
of the conclusions and arguments that have been introduced by these
analysts into the field of adult education.

Lawson (1975) makes it clear that his work is one of conceptual
analysis. He is concerned about the "lack of impact upon adult education of the growing volume of literature which deals with general
educational concepts from the standpoint of linguistic analysis" (7).
His work is an effort to redress this balance. Lawson asserts that
there are some special concepts in the field that require analysis,
for these concepts are different from those analyzed in general educational theory. Lawson (1998) concedes that the analytical tradition of philosophizing is not as prevalent in adult education as it is in
general education, but he thinks there is value in "an approach that
concentrates upon detailed argument within a narrow focus," which
deals in "conclusions which are provisional and revisable and which
lead to "a practice of debate and criticism" (14).

While Paterson's work is also clearly conceptual analysis that
both he and Lawson engage in, it is not the value-free analysis that
is most common in the field. Both men move from the analysis of
concepts to make normative statements about the issues that they
examine. The same can be said of Monette who sees his work partly
in the analytic tradition as making a case for "the critical examination of the values and assumptions underlying the technology which
is advocated by [many contemporary] theorists. He presents a case
for philosophizing in adult education" (1979, 92). In Monette's (1979)
view:

> Philosophy of education is basically a justification of the edu-
> cational endeavor in its various modalities. It is distinguished

from educational theorizing or educational research in that it oversees these processes, seeking to clarify, criticize and question them—to integrate them into wholeness and coherence which is one's own. (93)

In developing this section of the chapter, we follow the basic structure of Paterson's work. Into his outline it is easy to place the various issues that Lawson and Monette treat in their writings. The four parts of Paterson's work are: *Educational Concepts* (concepts of adult, adult education, and liberal adult education); *Educational Objectives* (communication of knowledge, advancement of reason, and moral education of adults); *Educational Processes* (teaching, learning, and adult maturity); *Adult Education and Society (*educational justice and education for democracy).

The Concept of Adult Education

Paterson begins his work with an analysis of the concept of "adult." He argues that adulthood is a normative concept based on chronological age and status in society. Adults have certain rights in society that are not afforded to children. They also have responsibilities to which they are held by society. Though adults may not be emotionally and morally mature, they are expected to be so (Paterson 1979, 10). The only adequate grounds that can be given for these expectations, according to Paterson, is that adults are older than children. The presumption is that in the passage of time, adults have developed the emotional and moral maturity expected of them.

A second concept analyzed by Paterson and Lawson is adult education. In their analyses, both men depend upon the work of the foremost British analytic philosopher of education, R. S. Peters. For Peters, the concept of education entails a number of requirements: that there is a transmission of what is valuable and worthwhile; that individuals care about what they learn; that they want to achieve the standards associated with what is learned, that there is an awareness of what is learned through a process voluntarily undertaken: that there is a cognitive element and an understanding of principles; that what is learned is cognitively connected with other areas of learning so that each area is seen in relation to other areas: and that what is learned shall be usable (Peters 1967b).

Given this definition of education it is obvious that a person's education is never complete and that lifelong education is a necessity for full human development. Yet if one accepts this definition of

p.203

education, a number of problems arise with regard to the usage of the term adult education by adult educators in the United States. Paterson makes a strong case that only liberal adult education can properly be called adult *education* because it alone fulfills all the requirements for an educational enterprise. He distinguishes liberal adult education from what is called vocational education, role education, and education for leisure. Only in cases where the education in these other forms is broadly liberal would they be classified as adult educational activities.

Lawson (1975) follows the line of reasoning that has been developed by Peters and Paterson. He makes a distinction between the education of adults and adult education. The former would include all kinds of activities where adults are involved in learning. The latter term—adult education—is a normative one and should be applied only where the strict criteria of an educational process, as Peters proposes, are met. Both Lawson and Paterson in these works reject the usage of the term adult education as it is used in this country to embrace all kinds of learning activities of adults. They contend this usage is an administrative usage without the necessary normative or evaluative meaning. In later writings Lawson has modified his position, as will be seen below.

Monette (1979) has been directly influenced by Lawson's work. He opposes the service-centered orientation that adult education has embraced in the United States. He prefers an approach that is based on values that he identifies as humanistic and personal. He feels that adult educators have been too excessively influenced by the technological model of curriculum theorists such as Ralph Tyler, and have ignored important value questions about society, the human being, and the nature of educational methodology.

The efforts of Lawson and Paterson to give some philosophical justification for adult education are well reasoned and demand more careful examination than can be afforded here. A number of weaknesses of this analysis, however, can be noted. The definition of education and the criteria that are presented cannot all be derived so easily from our ordinary usage of the term adult education. What Peters, Lawson, and Paterson are proposing is rather a programmatic definition. Adult education, at least as used in the United States, has a broader usage. In restricting the concept adult education to what amounts to liberal adult education, these writers were guilty of a rationalist bias toward cognitive education and a bias against education for training and skill development. In the argument be-

tween liberal educators and progressive educators, these particular
analysts take the side of the liberal educators//This restriction of
terminology, we feel, serves little purpose in justifying adult education, for it legitimates only a part of what is included under the
ordinary usage of the term adult education in the United States. To
call some things adult education and others the education of adults
is to bring elitism and rationalist bias into the field of adult education which has developed along different lines in this country. In
restricting the term adult education to liberal adult education, British analysts such as Peters, Lawson, and Paterson may be guilty of
essentialism, claiming that words have an essential meaning that
transcends all social contexts.

In his most recent collection of essays, Lawson (1998) broadened his concept of liberal adult education to include "both the progressive tradition of Dewey, Lindeman, Bergevin and others and
the humanistic tradition of such writers as Maslow, Rogers, and
Knowles" (14). He thus separates adult education from the traditional liberal studies. In his present view of liberal education, it
"does not imply a particular content but embraces any content that
is taught or learned in a liberal manner" (12). Liberal education is
thus defined more in terms of processes, procedures and rules.
Lawson, however, has not abandoned the centrality of rationality in
adult education for he still contends that "the concept of liberal education draws heavily upon the idea of disciplined thinking which is
implicit in the whole idea of knowledge-based curriculum and upon
academic disciplines" (43). Lawson now distances himself from his
fellow analyst R. W. K. Paterson when the latter claims that liberal
adult education is not a species of education, it is education. Lawson
contends that it cannot be assumed that liberal values are themselves universal. Such claims for Lawson can only be made within a
particular tradition, the liberal tradition (69).

The Objectives of Adult Education

Paterson's treatment of the educational objectives of adult education is an extensive analysis of the curriculum of liberal adult
education. Adult education has as its purpose the communication of
knowledge by bringing about a deepened awareness or consciousness in persons. Skill learning is included in the range of knowledge
only if the skills are intrinsically worth learning and not merely
instrumental skills. Little attention is given to skills learning and
affective learning in Paterson's discussion of educational objectives. An academic subject matter approach is central to his view of

educational objectives. Utilizing the forms of knowledge thesis developed by Paul Hirst, the subject matter of adult education is presented as entailing nine different kinds of knowledge: "namely the kinds of knowledge distinctive of mathematics, the physical sciences, history, the human sciences, languages, the arts, morals, religion and philosophy" (Paterson, 1979, 84). Paterson argues that the objective worth and richness of these disciplines has long been established.

In his treatment of the curriculum for adult education, Paterson faces the problem of how this curriculum differs from that of children and adolescents. He admits the educational objectives remain the same. He does contend, however, that certain aspects of these disciplines are more appropriate for adults because they presume an adult maturity, especially in moral, philosophical, and religious areas (1979).

The two other objectives for adult education that Paterson offers are the development of the virtues of reason and the learning of moral values. Developing the virtues of reason gives a person mental autonomy, and learning values gives moral autonomy. Both of these objectives, Paterson feels, can be realized in a particular manner in adults because of their mental and moral maturity. Paterson shows himself sensitive to the problems of what justifies one adult educating other adults in moral values. He is less sensitive to this problem in the case of children and adolescents, where it also needs justification. He concludes that the moral education of adults will be a more indirect education through art, literature, philosophy, etc., where the teacher does not impart values or doctrine, but discusses with adults the moral implications of situations found in these sources.

In discussing the objectives for adult education, Lawson makes a case for the learning of skills as a legitimate form of knowledge within adult education. Yet his inclusion of craft subjects and skills learning is based on reducing these to a form of knowledge and intelligent behavior. Insofar as the learning of skills demands intelligence, it can be considered an adult educational activity. A craft qualifies as education if it is a "system of skills, criteria, values, and cognitive knowledge" (1975, 67). Lawson also maintains a distinction between education and training. Training is involved with goals outside the process, goals of a utilitarian nature, while education is involved with values that are intrinsic to the very concept of education (Lawson, 1975, 99).

The treatment that the two British analysts give to the objectives of adult education is consistent with their analysis of the concept of education. If the cognitive, rational, and intellectual dimensions of education are the only dimensions worthy of being called educational, then only those objectives that foster this form of development can be appropriate objectives for adult education. It is not that these analysts believe other objectives and forms of human activity are not worthwhile, it is only that they should not be classified under adult education. They believe that confusion arises when adult education is used as the umbrella term to embrace all types of learning activities. When it is so used it is difficult, in their opinion, to give an educational justification for the field of adult education.

One can sympathize with the conceptual analysts in their attempts to give a more precise definition to education and educational objectives, but their excessive concentration on rationality and cognitive understanding has resulted in a narrow view of adult education. Human beings are much more than rational beings. They are emotional, intuitive, and practical. Human beings are parents, friends, workers, citizens, playmates, and activists. To say that what promotes human development in any of these other areas is not education, and to restrict the term merely to what can be reduced to cognitive understanding, is to base the educational enterprise on a narrow and elitist basis. Though it may be difficult to draw the distinction between education and recreation, education and training, education and social service, we feel certain that this distinction should not be based upon a relatively narrow concept of human rationality and understanding.

Lawson (1998) has somewhat softened his view about what is included within the objectives of adult education. However, he is still reluctant to call prescription, indoctrination or the development of employable skills and competencies adult education, preferring to see it as a process of enquiry and criticism. He recognizes that there is a legitimate debate on this issue, and there can be no premature closures to the debate. In his implied rejection of postmodernist thought, he maintains that there must be some points that are fixed and these include explanations of truth, meaning and rationality. For him these concepts cannot be dispensed with "if we are to retain social institutions of some kind, including adult education" (16).

Educational Processes

Paterson's analysis of the educational processes of adult education includes, first of all, an analysis of the concepts of teaching and learning//He rejects the behaviorist viewpoint that learning is a change in behavior. He considers learning a coming-to-know. Even in the learning of skills, the coming-to-know aspect is fundamental to the concept of learning (1979). In the analysis of teaching it is emphasized that

> Teaching is a collaborative process, involving exchanges, out-goings, and interaction between two separate and independent centres of consciousness, and converging on to some objective and accessible reality. . . . (Paterson, 1979, 172)

Teaching thus is an intentional activity in which communication is intended. Since Paterson is interested in separating teaching from indoctrination, this leads him to a discussion of the freedom of the student in the teaching-learning process.

Indoctrination is distinguished from teaching in that the former attempts to bring about an uncritical acceptance of beliefs. Paterson contends that there is no contradiction in the concept that adults can be indoctrinated. It is a matter of empirical study whether or not adults are actually indoctrinated. The harm with indoctrination in his view is that it narrows the breadth of vision and awareness of those being instructed (Paterson, 1979).

Since Paterson limits his view of education to liberal education, he does not consider the question of mandatory continuing education. This is certainly a limitation on the rights of adults to pursue or not pursue their own education. Complicating this issue, however, is the right of society to demand that persons in certain professions keep abreast of knowledge deemed necessary to be of service to others. In the chapter on radical adult education, this question has been considered in the light of Ivan Illich's and John Ohliger's opposition to mandatory adult education.

From his treatment of the concepts of learning and teaching, Paterson turns to a discussion of the criteria for determining genuine processes of adult education. These criteria are "wittingness, voluntariness, conscious control, interpersonal encounter, and active participation by the educator" (1979, 196). There is a general presumption that adults are *witting* or aware recipients of the learning in which they are involved. This is not always the case in the education of children and adolescents. The participation of adults is *voluntary* if they participate for the reason that the educational experience is worth having for its own sake. Paterson contends that adults involved in education will not suffer the harmful effects of schooling because their education is freely chosen, and they can easily remove themselves from it//For an educational process to be genuine, adults must also be in *conscious control* of the process. They must have the power to require instruction from the teacher. This learner control will result only if there is some *encounter between persons* in the educational process. This criterion is more realizable in the case of adults, for they are more likely to act toward one another in such a way as to respect the other persons. Finally, an educational encounter must involve *active participation* of the learners. Such participation must be in educationally relevant ways. Dialogue through class discussion is the most appropriate form of activity among adult educational processes, and real dialogue includes only those communications that are educationally significant. In Paterson's view, it is only in the education of adults that these criteria can be realized to the highest degree.

Lawson's approach to educational processes is an argument against a number of popular approaches proposed in theory and practice. He is critical of the service orientation of adult education that attempts merely to respond to the demands of students. He also argues against student-centered education, which he takes to refer to: "Forms of organization which place the emphasis on the requirements of the learner rather than upon those of the subject to be taught or upon the professional and personal values of teachers." (Lawson, 1975, 18)

Lawson critiques student-centered teaching that emphasizes private thought rather than public knowledge, and reduces the inputs and contribution of the teacher to a minimum (1975). He argues against viewing adult education in terms of learning situations rather than teaching situations.

The basis of Lawson's argument against these approaches lies in his analysis of education as a value-oriented or normative activity. Lawson views these various student-centered approaches as attempts to shift the responsibility of value judgment about what is educationally worthwhile from the teacher to the student. For Lawson, the task of the teacher in adult education is to make choices about those things that are educationally worthwhile.

The concept of needs assessment in adult education has been analyzed by Monette (1977) who arrives at conclusions similar to those reached by Lawson. Needs, in Monette's view, logically demand some standards or social norms against which they can be measured. Monette concludes that adult education should move from a technological approach to a more humanistic approach in which values and needs are collectively determined by students and teachers together//Monette advocates the Freire approach to needs assessment, and thus his view appears better balanced than the position of Lawson who sees the teacher as the sole determiner of what is valuable in educational activities.

Lawson's recent collection (1998) questions whether adult educators are still avoiding the value questions. He criticizes the fashionable view that adult education is about process, not content. For him adult education cannot do without some conception of purpose and what is worthwhile. His task in this well argued collection of essays is to redefine a philosophy of adult education "in a more meaningful way which respects individuals . . . [and] defines them as a part of a group and not independently of it" (41).

The concept of experiential learning in adult education has been subjected to conceptual analysis and classification in a mode similar to the work of analytic philosophers. Fenwick (2000) distinguishes five distinct currents of thought apparent in recent scholarly writing analyzing experiential learning. She recognizes the definitional problems that arise "when one tries to disentangle the notion of experiential learning from experiences commonly associated with formal education such as class discussion, reading and analysis, and reflection" (243, 244).

Taking the concept of experiential learning to mean a process of human cognition she has identified five meanings of the concept. She identifies *reflection* on lived experience (*a constructivist perspective*) in the work of Mezirow and Brookfield. Within a *psychoanalytic perspective* she describes experiential learning as *interference*, which deals with how the unconscious tends to disrupt learning by producing conflicts between personal myths from the outside and personal fictions from inside. A third perspective, which she terms *situative*, involves *participation* in a particular situation and leads to changing processes of human activity in a particular community. A fourth perspective, *critical cultural*, found among critical pedagogues and postmodernists, focuses on the *resistance* caused by the inevitable power relations in human cultural situations. Finally, *co-emergence* (*a enactivist perspective*) "assumes that cognition depends on the kinds of experience that come from having a body with various sensorimotor capacities embedded in a biological, psychological, cultural context (261)." Fenwick rejects the possibility of developing a synthesis of these perspectives since they describe different world views. She concludes by suggesting that "in contexts of adult education, discussion might explore possible roles for educators within different perspectives. . . ." (266)

Adult Education and Society

The last set of issues that are examined by Paterson concerns the relationship of adult education to the society in which it takes place. The first issue that Paterson considers is the right and duty of adults to pursue lifelong education. His treatment is thorough and balanced and thus not easily summarized. After analyzing such concepts as justice, rights, and duties, Paterson discusses the right of adults to education. Based upon the individual's right to deepen knowledge and develop personally, Paterson concludes that individuals have both rights and duties in pursuing lifelong education (1979). The process of establishing these general principles leads Paterson to a discussion of more precise educational rights.

Paterson discusses the specified share of educational resources to which adults are entitled. In general, every individual adult

> does have a right, it seems clear, . . . to some appropriate share, and neither more nor less than that share, of whatever overall resources a society finds that it can reasonably devote to the business of promoting the education of its adult members. (Paterson 1979, 239)

Some preferential treatment should be given to those who through no fault of their own are deprived of educational opportunities before they became adults. The responsibility of societies is limited in these areas, however, by the availability of resources.

Paterson's discussion of these issues is important for clarifying the concepts to be used in public policy arguments about the rights to continuing adult education. The past four decades have witnessed in the United States debates on these issues with regard to educational equality and compensatory education for children and adolescents. No comparable public policy debate has taken place with regard to adult education. Most funding in adult education from federal government sources is directed toward compensatory education, originating in the social programs of the 1960s. The issues raised by Paterson are cast philosophically, but they have practical implications with regard to funding in adult education.

The second issue that Paterson treats is the social purpose or social relevance of adult education. After an analysis of these terms, Paterson raises the question of what social purposes or goals should adult education address. In keeping with his position on adult education as serving the liberal purposes of education of the mind and reason, Paterson sees no direct social purpose for adult education. He concludes that

> it cannot be part of the purpose of education either to vindicate the status quo or to advocate social change, whether gentle and piecemeal or radical and sweeping. The commitment of education is to knowledge, understanding, insight, in whatever social directions these may happen to point. The commitment of education is always and necessarily to the truth, wherever it may lead. (Paterson, 1979, 256)

What education does to promote social progress is to educate persons liberally. In so doing, this education indirectly promotes a democratic society. Education cannot remain education if it allows itself to be used as an instrument for attaining noneducational goals, "however socially necessary or desirable these may often admittedly be" (Paterson, 1979, 268).

Paterson's argument for the neutrality of adult education is accepted and reinforced by Lawson. Besides the educational argument, Lawson brings out the practical consideration that if adult education were to become involved in social causes, it would run the risk of not receiving adequate public funds for its management. Another danger is that adult education could become so fluid that it becomes adaptable to every change with regard to social, political, and economic issues.

The position that Paterson and Lawson take on this issue is a well-argued one, but it is not one that all adult educators have maintained. In the chapter on radicalism and adult education, the views of Paulo Freire have been examined on this issue. It is Freire's contention that it is impossible for education to be value free when it comes to social purpose and relevance. The position of the two British analysts is also not one that has been accepted by all educators who espouse liberal education. What these analysts are proposing may be a purist concept of education that does not take into account the close connection between education and the society in which it takes place.

Lawson's Criticism of Radical Education and Postmodernism

Lawson (1982) continued his work in the analytic tradition by providing a well-argued criticism of radical adult education. While his criticisms are mainly directed at the theoretical assumptions of the new sociology of education in Britain, the logic of his argument also extends to radical educators who have made use of critical theory and feminist pedagogy.

Lawson attempts to show that the use of concepts in educational discourse is connected with values and assumptions associated with a philosophical tradition. Both he and Peters, whose work he draws on extensively, ascribe to the values and assumptions of classical liberal education. The definition of education used by analytic philosophers stresses intellectual understanding and organized bodies of knowledge. Lawson admits that in other traditions, education has a different meaning, one that often includes political action or vocational education.

Since conceptual analysis has come under attack from radical adult educators in Britain, Lawson tries to show the conceptual weakness of radical arguments. Radicals argue that the traditional liberal education is not objective, open, and truthful, but is biased in favor of elites. Their attempt, in Lawson's analysis, is to reconstruct or radicalize adult education by basing it on working class values and having it address working class experience. Thus in their view, education should be a cultural and political tool.

Lawson points out how the radical position is based on a relativism that rejects universal values and argues instead that "there are values which are so universal that they can be used to judge on issues . . . and they are used by members of many groups" (15). Lawson contends that the principle of rationality is such a universal, and it is on this principle that he bases his defense of liberal education and his rejection of the radical argument. A commitment in education to predetermined political goals such as socialism does not, in his view, respect the freedom and rationality needed in the educational process. Lawson prefers to base education on such universal values as rationality and understanding rather than on the values of particular classes in society.

In arguing against radical adult educators, Lawson rejects the new sociology of knowledge upon which their educational philosophy is based. He argues that this sociological theory, which is so insistent in pointing out the ideologies and myths of traditional education, has its own ideology, usually a form of Marxist theory. Thus Lawson argues that when radicals speak of false consciousness, they implicitly presume that they have a true consciousness or valid beliefs about society, social roles, and social relationships. Lawson contends that the radical critique is no more correct than the analyses presented by liberal educators.

In rejecting radical arguments, Lawson defends important aspects of liberal education. Against educational deschoolers he defends the autonomy of institutions to educate. He argues for the value of curriculum or subject teaching, made up of public forms of knowledge, to counter the views of educators who see teachers as mere facilitators or coordinators of student learning. Finally, he insists on the objectivity and timelessness of knowledge against excessive democratization of knowledge in which all are involved in making knowledge. Lawson questions all forms of political and community education as not only ideologically dangerous but also as diverting educational resources "away from the more traditional role of general cultural diffusion and personal development through studies on a broad perspective" (1982, 31).

In Lawson's conceptual analysis of all issues relating to adult education (e.g., lifelong learning, community education, the right to universal higher education, equal educational opportunity, training, relevance, teaching), the relevant criteria come from the philosophical traditions of British analytical philosophy and its justification of traditional liberal education. That there is no necessary connection between these two traditions is shown in the work of some North American analytical philosophers who espouse both progressive and radical standpoints in education.

In his latest collection, Lawson (1998) argues against both radicals and postmodernists in critiquing philosophies of individualism. He clearly defends the key concepts of a liberal approach to adult education: citizenship, autonomy, knowledge, truth, rationality and moral obligation. Lawson is in dialogue with both analytic and political philosophers. Lawson seems to move away from his previous position on the neutrality of adult education in the political sphere. He connects his conception of adult education with the tradition of political liberalism from John Locke to John Rawls, Robert Nozick, and Martin Dworkin. For him this tradition embodies a constructive tension between the concepts of individuality and society (16). It is unfortunate that adult educators in North America have not adequately engaged the arguments of this British philosopher of adult education who, throughout his long career, has offered penetrating and profound analyses of key concepts and arguments in adult education.

Assessment of Analytic Philosophy
of Adult Education

There is something challenging about the analytic philosophy of adult education that has appeared thus far. The writings of Lawson and Paterson, and to a lesser extent Monette, are precise and carefully reasoned//There is a conceptual clarity in these analyses that is unrivaled by other philosophical writings in adult education. Arguments and explanations are detailed. Possible objections to the positions taken are foreseen and answered in unambiguous and restrained argumentation.

These philosophical analyses are also a challenge because they introduce the readers to an influential tradition in contemporary philosophy of education. The clear and persuasive positions arrived at by the renowned British analyst R. S. Peters are related to adult education. Other analysts in both Britain and the United States have also produced writings of considerable merit. The conceptual analysis presented in this chapter represents a serious attempt to introduce adult educators to this tradition.

Analytic philosophy of education is a challenge to adult educators not only in the clarity and quality of the reasoning, but also because of some of the positions that have been arrived at through this philosophy. This philosophy is critical of some of the loose language and slogans that have prevailed in the writings of adult educators. Lawson's critique of the language of needs, adult education as a service-oriented field, and the emphasis on learning situations will help to sharpen the thinking of many adult educators. Though some of the conclusions that the analysts have arrived at will not be accepted, it is a useful exercise to have one's thinking challenged by these arguments. To maintain one's views in the face of their criticisms takes a comparable philosophical critique and analysis.

Though analytic philosophy of adult education has already made some contributions to developing a philosophy of adult education, it is not a philosophy without its faults and limitations. Some of these have been pointed out in the course of this chapter. One major limitation or problem with this method is that it may arrive at a false precision which then leads to unwelcome consequences. An example of this is the concept of education that has been adapted by Lawson and Paterson from Peters. This concept brings in a clarity that then eliminates much of what is ordinarily included by this term. This leads, as we have seen, to a devaluing of certain forms of education, specifically those that are utilitarian and pragmatic. The introduction of this concept of education into the field of adult education in the United States would most likely increase confusion rather than eliminate it. Recent essays by Lawson have attempted to deal with this criticism.

A second and perhaps more critical weakness of this approach to philosophy is the stance of some analysts in providing a methodology that is value free or neutral. The techniques employed by some analytic philosophers resemble the techniques of the social scientists who attempt to be value free in their inquiry. There is, however, a distinction between holding one's views in abeyance in a philosophical analysis and advocating neutrality in educational decision making. The arguments of Lawson and Paterson for value free adult education with regard to social purpose and relevance are examples of this confusion. It may be impossible to avoid value decisions in these areas. Although analysts often argue for taking neutral positions on social questions, the actual practice of education often makes this impossible.

Perhaps on this point we are asking too much of the analysts. Depth in one area may be achievable only by ignoring other areas of consideration. Perhaps the analysts can achieve language clarity, precision, and vigor only if they separate themselves to some degree from political, social, economic, and educational issues in society. This separation is not, we believe, a necessary one, but it is one that has characterized the work of many analysts. If analytic philosophy includes and moves beyond the conceptual analysis to a rational reconstruction of educational enterprise in its full dimension, it may well provide the strongest philosophical basis for contemporary philosophy of adult education.

// p. 216 is blank

(STOP 14)

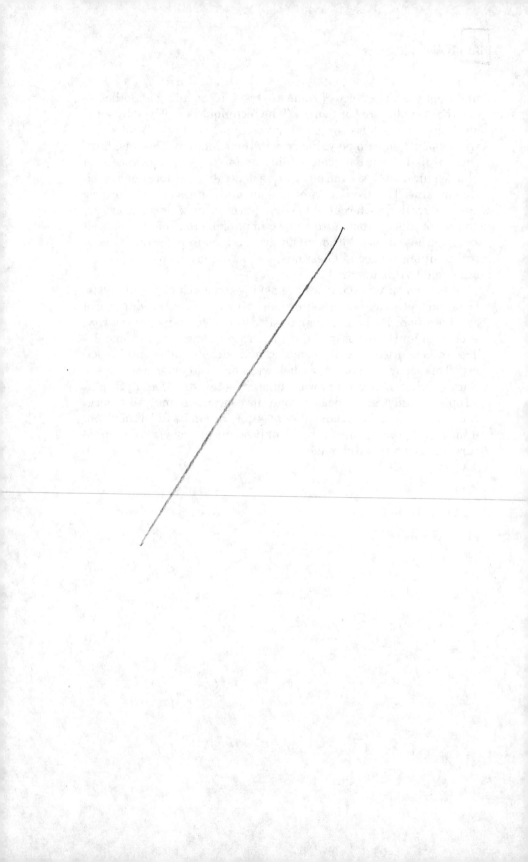

CHAPTER VIII

POSTMODERNISM AND ADULT EDUCATION

In the past two decades some educators, including adult educators, have begun to bring various forms of postmodernism to bear on the theory and practice of education. Many aspects of education have been subjected to criticism at the hands of thinkers who utilize the themes and insights of postmodernism. While some applaud these efforts, many see little value in such theorizing. The language utilized in these debates lacks the clarity found in other philosophical approaches, perhaps a sign that the movement is still in its beginnings.

The term postmodernism has been in use for many years. It is a difficult word to define since many often-conflicting meanings are attributed to it. In brief, the term serves to draw attention to the changes which some intellectuals, artists, and scholars see taking place in our societies and cultures. Postmodernists in the arts include architects, playwrights, writers, and photographers. In the academy, postmodernists are found in all fields of study, including education. The term is both fashionable and elusive. It almost appears that the word has different meanings in different academic disciplines.

Postmodernism may have its great appeal because it is open-ended and lacks specificity. The word may be used to describe almost anything that one approves or disapproves of. At its core the term may signal dissatisfaction with the present or modern situation. Some have interpreted its use as the product of desperation among many intellectuals and artists, particularly in Europe. On the other hand, postmodernism may reflect a disillusioned optimism about recent events in societies and cultures. What postmodern means in one context may not particularly illuminate its meaning in another area. Since the term has many meanings, this chapter will attempt to use the term as especially adult educators have used it in their writings.

Historical Perspectives and Origins of Postmodernism

Postmodern is a term that was first used in art and literature. As applied to the arts it has been described as "the overall character and direction of experimental tendencies in Western arts, architecture, since the 1940s or 1950s" (*The Harper Dictionary of Modern Thought*, 1988, 671). In architecture the postmodern introduces decorations used in surprising and even comic ways in contrast to the cool efficiency of twentieth century modern architecture. Postmodern literature is playful in stressing that stories are fiction and fragmentary.

The term postmodern has been broadened to designate a cultural phenomenon describing developments marked by "eclecticism, pluri-culturalism, and often a post-industrial marked frame of reference coupled with a skeptical view of technical progress" (*The Harper Dictionary of Modern Thought*, 1988, 672). Some scholars trace its rather recent cultural usage to the riots in Paris in 1964 when French scholars used the term to describe their cynicism and resignation after the failures of such movements as Marxism, feminism, and environmentalism to bring about radical change in society (Rosenau, 1992). Other analysts have broadened the moment of transition from the modern to the postmodern to include events in Chicago, Prague, Mexico City, Seoul, Tokyo, and Berlin when it appeared that

> it is almost as if the universal pretensions of modernity had, when combined with liberal capitalism and imperialism, succeeded so well as to provide a material and political foundation for a cosmopolitan, transnational and hence global resistance to the hegemony of high modern culture. (Harvey, 1989, 38)

Still other interpreters describe postmodernism as a rejection of the modern developments in science and technology that led to the death-events of the twentieth century: World War I, Soviet concentration camps, the Holocaust, World War II, Hiroshima and Nagasaki, the continuing threat of nuclear and ecological holocaust. For these interpreters, such events have ended the modern era and the continuation of a modernity that appears to threaten the very existence of the planet. (Inbody 1995, 529) Postmodernists thus share

p. 219

the mood of cultural pessimism found among the proponents of critical theory of the Frankfurt school, though there are many arguments between critical theorists and postmodernists on other issues.

The intellectual ancestors of postmodernists are many. The philosophies of Friedrich Nietzsche and Martin Heidegger contained similar cultural criticisms and pessimistic outlooks. Many postmodern themes are found in the existentialism of Jean Paul Sartre and others. From modern theories of hermeneutics, postmodern scholars have adopted criticism of empiricism, rationality, universal science, and mechanical causation. Postmodernists have also embraced romanticism's questioning attitude towards objective reality, its interest in fantasy, feelings, and emotions, as well as its attention to the metaphysical, the sacral, the exotic, the deviant, the primitive and the unusual.

The foremost postmodernists thinkers include the French scholars Michel Foucault, Jacques Derrida, Jean Lyotard, Jean Baudrillard, and the American Stanley Fish. Among its severest critics are the German Jurgen Habermas and the American philosophers Fredric Jameson as well as Richard Rorty, who, while once considered a postmodernist, has now dismissed the postmodernist label as not helpful for understanding contemporary culture and considers it just another grand narrative or overarching and totalizing explanation like those that postmodernists reject.

Modernism and Postmodernism

Postmodernism is best being/seen in contrast to modernity and modernism to which it is a reaction. Modernity refers to the many social, economic, and political systems that have developed in the West since the eighteenth century. For some scholars, modernity stretches from European Renaissance humanism in the sixteenth century to the present day. Renaissance humanism began the separation of the search for truth from dogma and tradition, which was continued in the Protestant Reformation and then especially in the Enlightenment. The rationalisms of Descartes bequeathed to modernism one of its major principles, the appeal to reason. Evolutionary Darwinism contributed the strong reliance on science that marks many modernists projects.

From a sociological perspective, the modern refers to the progressive economic and administrative rationalization and differentiation of the social world. Examples of differentiation are the separation of fact from value and the ethical from the theoretical sphere. Modernity includes the following: "the accumulation of Western civilization, industrialization, urbanization, advanced technology, and the nation state" (Rosenau 1992, 5)//Modernity refers to the rise of industry, cities, market capitalism, the bourgeois family, growing secularization, democratization, and social legislation (Hollinger, 1994, 25).

From a philosophical perspective, modernity can be identified with the Enlightenment worldview that embraces an entire body of attitudes and ideas. For the Enlightenment philosophes like Locke, Voltaire and Rousseau, the problem of knowledge was critical. For them, knowledge was to be achieved not through faith, tradition, or authority but

> through reason conceived by rationalists as deductive and empiricists as inductive or experimental. The Enlightenment quest was for certainty, for literal objectifying thought, for direct representation of reality in language, for comprehensiveness, and for certain imperatives for practical action, most notably the quest for individual human freedom and the demand to create history. (Inbody, 1995, 526)

The view of human nature espoused by the Enlightenment thinkers was mechanistic. Accordingly, they sought to control data in a rational manner, pursued single meanings and universal claims to truth, objective interpretations of data, and the value of sense perception. To these tenets they added beliefs in the certainty of knowledge and a fixed human nature, as well as a devotion to science and eventually technology, and the secularizing liberation of society and culture from the excessive power of a supernatural or revelation-based religion.

In the social sphere, the modernity of the Enlightenment stressed individual rights, multiple dualisms, a focus on human persons, a search for substances, European culture, progress in a straight line, centralization in social, political, and economic spheres, and a domination of nature. Enlightenment thinkers asserted that meaning and value are established by human subjectivity, which stresses the autonomous, self-consciously knowing and acting human subject. In academia the modern era fostered not only the natural sciences and new approaches to philosophy and religion, but also utilized new historical methods that gave rise to a historical consciousness which recognized the factors of change and novelty in history as well as differences between historical periods and cultures (Inbody, 1995).

The postmodern may be best interpreted as a critical response to the entire modern or Enlightenment project, though some theorists maintain some continuity between the two periods. One of the chief premises of postmodernism is that the second half of the twentieth century marked the end of the modern period in art, architecture, literature, science, philosophy, theology, media, and popular culture. Postmodernists consider changes in culture and society so great that the new epoch requires a new name. In their view, the present intellectual and cultural situation, especially in advanced capitalist countries, is in discontinuity with modernity. Thus postmodernity refers to all those cultural phenomena that are emerging with the present decline of modernity. Other terms used to describe this emerging culture include post-industrial, media society, information age, consumer society, and the bureaucratic society of controlled consumption. Some scholars (e.g., Sarup, 1989, 130) have presented the two cultures in a binary fashion:

modernity	*postmodernity*
autonomous subject	plural, polymorphous subject
coercive totalizing politics	pluralistic open democracy
certainty of progress	awareness of contingency
industrial technology	universal consumerism
Puritan asceticism	pleasure principle

Postmodernism thus is primarily a cultural movement in advanced industrial and capitalist societies. As such, it challenges many modern priorities: "career, individual responsibility, bureaucracy, liberal democracy, tolerance, humanism, egalitarianism, detached experiment, evaluative criteria, neutral procedures, impersonal rules and rationality" (Rosenau, 1992, 5-6). Postmodernism's attack on modernism rejects its moral claims, institutions, and interpretations. It does not view modern institutions as a force for liberation but rather as sources of subjugation, oppression, and repression. Postmodernism rejects the global, all encompassing worldviews that have marked the modern era: Marxism, certain interpretations of Christianity, Stalinism, capitalism, liberal democracy, secular humanism, feminism, Islamic fundamentalism, and modern science.

Although postmodernism has generally been portrayed as in opposition to the Enlightenment, the position of some postmodernists may be a bit more nuanced. Both Foucault and Derrida have made it clear that they do accept certain aspects of Enlightenment; they accept its ethos but not what they call its dogmas: the belief that knowledge in the empirical sciences can be automatically applied to increase human progress and happiness; that the human sciences can transform society into a totally rational culture; the belief in rational universal values and human progress toward a utopian goal; that knowledge will liberate people from oppression (Hollinger, 1994). What Derrida, Lyotard, and Foucault do is explore the limits of reason and in this way they continue the work of Immanuel Kant and others.

Forms of Postmodernism

Since postmodernism is a complex phenomenon embracing a wide spectrum of views, attempts have been made to identify different forms of postmodernism. Scholars have identified skeptical postmodernists as well as affirmative postmodernists depending on whether culture is viewed as primarily pessimistic or optimistic. A distinction has also been made between establishment postmodernism and radical critical postmodernism. Others identify deconstructive or eliminative postmodernism and constructive or revisionary postmodernism. Scholars also distinguish between hot and cool postmodernism, neoconservative postmodernism, and poststructural postmodernism, postmodernism of reaction and postmodernism of resistance (Rosenau, 1992). It should be noted that the analyses of postmodernism ironically all utilize some form of the dualism that postmodernists abhor. For purposes of this chapter we will distinguish two forms of postmodernism: deconstructive or skeptical postmodernism and constructive postmodernism.

Deconstructive or Skeptical postmodernism offers a pessimistic assessment of the modern age in analyzing the fragmentation, disintegration, malaise, and vagueness or absence of all moral parameters. This dark form of postmodernism is inspired by the writings of the existentialists Nietzsche and Heidegger. It stresses the impossibility of arriving at truth and often predicts disasters ahead for the human race. Representatives of this form of postmodernism are Jean Baudrillard, Michel Foucault, and Jacques Derrida.

Deconstructive postmodernism includes philosophers and intellectuals who deconstruct or break down the modern metanarratives of science and philosophy. Deconstructionists tend to look upon persons as subjects who are de-centered, who are inseparably involved with the unconscious and irrational and shaped through particular social relations, language, and culture. These thinkers deny the possibility of going beyond language to reality. They assert that our understanding of the world is fragmentary, that our knowledge is corrupted by power and domination, and that it is futile to search for sure foundations of our knowledge. What they propose is a pragmatic approach to living in a confused world. For deconstructionists, the very concept of reality is a fiction, a construction of the imagination. Deconstructionists challenge as mythical and even illusionary, the modern model of the enlightened rational thinker. The purpose of deconstruction is to demystify our basic assumptions about knowledge, reality and action. For deconstructive postmodernists, these modern concepts are responsible for the oppressive horrors of the twentieth century.

One of the principal tenets of deconstructive postmodernism is antifoundationalism. Deconstructionists are keen on undermining the foundations of the clear and certain knowledge that was dear to modern science and philosophy—the belief that there was some correspondence between our minds and objective reality. For deconstructionists, the social world is constructed through our use of language. For them there is no reality other than the reality that the mind tentatively constructs through its use of language.

Critics of deconstructive postmodernism have treated it harshly. They argue that the logical conclusion of this form of thought is absolute relativism, skepticism, cynicism, or even nihilism. They contend that this approach makes knowledge, moral judgment, and aesthetic theory impossible. It eliminates the possibility and desirability of any worldview. This theory provides little basis on which to construct any cultural or political life (Rosenau, 1992).

Constructive or Liberating Postmodernism recognizes that the postmodern period is either the decline of the Enlightenment or the beginning of its decline. The theologian Sallie McFague (1987) has tried to identify some of the elements of postmodern sensibilities:

> a greater appreciation of nature, linked with chastened admiration for technology, the recognition of the importance of language, and hence interpretation and construction in human existence; the acceptance of the challenge that other religious options present to the Judaeo-Christian tradition; a sense of displacement of the white, Western male and the rise of those dispossessed because of gender, race, or class; an apocalyptic sensibility, fueled in part by the awareness that we exist between two holocausts, the Jewish and the nuclear; and perhaps most significant, a growing appreciation of the thoroughgoing, radical interdependence of life at all levels and in every imaginable way. (x)

Constructive postmodernism begins with cultural analysis but moves to deal with political and economic realities. It is decidedly liberational and critical of social injustices. It calls for moving beyond European and North American political and economic power and social paradigms, to new paradigms and centers of power. In the decline of socialism and the problems of late capitalism, it envisions the possibilities of new alignments wherein women, ethnic minorities, and other groups long ignored by power elites can raise their voices and express a different experience and perception of the world.

For some interpreters, the term postmodern should be restricted to the deconstructive postmodernists. However, there are enough similarities between the two forms to give them both the same label. Both share a suspicion of the Enlightenment and modernity, and both develop approaches that are in contrast to the chief themes of the Enlightenment.

Constructive postmodernism has also been called cultural and liberational and can be interpreted as a revisionary modernism. It does accept some of the assumptions, values, and strategies of modernity in order to challenge them. It accepts the modern critical spirit, personal autonomy, individual rights, political equality, and other modern notions. But at the same time it does expose the self-contradiction, illusions, failures, repressions, and the ideological agenda of modernity. It is thus involved in a chastening and refinement of the characteristic values of modernity. This approach to the modern world is both revisionary and affirmative. It defines

> a vision of the world that refines and enriches the positive contributions of the modern view of the world but is more in accord with emerging paradigms, which see the world more as rich, open, subtle, complex, complementary and interrelated than the truncated view of modernity. (Inbody, 1995, 536)

Themes of Postmodernism

Since postmodernism includes such a wide range of ideas and differences of opinion, it is difficult to identify the chief themes in understanding language and the world. Using Rosenau (1992) as a guide we will attempt to isolate what are considered the chief themes in postmodern theory. Though not all of these themes have relevance to education, some overall perspective on this complicated theory will assist in grappling with its implication for adult education.

Interpretation: Author, Text and Reader

Postmodern theory diminishes the authority of the author of texts while increasing the privileges of the text and elevating the reader. Texts are open to readers defining and creating meaning. Everything is defined as a text, not only the written word but all phenomena. In postmodern theory, authors say more than they intend to say and readers understand more than the authors intended. Thus the text means more than both the reader and author think. Meaning comes not from what the speaker wants to say but from the linguistic system as a whole, which produces it. A dramatic way of expressing this aspect of postmodern theory is found in Umberto Eco's statement: "The author should die once he has finished so as not to trouble the path of the text"(1983, 7). According to Derrida (1976) the reading of a text has "nothing to do with the author as a real person" (158). The meaning of a text does not inhere in a text but in the interaction between the text and the reader. Thus the text can have different meanings for different readers and even for the same reader at different times. A definitive meaning of a text cannot ever be arrived at.

There is some difference between deconstructive and constructive postmodernists on this issue of author, text, and reader. The constructionist postmodernists do not speak in terms of wholly eliminating the role of the author, but rather of reducing the author's authority. The author's influence remains but in a diminished fashion. The interpreter's view is important but does not have universal validity.

The postmodernist most closely connected with the death of the author is Jacques Derrida (1930-), a philosopher and literary critic who is most often associated with deconstructive postmodernism. His work focuses on language and a style of reading texts. Derrida contends that texts should be deconstructed or broken down to get at their meanings. Deconstruction challenges the idea that a text has an unchanging, unified meaning. Derrida argues that multiple layers of meaning are at work in language.

Derrida is largely responsible for the famous death of the author proclaimed by postmodern critics. For him, what authors write is generally not what they mean (1976). He also asserts that "the text is all and nothing exists outside it" (1976, 158) Rather than

p 226

concentrate on authors, postmodern critics like Derrida focus "on language, free floating signs, symbols, readings, and interpretations, all of which escape the concrete definitions and reference points required by the subject" (Rosenau, 1992, 43).

Start ————————→ The Self: Subverting the Subject

Postmodernists in the humanities call for the death of the subject and in so doing they present a radically different view of human nature than usually presented in philosophy. Postmodernists resist the unified, coherent subject as a human being. They dispute the subject's stable identity, the assumptions ensuring its free will, and the philosophical humanism the subject's existence implies. What they oppose is the subject as an agent independent of social relations. Emphasis is to be placed outside subjects or factors in all fields of endeavor. Leaders are to be understood from situations and not from personal choices and decisions. Affirmative postmodernists speak of a new type of individual who is closely in tune with the world.

In literature, postmodernists are not interested in long and detailed descriptions of characters. In *The Name of the Rose,* Umberto Eco declares that "in the pages to follow I shall not indulge in descriptions of persons . . . as nothing is more fleeting than external form, which withers and alters like the flowers of the field at the appearance of autumn" (1980, 7). Thus in postmodern literature, characters and character development are not important.

Postmodernists are in opposition to all forms of humanism, including classical, scientific, Renaissance, Christian, Marxist, and Enlightenment. For them the philosophy of humanism has been used to justify Western superiority and cultural imperialism, which are manifested in a special way in Western education. This Western humanism has also led to environmental destruction.

The postmodern individual, according to deconstructive postmodernists, is not free, conscious, and self-determining. The postmodern individual is relaxed, flexible, oriented toward feelings and emotions, and holds a "be yourself" attitude. This person looks to fantasy, humor, the culture of desire, and immediate gratification. The postmodern individual is

> fascinated with tradition, the antiquated (the past in general), the exotic, the sacred, the unusual, and the place of the local rather than the general or universal. Postmodern individuals are concerned with their own lives and less con-

cerned with old loyalties such as marriage, family, church and nations. (Rosenau 1992, 55)

Constructive postmodernists call for the return of the subject as a changed person. This person will be decentered and emergent, living at the margins and rejecting total explanations of human phenomena. This person may be politically involved and engaged in resistance to oppressions in society. The postmodern person in this view will not be domineering, looking to master and reduce others to submission. Julia Kristeva writes of this person as a work in progress, a speaking subject (1984).

Knowledge of History, Time, and Geography.

Postmodernists are skeptical of efforts concerned with knowing and representing the past. They question that there is a knowable past, that historians can be objective in writing history, that reason enables historians to explain the past, and that history can interpret and transmit cultural and intellectual heritage from generation to generation. For them, history is the instantaneous second between yesterday and tomorrow; time is disparate, crisscrossed, layered, and misaligned rather than homogeneous, evolutionary, purposive, and regular. Postmodernists are especially critical of humanist history, which contends that human agents form individuals and their societies. For them the only value of history is the traces that it leaves on the present. They do, however, have a respect for the primitive and for tradition.

Constructive postmodernists look to new forms of history such as micro-narratives and genealogies to replace current history. Priority is given to local and regional history, time, and space.

Theory and Truth

Deconstructive postmodernists seek to abandon truth and theory and accept relativism and pluralism of truths. For them it is impossible to say anything with confidence. "There is no such thing as truth in itself. But only a surfeit of it. Even if it should be for me, about me, truth is plural" (Derrida, 1979, 103). For Foucault truth cannot be separated from power and ideology. He states that "we are subjected to the reproduction of truth through power, and we cannot exercise power except through the production of truth"(1976, 14). In rejecting truth, postmodernists reject the Enlightenment and certain concepts connected with it: order, rules, values, and dependence on logic, rationality and reason//Truth for radical postmodernists is a form of distorted rhetoric or propaganda.

Deconstructive postmodernists reject theory as alienating, disparate, and dissonant. They are not interested in meta-narratives or all embracing explanations, seeing no value but rather dangers in them.

Constructive postmodernists view truth as personal and community-specific. Thus each person or each community may have its own version of truth. According to Rosenau (1992, 81) constructive postmodernists contend that a community of knowledge may establish a consensus of language and values, making it possible to communicate certain truths, though they are not universal, but true for a community at a certain time in its history.

Deconstructive postmodernists reject modernists' theories as totalizing, logocentric projects. They contend that theory conceals, distorts, and obfuscates reality. Theories do not fulfill the purposes for which they are constructed; they neither give direction nor are a basis for action. Rather than speak of theory, deconstructive postmodernists write about "instantaneous lightening flashes of paradoxical illumination" (Rosenau, 1992, 82).

Constructive postmodernists do not totally reject the value of theory but diminish its importance. Rather than guiding one's life and work by theories, individuals should understand everyday life as intuitive, based on feelings, and nearly spiritual. These postmodernists see value in trying to transform everyday life. Rather than focus on theories they privilege small narratives, community-based narratives, and dismiss grand theories or narratives. Whenever an explanation is given, it is only one possible explanation. Grand theories are rejected because they claim that there is a beginning, and end, and a definitive theory, all of which are impossible in a postmodern world.

Representation

Deconstructive postmodernists consider all representations as fraudulent forms of knowledge. They do not believe that it is "possible to present something over again, to replace one concept, person, place, or time with another, without loss of content or violation of intention" (Rosenau, 1992, p. xiv). They reject representation in language, politics, epistemology, and methodology. The superb, the non-general, the unique, the idiosyncratic, the sublime, the eccentric cannot be represented. Representation is a copy of a copy, a copy for which there is no original.

Affirmatives see representation as possible but in new forms. Representation in democracy is a source of debate with skeptics rejecting it and affirmatives demanding more authentic representation. Constructive postmodernists still believe that it is possible to represent the social world though not with the certainty that was once thought possible.

Epistemology and Methodology

Postmodernists practice deconstruction and intuitive interpretation. The goal of deconstruction is to undo all constructions. It tears a text apart, reveals its contradictions and assumptions without attempting to improve, revise, or offer a better version of the text (Rosenau, 1992). Its methods attack scientific claims of objectivity, causality, materialist reality and universal rules of inquiry. Relativism and uncertainty characterize these methods. Affirmatives are more constructive and contextual, depending on emotion, intuition, and imagination.

Political Orientations and Social Sciences

Deconstructive postmodernists tend to be political agnostics, rejecting all political views. Some argue for nonparticipation and reversion to play and euphoria. They also speak of terror, suicide and violence as the only alternatives. Constructive postmodernists are more optimistic in advocating new special movements around peace, ecology and new age. In the Third World they tend to be populist, fundamentalist, and nationalist.

To summarize such a vast intellectual movement as postmodernism is almost an impossible task. Perhaps Atkinson's (in Rikowski and McLaren, 2002, 20-21) portrayal might be an apt description. Postmodernism resists certainty and resolution. It rejects fixed notions of reality, knowledge or method. It accepts complexity, lack of clarity, and multiplicity. Postmodernism acknowledges subjectivity, contradiction, and irony. It manifests an irreverence for traditions of philosophy or morality. Postmodernism make a deliberate attempt to unsettle assumptions and presuppositions. It refuses to accept boundaries or hierarchies in ways or things. Finally, it disrupts binaries that define things as either/or. This portrayal could be expanded but these appear to be some of its major features.

The Postmodern Critique of Philosophies
of Adult Education

For the past decade educators, including adult educators, have attempted to relate postmodernist thought to the field of adult education. One thing that has resulted from these efforts is a criticism of all previous philosophical theories of adult education. These philosophies, though found in some form among the ancients, took shape and have had influence in the modern era. This section covers the postmodern critique of the philosophies of adult education presented in this book. The chief source for this critique is *Adult Education and the Postmodern Challenge* (Usher, Bryant, and Johnston, 1997), though other sources will also be used. The brand of postmodernism utilized in this text, as in the work of many others who apply postmodernism to education, is much closer to constructive postmodernism than to the deconstructive version.

From the perspective of postmodernism, the previous six theoretical approaches to the philosophy of adult education were conceived within the modernist framework, which is to mold "individuals into appropriate functional roles within the project of modernity" (Bagnall, 1999, 35). The approaches are examples of grand theories that attempt to interpret and recommend what education is or should be like. All these theories have a view of what individuals should be and what type of society they are educated for. Liberal adult education and analytic adult education are united in promoting the intellectual freedom of individuals by placing the modernist disciplines of the liberal arts at the center of education, and by their stress on a rational approach to education. Progressive education centered attempts to educate persons for social and economic progress by infusing the content and method of education with notions of science and progress, and by connecting education to one's vocation or work in the industrial society. Behavioral adult education promotes molding individual behavior to both individual and social needs. Humanistic adult education attempts to release the inner potential of individuals. Radical adult education, which includes critical theory, has as its aim emancipation and empowerment of individuals and groups from oppressive situations or forms of government.

Liberal Adult Education and Analytic Philosophy of Education

Liberal adult education is critiqued by postmodernists as being directed to the fulfillment of the project of modernity. The purpose of this education is to shape a certain type of subject or person with definite qualities and attitudes/This education "was an important instrument in the formation of the 'liberal' citizen, individualistic, rationalistic, with a faith in benevolent progress through science and 'truth'" (Usher et al., 1997, 11). The goals, definition of needs, curriculum, methods, and organization are carriers of the values of modernity.

Liberal education's stress on truth, the value of theory, the autonomous self, and human freedom go counter to the principal tenets of postmodernism. Postmodernists reject the very concept of adulthood that underpins the liberal adult tradition, which stresses the self's capacity for ever-increasing autonomy and social action.

Liberal adult education is deeply committed to the grand narratives of the past and of modernity. These are the carriers of the great truths of Western civilization. Postmodernists are not alone nor are they the first to point out this weakness of liberal education. Liberal education's battles with the progressives and radicals have engendered similar criticisms. But the wholesale rejection of the truths in the Western tradition is particularly pronounced in postmodernism. For them a study of the Great Books is engaging in ideological indoctrination not an opening of the mind to the reality of everyday life.

Postmodernism's attack on academic disciplines is in a special way directed at liberal education. For postmodernists, since there are no foundational truths, the legitimacy of discipline-based education is rejected. It is contended that:

> If there are no sure foundations and no Archimedean points from which knowledge is generated and assimilated but instead a plurality of partial knowledges, then the very foundations of discipline-based education are themselves undermined. (Usher et al., 1997, p. 12)

Postmodernists have been especially critical of liberal adult education for citizenship in the world. Although this education speaks about the education of adults for self-development and the development of a critical sense of citizenship, it has in reality been an elitist education in distinguishing between knowledge for its own sake and utilitarian knowledge. This education has not dealt adequately with the connection between knowledge and power. It has also attracted a disproportionate number of learners who are middle class and affluent. What it has failed to do is connect the private sphere to the public sphere. It is also charged with reinforcing a common culture of sameness (Keddie, 1980).

(STOP 15)

Postmodernist educators repeat the charges against adult liberal education that have been offered by critical pedagogues. This education too often fails to examine the social, political and economic contexts and problems that are involved in active citizenship. Liberal educators have been insufficiently critical of how their education advances the cause of capitalist elites.

The criticisms made by postmodernists of liberal education extend to the work of analytic philosophers of adult education who have argued for a definition of adult education that privileges liberal adult education. Postmodern adult educators are especially critical of the modernist dichotomy that such analysts as Peters, Lawson, and Paterson have made between education and training. This sharp dichotomy permeates all aspects of education: curriculum, teacher recruitment, institutions, and vocational outcomes. It also has led to wide differences in social status (Bagnall, 1999).

Progressive Adult Education

Since progressive adult education had its intellectual origins in the Enlightenment, postmodernist criticisms of its principal tenets are deep and extensive. Progressivism builds on the empiricism and rationalism that arose in the Western world and the education that it spawned.

At the center of progressive education is a commitment to science and the scientific method. Postmodernists consider modern science one of the principal culprits for perpetrating ills in today's society. Postmodernism

> enables a *questioning* of the scientific attitude and scientific method, of the universal efficacy of technical-instrumental reason, and of the stance of objectivity and value neutrality in the making of knowledge claims. (Usher et al., p. 7)

Postmodernism's criticism of the scientific method extends to scientific research. It questions the assertion that knowledge is established through systematic empirical observation and experiment and rational processes of induction and deduction.

At the heart of progressive adult education is the notion of learning from experience. Progressives tend to privilege experiential learning over the discipline based learning advocated by liberal educators. Postmodernists question whether this is an advance. The danger with learning from experience is that it may be uncritical and merely integrate the individual into a more formal educational or employment system and technology of control (Usher et al., 1997). Postmodernists advocate locating individual experience within a wider critical social context.

Many have taken issue with the emphasis in progressive adult education on education for vocation. Even in John Dewey's time, progressives had to defend themselves against the charge that they were advocating a limited and limiting education that would suit the needs of the national economy rather than the real and felt needs of individuals. As in other areas, postmodernist educators adopt the criticism and proposals of critical pedagogy in calling for a critical vocationalism that seeks "to help learner/citizens engage critically and productively with their private interests in securing and retaining work and gaining personal meaning and worth from it" (Usher et al., 1997, 46-47). This education would focus on providing learners with knowledge about how industries work and thus lead to a more enlightened citizenry and work force.

Behaviorist Adult Education

Postmodern educators have repeated many of the criticisms of behaviorism that have been made by humanists and radicals. Their criticisms of the scientific orientation of modernity lead them to oppose a form of education that is based so strongly on the behavioral sciences. Even such skills as reading, writing, and numbering were treated as skills in which persons were to be trained. The postmodernist emphasis on freedom leads them to oppose what they consider the manipulation of individuals to conform to the demands of societies.

Postmodern adult educators oppose the regulation of individuals by variables defined either as instruction or as rewards for correct behavior. This molding of individuals leads to the sorting of individuals into their places in society. Those with a weak intellect are judged suitable for "non-intellectual pursuits of the body: for manual or routinized occupations which required not a liberating education of the intellect but a training of the senses, the body" (Bagnall 1999, 36). Those judged inferior are not educated but trained for certain roles in society. The training advocated by behaviorists is criticized for accepting

> intellectual limits that nature had imposed or the possibility
> of many individuals gaining significant autonomy, or at least
> of doing so within particular spheres of their lives. It sought
> to ameliorate the effects of such deficiencies through pro-

viding for the developing of functional routines by the af-
flicted individuals, sufficient for them to be happy and grateful in their work, social intercourse, and other spheres of
civilized existence. (Bagnall, 1999, 36-37)

Postmodern adult educators join others who have criticized the
competency-based approach to teacher education that attempts to
reduce teaching to a set of behavioral skills. They contend that "to
be a teacher is not to apply a set of skills derived from theoretically
based knowledge, for example of behavioural psychology. It is certainly not a matter of acting in repeated and predictable ways learnt
from . . . theoretical knowledge" (Usher et al., 1997, 127). A
postmodern approach to teacher education would place an emphasis
on diversity and on many different forms of knowledge and many
different contexts.

The pedagogy of behaviorist adult education is criticized for ignoring the particularities of learners, notably their gender, ethnicity
and class. The pedagogy focuses on preplanned inputs and determined outputs wherein learning becomes a neutral process. They
note that

> the self that is operative here is the classical scientific self--
> individualised, undifferentiated, an essentially abstract
> entity, the monological self, the self-contained individual
> having no transactions with and unaffected by anything other
> to itself—a kind of pure learning machine. (Usher et al.,
> 1997, 95)

In this pedagogy learners appear to have control, but this control is
illusory because of the predetermination of the learning outcomes
that are socioculturally constructed and thus viewed as problematic
by postmodernists adult educators (Usher et al., 1997).

Humanistic Adult Education

Postmodernist adult educators recognize how essential the humanistic psychology of Rogers, Maslow, May and others has been to
adult education theory and practice. Its principles are at the basis of
what has been the most influential theory of adult learning and
teaching. They also recognize that

> many unconscious reference points and implicit frameworks
> of understanding are constituted by its language of person-

centeredness, self-directness, empowerment, student-centredness pedagogy and its equation of the educational experience, adult learning and self-development. (Usher et al., 1997, 75).

Andragogy, based as it is on the scientific findings of humanistic psychology, has served to give professional status to adult education as a distinct academic discipline and profession. To humanistic psychology has been added the related theory and research from cognitive psychology and developmental psychology.

Drawing on the insights of Michel Foucault, postmodernists have tended to question the equation of social progress with the growth of scientific knowledge. Such knowledge in their view is a form of power and control, based on the assumption that the more we know about something the better we will be. Postmodernists are suspicious of psychology's contention that it is a human technology that will lead to better individuals and a better society. (Of course, these same critical questions are posed to forms of adult education that depend on behaviorist psychology.)

Again, relying on Foucault's analysis, postmodernist adult educators are critical of humanistic adult education which relies on "technologies of the self where people can effect by their own means or with the help of others a number of operations on their own bodies and souls, thoughts, conduct, and ways of being, so as to transform themselves" through vocational and confessional practices" (Usher et al., 1997, 83). While vocational practices are prevalent in behaviorist adult education, it is confessional practices that are a key element of humanistic adult education.

Through confessional practices or self-talk, people regulate themselves by allowing the autonomous self to become the center and focus of activity, thus leading to empowerment. Postmodern educators question the belief that people can gain power over themselves merely through confession or talk, as humanistic psychologists and psychoanalysts contend. They extend their criticism to forms of adult guidance and counseling that depend on confessional talk. What postmodern educators and counselors find objectionable in reliance upon these techniques is that they do not empower people but rather force them to evaluate themselves according to criteria provided by others though subtle forms of manipulation. The entire process forms a connection between individual desires and self-fulfillment and political, economic and social goals.

In the view of postmodern critics of adult education, common practices in both behaviorist and humanistic education, depending as they do on the discipline of psychology, are not empowering of individuals but rather under the cloak of objective knowledge they have become forms of a

> power which has become particularly influential in adult education in a wide range of practices such as guidance and counseling, action planning, recognizing prior learning, portfolio-based assessment, learning contracts, records of achievement and self evaluation. (Usher et al., 1997, 87)

Postmodern educators have directed their criticism at andragogy, the most prevalent form of humanistic adult education. Although they repeat some of the criticisms that this theory has received in the past thirty years, they add their own particular criticisms based on what they believe is a faulty view of the self, experience, and culture. They are particularly critical of the influence that Carl Rogers's psychology has had on andragogy and other forms of humanistic adult education.

Postmodern critics question the use of the experiences of adults to give them a more authentic status as learners over the experience of children. They reject the anti-schooling bias that this position has engendered among adult educators. They question whether knowledge from the real world is necessarily better than other forms of knowledge. Seeming to reject or at least to minimize knowledge from other sources while extolling knowledge from personal experience, humanistic adult educators and advocates of andragogy lack "a conception of experience as culturally constructed, pre-interpreted, complex and multistranded," which is a central belief of postmodernism (Usher et al., 1997, 96).

The view of the self assumed in humanistic adult education which emphasizes that individuals make meaning, fails to recognize to what degree the self is determined by the culture in which it is formed. The self implied here is "the transcendental self of the Enlightenment" (Usher et al. 1997, 96). This self is pre-given and decontextualized and there is an assumption that persons can be largely unaffected by the culture in which they were raised. This view of the autonomous self, the value of personal experience in learning, and the lack of attention to culturally based knowledge has led to an over psychologized andragogical tradition in which "learners are thrown back on their personal resources which determine the path of their learning—a seeming control by the learner which, in practice turns out to be illusory." (Usher et al., 1997, 96)

Thus it is the lack of attention to the social self that post-modernists fault the humanistic tradition. Humanistic educators show little awareness that persons are constituted through social relationship and that learning is more than learning about oneself and getting in contact with one's authentic self and acting in accordance with what one feels. Humanistic educators seem to view the social as oppressive and fearful, an area from which one must be liberated through authentic educational experiences in which the self affirms itself by privileging its own experiences. In the view of postmodern adult educators, the excessive psychologism and individualism of humanistic adult education

> can lead ultimately and paradoxically to a dehumanization through the substitution of covert for overt regulation under the guise of being human, enabling learners to open up and provide access to their inner world. This is an infiltration of power by subjectivity and a complementary infiltration of subjectivity by power. (Usher et al., 1997, 98)

Radical and Critical Adult Education

Radical adult education is a modernist form that "attempts a transformative release from oppressive and exploitive cultural structures, by educationally empowering individuals and groups with the authentic knowledge of their contingent realities" (Bagnall 1999, 35). Various forms of radical education have been identified: Marxist or neo-Marxist education, critical pedagogy, and radical feminist pedagogy. Each of these theoretical approaches challenges current forms of education by offering alternative realities and possibilities.

The postmodern critique of radical adult education is rooted in criticisms of radical thought, especially Marxism. It views the embrace of Marxism as just another acceptance of a meta-narrative or totalizing effort to achieve large-scale social, economic, and political change. Postmodernists reject the dream of a future utopia in favor of a politics that attempts to deal with local situations, the here and now. The postmodern approach to social change is to embrace temporary actions of resistance within a limited situation. Also, postmodernism rejects the worldview of Marxism since it believes that principles are constantly in the process of change. It sees no time when the process will end.

Postmodern adult educators have directed their criticisms particularly at critical pedagogy that is influenced by the Frankfurt

School of Social Research and has blended with Freire's pedagogy. Usher et al. (1997) find many aspects of critical pedagogy attractive, especially its emphasis on empowering democratic citizenship but it questions the translation of these goals into practice. Critical pedagogy in their view, however, does not adequately relate "these goals to contemporary educational contexts, the political realities of existing educational policies and practice and the predominant cultural influences on the lives and interests of different learner citizens" (40). Postmodernists contend that critical pedagogy does not respond to the existence of a fragmenting postmodern world. Critical pedagogy is thus viewed as a utopian opposition to the educational status quo which may have become a hindrance or stumbling block to exploring and negotiating with the new social and educational context (Usher et al., 1997, 40).

Some educators have attempted to combine critical pedagogy with postmodernism or as Edwards (1997) assumes, the mantle of postmodernism. Michael Collins (1995) considers postmodernist thought as a contributor to the critical turn in modern adult education. Postmodernist emphasis on power relations and on the will to power as a strong motivating force within society finds resonance with critical or radical educators. Critical theorists have also embraced the postmodernist desire to unsettle authoritative texts as guidance for acting in the world. The acceptance of many points of view, especially voices of those neglected in the past, are valued in critical thought "to destabilize the dominant discourse of status quo interests, creating possibilities for disempowered groups and individuals in society to assert themselves" (92). Collins, however, distances himself from the postmodernist tendency to reject rational criteria for how persons should act in the world. He concludes his analysis by remarking that

> for critical adult education, perhaps the juncture between postmodernist thought and critical theory is most usefully effected around a concern for both ethical and political commitments, leaving aside any preoccupation with resolving ontological differences. (Collins, 1995, 92)

Donovan Plumb (1995) has also taken up the challenge of assimilating postmodern critique within critical theory. He openly admits that "critical adult education is confronted with the uncomfortable prospect of finding new ways to constitute itself as a viable cultural enterprise in postmodern times" (184). Postmodern rejection of rationality, truth, and theory challenge the certainties that are embedded in critical adult education, especially in its Marxist versions/The movement toward a nonverbal culture also challenges the logocentrism of critical adult education. Thus the postmodern rejection of the notion of a rational culture in which communicative discourse is possible and necessary, undercuts the very nature and purpose of critical adult education. For Plumb, what is left for critical adult educators is to "absorb the magnitude of postmodernity's implications without rushing to find answers" (189). Plumb concludes on an optimistic note, based it appears more on faith than reason, that "critical adult education already possesses resources to sustain the tension of discourse and action, of openness and resolve, of the variegated boundaries, of the heterogeneity that prevail in postmodern times" (190)

Tendencies in Postmodern Adult Education

The postmodern critique of philosophies of adult education has revealed a number of tendencies that might constitute elements in a postmodern adult education. Bagnall (1999) and others identified these tendencies. Although they cannot in any way constitute a coherent philosophy of adult education, which would be contrary to the very spirit of postmodern thought, they do give some indications of the directions of postmodern thought. These tendencies represent at most divergences from the various forms of modernist education.

Heterodoxy

The postmodern in education tends toward what is different from the traditional and conventional. This tendency arises from the postmodern privileging of what is different and spontaneous in contrast to what comes from restraint or control. The postmodern recognizes that there are many social contexts that call for different responses. There are many different groups whose voices need to be heard. Postmodern adult education thus fosters a decentered responsibility that embraces "emotive, nonrational, unconscious impulses to human action, . . . an alluring freedom that is minimally constrained by convention, responsibility for consequences, the demands of rationality, or common sense" (Bagnall, 1999, 134). This tendency leads to a variety of forms of adult education, none of which is destined to remain or even be unique.

This tendency of postmodern adult education is stressed by Hemphill (2001) who argues that adult educators should include many perspectives in their work including race, class, gender, and language. A goal for adult educators should be dealing with the marginalization of many adult students' experiences to "develop adult education practices that respectfully legitimize adult learners' lives, perspectives, discourses, and voices" (29, 21). Hemphill also argues for increased attention to popular culture and media, which have remained marginalized from the mainstream adult education thinking.

Expressiveness

The expressiveness of postmodern adult education leads it to reject overly planned events and needs-based programming in favor of being responsive to "the noncognitive, emotive interests, inclinations, and preferences of its participants" (Bagnall 1999, 135). It is thus a contrast to the set curriculum of liberal education, behavioral modification, problem-posing education, and other rational forms of program development. This tendency results from the postmodern belief that all human actions are underdetermined, unpredictable, and ambiguous. It recognizes the power of the unconscious in human actions as well as the importance of feelings, emotions and nonrational inclinations. This tendency leads to less emphasis on propositional knowledge and a greater sensitivity to beauty, rhythm, and harmony. The postmodern adult educator fosters "the upgrading of the value of the nonrational, the spontaneous, and the *ad hoc*, both in curriculum and in the form of educational engagement itself" (Bagnall 1999, 136). The evaluation, justification, and appraisal of adult education employ diverse criteria, especially those that stress the aesthetic, spiritual, affective, and experiential.

Reflexive Contextualization

Postmodern adult education in its goals, curriculum, procedures, and programs is partially determined by its cultural context and is partially undetermined. This is in contrast to modernist theories or philosophies that determine educational events. This situation arises because of the postmodern tenet of not privileging any particular discourses as necessarily leading to the true, the good, the authentic and the beautiful, and the contingency of all beliefs (Bagnall, 1999). This tendency produces great diversity in the field of adult education in goals, curriculum, procedures, and participants. This diversity recognizes many forms of knowledge, including the ethical, the technical, the existential, and the aesthetic. Postmodern adult education is thus open to influences that may have been suppressed in the past through centralized planning, systematization, outcomes-based education, and evaluation. The role of the state in regulating adult education is rejected. The tendency also favors a short-term perspective in program planning, remaining open to all contingencies. Finally, this tendency privileges experiential learning including the recognition of prior learning.

Revisionism

Postmodern adult education remains open to radical reinterpretation, deconstruction, and revision from any contemporaneously and contextually cultural perspective be it feminist, black, physically handicapped, or whatever. This tendency arises from the loss of foundational knowledge in postmodern belief itself. As a result of this tendency, all norms of belief are subject to radical criticism and educational events are "optimally responsive to the cultural situation of its generation, conduct and appraisal" (Bagnall 1999, 149).

Indeterminacy

Postmodern adult education is uncertain, indefinable and unpredictable in where it locates authority or responsibility for educational decisions since such are dispersed to the "shifting plethora and confusion of intersecting and interacting cultural traditions that determine, yet undetermine, and partially constitute the individual, social, and institutional identity of humanity" (Bagnall, 1999, 140). This tendency arises from the fragmented individual identity and the importance of nonrational influences on human actions, which leads to a decentering of authority away from particular individuals or groups. The locus of authority thus remains problematic and contested. This opens the possibility for marginalized groups to have power and authority. Postmodern adult education discourages the state to assume responsibility for adult education except in rare and clear-cut places, thus advocating minimal state support.

Privatization

Postmodern adult education favors moving involvement and control to the participants, who will determine the goals, curriculum, processes. In this way they will be independent of educational institutions that sponsor the events. This tendency counters the controlling effects of theories of adult education that foster passivity on the part of participants. Privatization also allows participants the choice of whether or not to participate, without the existential burden of active involvement in and contributory control over the educational event. Furthermore, participants have the alternative of complete withdrawal from the educational event.

Phenomenalism

Postmodern adult education places emphasis on the intrinsic value of the educational experience. It goes against the utilitarian and pragmatic goals of modernist education and fosters valuing education for the quality of the learning experiences whatever they might be: "the joy of new understanding, the elation of transformative change to one's perspective, the satisfaction of successfully mastering a skill, the exhilaration of a new aesthetic experience" (Bagnall, 1999, 143). The emphasis on intrinsic learning goals makes this approach similar to liberal adult education, differing from it, however, in that postmodern adult education does not ascribe to any ideological position such as espoused by liberal adult educators. Phenomenalism, which derives from the unpredictability, changeability, uncertainty, and ambiguity of postmodernity, fosters an adult education that counters the emphasis on credentials and outcomes-education fostered by modernist education.

Dedifferentiation

Postmodern adult education does not differentiate itself from other related human activity such as research, social work, political action and recreation, but is immersed in all of these activities. This view of adult education sees it everywhere in society and has difficulty isolating it as a separate identity. This tendency arises from the postmodern emphasis on impermanence, ephermerality, flexibility and changeability of reality. This characteristic entails to a degree the deprofessionalization of the field whereby the responsibility for adult education becomes diffused through society. There are many ways of becoming an adult educator. The curricula and goals of postmodern adult education tend to be "opaque, multilayered or diffuse, and resistant to deterministic analysis, criticism, and understanding" (Bagnall 1999, 146).

Though Bagnall recognizes that his attempt to isolate these features of postmodernism may ultimately fail, his attempt does uncover important values entailed in the postmodern critique of mod-

ernist forms of adult education. Some of these features are found in
the work of earlier critics of the adult education enterprise. But
drawing them together does give at least a feeling for what a
postmodern adult education might appear to be.

Evaluation of Postmodernism

There is much to commend in the postmodern project. It presents a challenging critique of many destructive and limiting aspects of the modern world and culture. It offers a scathing criticism
of practices and theories in all academic disciplines. Postmodernism
has uncovered many of the weaknesses in the Enlightenment project
for bettering humanity socially, politically, and educationally. One
can commend its reaction to the overconfidence in modern science
and other forms of knowledge and to the assumption of a false certainty that many have in the face of human complexity.
Postmodernism is often a healthy counter to the exaggerated confidence and optimism that is found in many areas of modern society.
One can also admire the efforts of postmodernists to deal with the
marginal, the ignored, the powerless, and the ostracized in all societies.

Postmodernism, however, has not been without its serious
critics who have pointed out its many contradictions and unresolved
problems. Those who criticize postmodernism pay the price of
being accused of being reactionary and out of date. One critic notes
that

> quite simply, any talk of truth, reason, valid argument, cri-
> tique or other such "Enlightenment" notions is enough to
> mark one out as hopelessly *derriere-garde*, or as a last-ditch
> defender of some obsolete creed . . . whose deplorable ef-
> fects are witnessed everywhere around us, and whose im-
> minent demise must surely be welcomed by all right-
> thinking persons. (Norris, 1993, 285)

Critics of postmodernism become defenders of the accomplishments
of the Enlightenment, which is viewed as the point of the modernist
achievement. While they recognize the flaws of the Enlightenment,
they stress its many significant achievements such as:

> the tradition that has given us the impressive corpus of
> modern science (including medicine) and mathematics, mod-

ern technology; (with its contribution to modern health, transportation, communications, and agriculture) and ideals of justice and freedom for the individual (those ideals, for example, that are embodied in the U.S. Bill of Rights). (Phillips, 1995, 36)

Critics of postmodernism have pointed out a number of contradictions to be found in their work (Rosenau, 1992). The anti-theory bias of postmodern thinkers is actually in a contradictory way a theoretical and ideological stand. In stressing the irrational in human life and culture, postmodernists often employ the very rational tools of discourse that they say they are rejecting. The postmodern emphasis on the marginal in all cultures is in itself an evaluative judgment that the theory is supposed to avoid. The fact that postmodernists reject truth claims undercuts the truth of their own theories.

It must be granted that postmodern thought has also made important contributions to debates in education, including adult education. Postmodern doubt and suspension of belief requires us to question many conventional beliefs about education. Postmodern questioning may provide opportunities to move beyond the realms of knowledge that are now accepted. For example, Edwards et al. (2002) question the technical objectivity of research in adult education. They "interrogate" the text about

> the link between the accounts collected by researchers and the reality they purport to represent; about the ways in which researchers work on these accounts, fashioning their own representations of reality while erasing their own authorial presence. . . . This interrogation has opened up different research terrains and put in question certain traditions of study. (129)

The postmodern emphasis on inclusion and diversity challenges our notions of a set curriculum for all persons, without respect to their differences. Greene (1995) has used postmodern thought to uncover the patriarchal, colonialist, hierarchical, and repressive nature of much of the discourse in philosophy of education.

Sadovnik (1995) has made an appraisal of the effort of postmodernism in education. Though he judges some forms of educational postmodernism to be close to progressive and reconstructionist theory, he does commend it for some new insights.

The rejection of meta-narrative brings out the importance of local and situated meanings. The emphasis on difference makes possible dialogue among different groups. Postmodernism has the potential of connecting critical and feminist interpretations of education to the field of practice.

Despite these strong points, Sadovnik (1995) offers the following criticism. The language of postmodernism is abstract and rather impenetrable, setting up a distinctive club. In the social sciences, postmodernists are short on empirical research, due perhaps to their anti-scientific bias. Also, they fail to connect theory to practice in any meaningful way, assuming that their political positions are correct and that the only issue is how educators are to implement the ideas. He concludes that if postmodernists do not connect theory to practice in any meaningful way, they run the risk of becoming increasingly irrelevant to practitioners and policymakers.

The most severe criticisms of postmodernism in education have come from educators with a Marxist orientation. (Hill, McLaren, Cole, and Rikowski, 2002.) Marxist educators argue that Marxist educational theory has greater power in generating challenges to educational orthodoxies and in bringing about a transformation of society. For them, postmodernist education cannot generate a vital politics of human resistance to current educational polities. Postmodernism is a sterile, theoretical cul-de-sac with no political program for transformative change. Carried to its logical conclusion, it ends in the celebration of an aimless anarchism.

Marxist theorists admit that postmodern education has made significant contributions to our understanding of the power of mass media, the dark side of the technological revolution, the ideological dimensions of education's connections with capitalism, as well as the racial, gender, sexual, and national prejudices within educational policies and practice. Yet Marxist educators find dangers in the lack of collective memory and the lack of close analysis of economic, political, and cultural forces that they feel that Marxist analysis can bring to educational theory, research, and practice.

No final appraisal of postmodernist adult education can be given at this time. Adult educators need to remain open to the criticisms that postmodern philosophers and educators level against even the most cherished traditions and theories of the past and present. But these criticisms also need to be subjected to serious thought and questioning. It is not certain at this time whether the postmodern critique ushers in a whole new era and way of thinking, or is merely a critique and correction of the rich and complex modernist and

Enlightenment tradition in philosophy and education. This debate is important for adult educators to engage in because it raises crucial questions about the world we live in, and the enterprise that engages us.

We tend to share the conclusion of David Hemphill (2001) who, while recognizing the weaknesses and limitations of postmodern discourses, argues that these discourses

> offer a path—albeit a frustrating and convoluted one—to understanding present and future phenomena that are no longer well suited to modernist, rational explanations. Adult education is too important an enterprise to be left to ossify in a decaying paradigm of postmodern discourse. (27)

CHAPTER 9

EPILOGUE

PHILOSOPHY OF ADULT EDUCATION: RETROSPECT AND PROSPECT

The quest for truth in philosophy is a continuing one. The answers given by one philosopher or system of thought often provide the questions for the next philosopher or system. This quest continues because there is change in human life. People change, societies change, cultures change. These changes call for new explanations, new theories, and often new systems of thought. Philosophical questions can also never be fully answered because they touch the deepest human realities.

Adult education participates in the general philosophical quest. Over time it appears that various theoretical positions emerged in order to attempt to develop principles by which adult educators can better understand the enterprise they are engaged in and to determine what stances and roles they should take in the enterprise. As we have seen in this work, these principles generally relate to the nature of education, the concept of adulthood and adult education, the teaching-learning process, and the relationship between education and society.

While there is an admitted artificiality in incorporating into one classification schema centuries of Western thought, the attempt can be justified as a helpful way to introduce new students into the vocation of adult education. Exploring what many consider the best thinking in adult education is not an end in itself but should lead to further questioning and critical analysis. All philosophers learn something about the tradition of philosophy before they make their own particular contribution or raise their own questions.

In presenting the various principles of seven philosophies of adult education, we have left two issues to the concluding epilogue: how can the relationships among these various theories be clearly and simply understood, and what stance should the adult educator adopt in his or her personal philosophy of adult education?/The first question is retrospective looking back over the various philosophies presented in this book. The second question is prospective, for it involves looking ahead to the future work of adult educators challenged by the philosophical questions raised in this book.

Retrospect

There is a certain logic in the order in which the seven philosophical approaches are presented in this book. The order is loosely chronological and shows how theoretical approaches give rise to others in a dialectical fashion. Liberal adult education was the predominant Western philosophy of education from the time of the early Greeks to the rise of modern science and academic disciplines in the eighteenth and nintheenth centuries. The aims, methods, and content of this education were clearly established and have remained constant over the years. Truth was viewed as absolute and educational values were found in circumscribed disciplines and studies. This educational philosophy corresponded to a static conception of society in which truths, values, and structures were considered authoritative and immutable.

The great challenge to this system came with the rise of modern science, both natural and social, and modern philosophy. Change, relativity, and pluralism intruded themselves into human consciousness. A new educational theory developed to cope with this changed view of the world. Though some of its ideas were known by the ancient Sophists and other philosophers over the years, it was only in the progressive and pragmatic writings of William James, John Dewey, Eduard Lindeman and others, that this view of the world and the education based on it found their most eloquent advocates. At the beginning of the twentieth century progressive adult education became the philosophical positions of adult educators in the United States.. While liberal adult education still prevailed in other Western countries, it had an increasingly smaller role to play in this country. Progressive education placed the experience of learners at the heart of the educational process, called for a changed role for teachers, expanded the curriculum of education of education to include practical knowledge and concerns, and forged a close connection between education and societal change.

The richness of progressive adult education is seen in its powerful influence in one way or another on other philosophies of adult education. One way in which these philosophies can be understood is by examining their relationship to progressive adult education, from which some historically developed and others are closely related.

Behaviorist adult education is indebted to progressive thought for some of its basic principles. Progressives bequeathed to behaviorists their great emphasis on the scientific method and the importance of experimentation in arriving at truth. Scientific observation, problem-solving, hypothesis testing, and control are features that progressives and behaviorists have in common. Behaviorism departs from progressive thought, however, in its view of the possibility and desirability of controlling human behavior. The foremost behaviorist to apply principles of behaviorism to adult education was B. F. Skinner. This philosophy has inspired many practices in adult education, even though philosophers of adult education have for years been critical of the philosophical principles behind these practices. Furthermore, many practitioners engage in the practices inspired by behaviorism without explicitly embracing many of its philosophical tenets. The relationship between philosophy and practice has always been a complex one.

Humanistic adult education is related to the first phase of progressive education, that which placed an emphasis on the growth experiences of learners. Significantly, the best known humanistic educator, Carl Rogers, studied progressive thought at Columbia in the 1930s. Humanistic adult educators have concentrated upon the human potential for growth in both cognitive and affective areas of life. Much recent work in adult education has been influenced by humanistic and existential approaches to education. The group work that strongly characterizes humanistic adult education was first brought into prominence by the progressives. Also, both progressives and humanistic educators are optimistic in their approach to personal and societal change.

The emphasis on social change so central to radical and critical adult education can also be traced back to progressive thought. Social reconstructionists like George Counts and Theodore Brameld accept many basic progressive principles. Even the Brazilian educator, Paulo Freire, has acknowledged his indebtedness to John Dewey. Both progressives and radicals promote education as a powerful force for bringing about change. The two theories part company when it comes to the explicitness of the vision of the new society and the means to bring about social and political change. Radicals are more willing to adopt utopian visions of society and boldly espouse education as a legitimate vehicle for reshaping society. Though critical adult pedagogy owes its origins to the critical social theory of the

Frankfurt school, many of its advocates make explicit connections with the social pedagogy of John Dewey.

The relationship between analytic philosophy of adult education and progressive adult education is not as clear as in the above three cases. A definite connection does exist, however, in that many of the concepts, slogans, metaphors, and positions of the progressives have been the subject of conceptual analysis. The conclusions that analysts arrive at on such basic issues as education, learner-centered education, needs and interests, and so on, are often opposed to the views of progressives and closer to those of liberal educators. However, in his most recent writings Ken Lawson strives to broaden the liberal tradition to include many elements of progressive thought.

Postmodern thought, which has in recent years influenced a growing number of adult educators, has as one of its foremost targets the scientific and modern worldview espoused by progressives. However, postmodern adult education extends its critique to all philosophies of adult education. Postmodernist educators have raised questions about the certitudes espoused by liberal educators. They subject to keen criticism progressives and behaviorists reliance on science and the scientific method. Postmodernists reject many elements of the humanistic project: concern for the development of an autonomous self is rejected by the principles of change, flexibility, and contingency espoused by postmodernists. Though closer in many ways to radical and critical adult educators, postmodernists reject the meta-narratives of Marxism and socialism promoted by many radicals and critical adult educators. Finally, the quest for rational clarity and precision so dear to analytic philosophers is subjected to the charge of logocentrism and hyper-rationality.

In retrospect, a word can also be said about the relationship between progressive adult education and liberal adult education. Though progressivism developed in opposition to liberal education, liberal education has been rejuvenated to a degree through its confrontation with progressive thought. Liberal adult education has had to rethink its position on the place of science in the curriculum, the absoluteness of its views of truth and values, and the rigidity of its curriculum of studies. Progressive adult education has also benefited from its battles with liberal adult education. The importance of subject matter, the cultivation of the mind, and the value of tradition emphasized in liberal adult education provide a balance to the pragmatic and vocational thrust of progressive thought. There are also a number of examples where philosophers have attempted to combine features of liberal and progressive thought.

Prospect

The final question to be considered in this book may ultimately be the most important one: what stance should the adult educator adopt as his or her personal philosophy of adult education? Whatever the position adopted, it must be held critically. The professional adult educator should be constantly examining, evaluating, and perhaps rejecting or modifying what has been received from the past. A study of philosophies of adult education should produce professionals who question their own theories, practices, institutions, and assumptions as well as those of others.

In deciding upon a philosophy of education, one is faced, we believe, with three options. The first option is to choose one of the philosophies, or to determine that one has already espoused, perhaps implicitly, one of the philosophies discussed in this book. The advantage of this stance is that the educator has a clearly articulated approach that possesses a great degree of consistency. In addition, the criticisms offered of the various philosophies provide the educator with the opportunity to critically examine the assumptions underlying his or her chosen philosophical position.

A second stance is to opt for an eclectic approach to one's philosophy of adult education. In this approach, one chooses certain elements and values from different theories and operates according to those principles. This alternative has the advantage of flexibility and the possible disadvantage of inconsistency. Yet many persons see themselves as truly eclectic, constantly working toward a synthesis and integration of views.

This eclectic approach seems to be similar to the core values approach advocated by Day and Amstutz (2003). They propose that adult educators commit themselves to values apparent or implied in adult education practice. We note, however, that their core values are quite similar to those found in the theories treated in this book: cultural custodianship (liberal adult education), useful knowledge (progressive adult education), spiritual connectedness (religious version of adult liberal education), personal existence (humanist adult education), individual growth (humanist adult education), social reconstruction (radical or critical adult education), and scientific scholarship (behaviorism).

A third stance is to choose one particular theory as a framework upon which one builds a personal educational philosophy. Within this structure, views from other theories can be incorporated that are not inconsistent with the basic position. This approach gives a certain consistency to one's theory and practice, yet does not close off the possibility of influence from other viewpoints.

In the practice of adult education it must be recognized that persons can be rather flexible in their philosophical approaches. One's philosophy may be shaped by the context within which one is working. The nature of the organization or institution, the goals of the enterprise, the types of persons involved may influence one's theoretical and practical approach. There is much truth in Tisdell and Taylor's (2001) observation that "practitioners in the field actually straddle several orientations each emerging to the fore as the teaching context shifts and changes" (10).

Whatever the philosophical stance one adopts, it is important that the continuing philosophical quest is not abandoned. The study of philosophies of adult education is not a means of settling, once and for all, theoretical and practical issues. While inventories of one's philosophy of adult education might serve an important diagnostic purpose, they run the risk of a rigid categorization which is inimical to philosophical inquiry and criticism. In the end, the study of philosophy of adult education is to enable persons to gain insight into their personal and cultural past, and to refine their personal tastes and powers of judgment. The continuing reflection on philosophical issues in adult education should serve to develop methods of critical thinking that aid individuals to ask better questions, and expand the visions of educators beyond their present limits.

(STOP 16)

//REFERENCES

Adams, Frank. (1972). Highlander Folk School: Getting Information, Going Back and Teaching It. *Harvard Educational Review*, 2, 497-529.

Adler, Mortimer. (1937). *The Revolution in Education*. Chicago: University of Chicago Press.

Adler, Mortimer. (1949). *How to Read a Book*. Chicago: University of Chicago Press.

Adler, Mortimer. (1982). *The Paideia Proposal*. New York: Macmillan.

Adult Learning. (2001). Bringing Our Philosophies Into Practice, 11, 2.

Adult Performance Level Staff. (March 1975). *Adult Functional Competency: A Summary*. Austin, TX: University of Texas.

Askov, Eunice N. (2000). Adult Literacy. In Arthur L. Wilson & Elisabeth R. Hayes (Eds.), *Handbook of Adult and Continuing Education*, (247-262). San Francisco: Jossey-Bass

Ayer, A. J. (1959). Editor's Introduction. In A. J. Ayer (Ed.), *Logical Positivism*. New York: Macmillan.

Bagnall, Richard G. (1999). *Discovering Radical Contingency: Building a Postmodern Agenda in Adult Education*. New York: Peter Lang.

Baudrillard, Jean. (1975). *The Mirror of Production*. St. Louis, MO: The Mirror of Production.

Baumgartner, Lisa A. (2001). An Update on Transformational Learning. In Sharan B. Merriam, (Ed.), *The New Update on Adult Learning Theory*, San Francisco: Jossey-Bass.

Beck, George A. (1964). Aims in Education: Neo-Thomism. In T. H. B. Hollins (Ed.), *Aims in Education: The Philosophic Approach*. Manchester, Eng: Manchester University Press.

Belenky, Mary F., Clinchy, Blythe M., Goldberger, Nancy R., & Tarule, Jill M. (1986). *Women's Ways of Knowing: The Development of the Self, Voice, and Mind*. New York: Basic Books.

Bellah, Robert, Madsen, Richard, Sullivan, William M., Swidler, Ann, & Tipton, Steven M. (1985). *Habits of the Heart: Individualism and Commitment in American Life*. New York: Harper & Row.

Bellah, Robert, Madsen, Richard, Sullivan, William M., Swidler, Ann, & Tipton, Steven M. (1991). *The Good Society*. New York: Knopf.

Benne, Kenneth. (1957). Some Philosophical Issues in Adult Education. *Adult Education*, 7, 67-82.

Berger, Brigitte. (1993), Multiculturalism and the Modern University. *Partisan Review*, 60, 4, 526-534.

Bergevin, Paul. (1967). *A Philosophy for Adult Education*. New York: Seabury.

Bergevin, Paul & McKinley, John. (1958) *Design for Adult Education in the Church: The Indiana Plan*. New York: Seabury.

Bergevin, Paul & McKinley, John. (1965). *Participation Training for Adult Education*. New York: Seabury.

Bergevin, Paul, Morris, Dwight, & Smith, Robert. (1963). *Adult Education Procedures: A Handbook of Tested Patterns for Effective Participation*. New York: Seabury.

Blakely, Robert J. (1958). *Adult Education in a Free Society*. Toronto: Guardian Bird Publications.

Blakely, Robert J. (1965). *Toward a Homeodynamic Society*. Boston: Center for the Study of Liberal Education for Adults.

Bloom, Allan. (1987). *The Closing of the American Mind*. New York: Simon and Schuster.

Blundell, Sue. (1992). Gender and the Curriculum of Adult Education. *International Journal of Lifelong Education*, 11, 3, 129-216.

Boone, Edward J. et al. (1971). *Programming in the Cooperative Extension Service: A Conceptual Scheme*. Raleigh, NC: The North Carolina Agricultural Extension Service. Misc. Extension Publication 73.

Boone, Edward J., Safrit, R. D., & Jones, J. (2002). *Developing Programs in Adult Education* (2nd ed.). Prospect Heights, IL: Waveland Press.

Bowers, C. A. (1969). *The Progressive Educator and the Depression: The Radical Years*. New York: Random House.

Bowles, Samuel & Gintis, Herbert. (1976). *Schooling in a Capitalist Society*. New York: Basic Books.

Boyle, Patrick & Jahns, Irwin. (1970). Program Development and Evaluation. In Robert M. Smith, George F. Aker & J. R. Kidd (Eds.), *Handbook of Adult Education*. New York: Macmillan.

Brameld, Theodore. (1956). *Toward a Reconstructed Philosophy of Education*. New York: Dryden Press.

Bridenbaugh, Carl & Bridenbaugh, Jessica. (1962). *Rebels and Gentlemen* (2nd ed.). New York: Oxford University Press.

Brockett, Ralph G. (Ed,). (1988). *Ethical Issues in Adult Education*. New York: Teachers College Press.

Brockett, Ralph, G. & Hiemstra, Roger. (2004). *Toward Ethical Practice*, Malabar, FL: Krieger.

Brookfield, Stephen. (1986). *Understanding and Facilitating Adult Learning*. San Francisco: Jossey- Bass.

Brookfield, Stephen. (1987). *Developing Critical Thinkers*. San Francisco: Jossey-Bass.

Brookfield, Stephen. (2001). Repositioning Ideology Critique in a Critical Theory of Adult Learning. *Adult Education Quarterly*, 52, 1, 7-22.

Brookfield, Stephen. (2002). Overcoming Alienation as the Practice of Adult Education: The Contribution of Erich Fromm to a Critical Theory of Adult Learning and Education. *Adult Education Quarterly*, 52, 2, 96-111.

Brookfield, Stephen. (2003). Racializing Criticality in Adult Education. *Adult Education Quarterly*, 53, 3, 154-169.

Broudy, Harry. (1967). *Aims in Adult Education: A Realist's View*. New York: Seabury.

Broudy, Harry. (1981). Between the Yearbooks. In Jonas Soltis (Ed.), *Philosophy of Education*. Chicago: University of Chicago Press.

Broudy, Harry & Palmer, John. (1965). *Exemplars of Teaching Method*. Chicago: Rand McNally.

Brown, Ted, Hall, Helen, Harnish, Dorothy & Lynch, Richard L. (August 2001). Industry Skill Standards: Current Information on their Development and Uses Nationally and Internationally. Occupational Research Group, University of Georgia. www.coe.uga.edu/ORG.

Bugental, James F. T. (1967). *Challenges of Humanistic Psychology*. New York: McGraw-Hill.

Caffarella, Rosemary S. (1993). Self Directed Learning. In Sharan B. Merriam (Ed.), *An Update on Adult Learning Theory*. New Directions for Adult and Continuing Education, No. 57. San Francisco: Jossey-Bass.

Caire, Kaleem, M. S. (2002). The Truth About Vouchers. Educational Leadership, 59, 7, 38-43. http://www.ascd.org/publications/ed_lead/200204/caire.html.

Candy, Philip C. (1991). *Self-Direction for Lifelong Learning: A Comprehensive Guide to Theory and Practice*. San Francisco: Jossey-Bass.

Carlson, Robert. (1989). Malcolm Knowles: Apostle of Andragogy. *Vitae Scholasticae*, 8, 1, 217-233.

Carnavale, Anthony P., Gainer, Leila J. & Villet, Janice. (1990). Training in America: *The Organization and Strategic Role of Training*. San Francisco: Jossey-Bass.

Casement, William. (1991). The Great Books and Politics. *Perspectives on Political Science*, 20, 3, 133-141.

Cervero, Ronald M. (1989). Continuing Education for the Professions. In Sharan B. Merriam & Phyllis M. Cunningham (Eds.), *Handbook of Adult and Continuing Education*, (512-524). San Francisco: Jossey-Bass.

Clark, M. Carolyn & Wilson, Arthur L. (1991). Context and Rationality in Mezirow's Theory of Transformational Learning. *Adult Education Quarterly*, 41, 2, 75-91.

Collard, Sue, & Law, Michael. (1989). The Limits of Perspective Transformation: A Critique of Mezirow's Theory. *Adult Education Quarterly*, 39, 2, 99-107.

Collins, Michael. (1991). *Adult Education as Vocation: A Critical Role for the Adult Educator.* New York: Routledge.

Collins, Michael. (1995). Critical Commentaries on the Role of the Adult educator: From Self-Directed Leaning to Postmodernist Sensibilities. In Michael R. Welton. (Ed.), *In Defense of the Lifeworld: Critical Perspectives on Adult Learning.* Albany, NY: State University of New York Press.

Collins, Michael. (1998). *Critical Crosscurrents in Education.* Malabar, FL: Krieger.

Combs, Arthur, Avila, Donald L. & Purkey, William W. (1971). *Helping Relations: Basic Concepts for the Helping Professions.* Boston: Allyn and Bacon.

Comenius, John Amos. *Great Didactic of Comenius.* Translated by M. W. Keatings. Whitefish, MT: Kessinger Publishing.

Comings, John P. (2003). *Establishing an Evidence-Based Adult Education System.* NSCALL Occasional Paper. Cambridge, MA: National Center for the Study of Adult Learning and Literacy.

Competency-Based Vocational Education: Participants Guide for Inservice Teaching. (1977). Richmond, VA: Division of Vocational Education: Virginia State Department of Education.

Conant, James. (1961). *Slums and Suburbs,* New York: McGraw-Hill.

Cookson, Peter S. (1998). *Program Planning for the Training and Continuing Education of Adults: North American Perspectives.* Malabar, Fla.: Krieger.

Cremin, Lawrence. (1961). *The Transformation of the School: Progressivism in American Education,* 1876-1957. New York: Random House.

Cremin, Lawrence. (1970). *American Education: The Colonial Experience,* (1607- 1783). New York: Harper & Row.

Cross, K. Patricia. (1981). *Adults As Learners.* San Francisco: Jossey-Bass.

Cuban, Larry. (1984). *How Teachers Taught: Constancy and Change in American Classrooms,* (1890-1980). New York: Longmann.

Cunningham, Phyllis M. (1988). The Adult Educator and Social Responsibility. In Ralph G. Brockett (Ed.), *Ethical Issues in Adult Education,* (133-145). New York: Teachers College Press.

Daley, Barbara J. & Jeris, Laurel. (2003). Boundary Spanning. *Advances in Developing Resources,* 6, 1, 5-8.

Darwin, Charles. (1859/2003). *The Origin of Species.* Peterborough, Canada: Broadview Press.

Davidson, Thomas. (1959). Education for All: Problem for the 20th Century. In Clinton Hartley Grattan (Ed.), *American Ideas about Adult Education,* (1710-1951). New York: Teachers College Press.

Day, Michael and Amstutz, Donna D. (2003). Beyond Philosophical Identification: Examining Core Values in Adult Education. *Proceedings of the 44th Annual Adult Education Research Conference,*(91-96). San Francisco: San Francisco State University.

de Lima, Agnes. (August 3, 1932). Education for What? *The New Republic.* LXXI, 922.

DeMao, Alisa. (February 22, 2004). Clarke Schools Not Alone in Failing 'Progress' Test. *Athens Banner-Herald*, 172, 53, A1, A7.

Denzin, Norman K. (1995). Postmodern Social Theory. In Donald McQuarie (Ed.), *Readings in Contemporary Sociological Theory: From Modernity to Post-Modernity*. Englewood Cliffs, NJ: Prentice Hall.

Derrida, Jacques. (1976). *Of Grammatology*. Trans. G. Spivak. Baltimore: Johns Hopkins Press.

Derrida, Jacques. (1979). *Spurs: Nietzsche's Styles*. Chicago: University of Chicago Press.

Dewey, John. (1910). *How We Think*. Chicago: University of Chicago Press.

Dewey, John. (1916). *Democracy and Education*. New York: Macmillan.

Dewey, John. (1938). *Experience and Education*. New York: Macmillan.

Dewey, John. (1939). *Logic: The Theory of Inquiry*. New York: Henry Holt.

Dewey, John. (1956). *The Child and Curriculum and The School and Society*. Chicago: University of Chicago Press. (Originally published as *The School and Society*, 1900, and *The Child and the Curriculum*, 1902.)

Dewey, John. & Dewey, Evelyn. (1915). *Schools of Tomorrow*. New York: Dutton.

Dubois, David D. & Rothwell, William J. (2004). *Competency-Based Human Resource Management*. Palo Alto, CA: Davies-Black Publisher.

Eco, Umberto. (1980). *The Name of the Rose*. New York: Warner Books.

Eco, Umberto. (1983). *Postscript to the Name of the Rose*. Orlando, FL: Harcourt Brace and World.

Edwards, Richard. (1997). *Changing Places? Flexibility, Lifelong Learning and a Learning Society*. London: Routledge.

Edwards, Richard, Clarke, Julia, Harrison, Roger, and Reeve, Fiona (2002). Is There Madness in the Method? Representations of Research in Lifelong Learning. *Adult Education Quarterly*, 52, 2, 128-139.

Eisenhart, Margaret and Towne, Lisa. (2003). Contestation and Change in National Policy on "Scientifically Based" Education Research. *Educational Researcher*, 32, 7, 31-38.

Elias, John L. (1979), Neither Andragogy nor Pedagogy, but Education. *Adult Education*, 29, 525-526.

Elias, John L. (1982). The Theory-Practice Split. In Sharan Merriam (Ed.), *Linking Philosophy and Practice*. San Francisco: Jossey-Bass.

Elias, John. L. (1993). *Foundations and Practice of Adult Religious Education* (2nd ed.). Malabar, FL: Krieger.

Elias, John L. (1994). *Paulo Freire: Pedagogue of Liberation*. Malabar, FL; Krieger.

Fass, Paula S. (1989). Outside. In *Minorities and the Transformation of American Society*. New York: Oxford University Press.

Fenwick, Tara J. (2000). Expanding Conceptions of Experiential Learning: A Review of the Five Contemporary Perspectives on Cognition. *Adult Education Quarterly*, 50, 4, 243-272.

Ferrer, Francisco. (1913). *The Origin and Ideals of the Modern School*. New York: Putnam.

Finger, Matthias. (1989). New Social Movements and their Implications for Adult Education. *Adult Education Quarterly*, 40, 1, 15-21.

Fischer, Joan K. (1978) A Review of Competency-Based Adult Education. *Report of the USOE Invitational Workshop in Adult Competency Education*. Washington, DC: US Government Printing Office.

Florence, Namulundah. (1998). *bell hooks's Engaged Pedagogy. A Transgressive Education for Critical Consciousness*. Westport, CT: Bergin and Garvey.

Foltz, Nancy. (Ed.). (1986). *Handbook of Adult Religious Education*. Birmingham, AL: Religious Education Press.

Frankena, William K. (1970). A Model for Analyzing a Philosophy of Education. In Jane R. Martin (Ed.), *Readings in the Philosophy of Education: A Study of Curriculum*. Boston: Allyn and Bacon.

Franklin, Benjamin. (1964). The Autobiography of Benjamin Franklin. In Leonard Laboree (Ed.), *The Writings of Benjamin Franklin*. New Haven, CT: Yale University Press.

Freire, Paulo (1970a). Cultural Action for Freedom. *Harvard Educational Review and the Center for the Study of Development and Social Change*. Cambridge, MA.

Freire, Paulo. (1970b). *Pedagogy of the Oppressed*. New York: Seabury.

Freire, Paulo. (1970c). The Political Literacy Process—An Introduction. Mimeographed manuscript prepared for publication in *Lutherische Monatschefte*. Hanover, Germany.

Freire, Paulo. (1972). *Conscientization and Liberation*. Geneva, Switzerland: Institute of Cultural Action.

Freire, Paulo. (1973). *Education for Critical Consciousness*. New York: Seabury.

Freire, Paulo. (1985). *The Politics of Education: Culture, Power, and Liberation*. South Hadley, MA: Bergin and Garvey.

Freire, Paulo. (1977). *Pedagogy in Process: The Letters to Guineau-Bissau*. New York: Seabury.

Freire, Paulo & Faundez, Antonio. (1989). *Learning to Question: A Pedagogy of Liberation*. New York: Continuum.

Freire, Paulo & Macedo, Donaldo. (1987). *Literacy: Reading the Word and the World*. South Hadley, MA: Bergin and Garvey.

Friedenberg, Edgar. (1956). Liberal Education and the Fear of Failure. *Leader Digest*, 3, 51-54. Washington, DC: Adult Education Association.

Friedenberg, Edgar. (May 1958). The Purpose of Liberal Study versus the Purpose of Adult Students. *Adult Leadership*.

Gates, Henry Louis. (1992). The Master Pieces: On Canon Formation and the African-American Tradition. In Darryl J. Gless & Barbara H. Smith (Eds.), *The Politics of Liberal Education*. Durham, NC: Duke University Press.

Gelpi, Ettore. (1979). *A Future for Lifelong Education*. Manchester, Eng.: Manchester University, Department of Adult Education.

Gilley, Jerry W. & Eggland, Steven A. (1989). *Principles of Human Resource Development*. Reading, MA: Addison Wesley.

Giroux, Henri A. (1988). *Schooling and the Struggle for Public Life: Critical Pedagogy in the Modern Age*. Minneapolis, MN: University of Minnesota Press.

Giroux, Henri. A. (1992). Liberal Arts Education and the Struggle for Public Life: Dreaming about Democracy. In Darryl J. Gless & Barbara H. Smith (Eds.), *The Politics of Liberal Education*. Durham, NC: Duke University Press.

Gleason, Barbara. (2000). Policy Link / Pay for Performance, Educational Leadership, 57, 5, 82-83. http://www.ascd.org/publications/ed_lead/200002/gleason.html.

Gramsci, Antonio. (1971). *Selections from the Prison Notebooks*, Edited by Q. Hoare and G. Nowell Smith. New York: International Publishers.

Gramsci, Antonio. (1995). *Further Selections from the Prison Notebooks: Antonio Gramsci*. Edited and translated by D. Boothman, Minneapolis: University of Minnesota Press.

Gray, J. Glenn. (1968). *The Promise of Wisdom: A Philosophical Theory of Education*. New York: Harper & Row.

Green, Thomas F. (1971). *The Activities of Teaching*. New York: McGraw-Hill.

Greene, Maxine. (1973). *Teacher as Stranger: Educational Philosophy for the Modern Age*. Belmont, CA: Wadsworth.

Greene, Maxine. (1995). What Counts as Philosophy of Education. In Wendy Kohli (Ed.), *Critical Conversations in Philosophy of Education*. New York: Routledge.

Griffin, Colin. (1983). *Curriculum Theory in Adult and Lifelong Learning*, New York: Nickols Publishing.

Griffin, Colin. (1987). *Adult Education As Social Policy*. London: Croom Helm.

Griffith, William S. & Cervero, Ronald. (1977). The Adult Performance Level Program: A Serious and Deliberate Examination. *Adult Education*, 27, 209-224.

Gross, Ronald. (1977). *The Lifelong Learner*. New York: Simon and Schuster.

Guy, Tal. (Ed.). (1999). *Providing Culturally Relevant Adult Education: A Challenge for the Twenty-First Century*. New Directions for Adult and Continuing Education, No. 82, San Francisco: Jossey-Bass.

Hansen, Kenneth. 1963. *The Educational Philosophy of the Great Books Program*. Unpublished doctora; dissertation, University of Missouri, 1949. A lengthy abstract appears in Lawrence Little (Ed.). *Toward Understanding Adults and Adult Education*, Department of religious Education, University of Pittsburgh.

Hansman, Catherine A. & Mott, Vivian W. (2001). Philosophy, Dynamics and Context: Program Planning in Practice, *Adult Learning*. 11, 2, 14-16.

The Harper Dictionary of Modern Thought. (1988). New York: Harpers & Row.

Harrington, Ann (2003). The 100 Best Companies to Work For. *Fortune*, 147, 1, 128-152.

Hart, Mechthild U. (1990). Critical Theory and Beyond: Further Perspectives on Emancipatory Education. *Adult Education Quarterly*, 40, 3, 125-138.

Hart, Mechthild U. (1992). *Working and Education for Life: Feminist and International Perspectives on Adult Education*. London: Routledge.

Harvey, David. (1989).*The Condition of Postmodernity*. Cambridge, Eng.: Basil Blackwell.

Hayes, Elizabeth R. (1989). Insights from Women's Experience for Teaching and Learning. In Elizabeth R. Hayes (Ed.), *Effective Teaching Styles*. (55-65). New Directions for Continuing Education, 43. San Francisco: Jossey Bass.

Hayes, Elisabeth R. & Smith, Letitia. (1994). Women in Adult Education: An Analysis of Perspectives in Major Journals. *Adult Education Quarterly*, 44, 3, 201-221.

Heaney, Thomas. (1996). Adult Education for a Change: From Center State to the Winds and Back Again. ☐ HYPERLINK "http://www.nl.edu/ace/Lindeman." http://www.nl.edu/ace/Lindeman.

Hemphill, David F. (2001). Incorporating Postmodernist Perspectives into Adult Education. In Vanessa Sheared and Peggy A. Sissel (Eds.), *Making Space: Merging Theory and Practice in Adult Education*. Westport, CT: Bergin and Garvey.

Henle, Robert. (1965). A Roman Catholic View of Education. In Philip Phenix (Ed.), *Philosophies of Education*. New York: Wiley.

Herman, Therese M. (1977). *Creating Learning Environments: The Behavioral Approach to Education*. Boston: Allyn and Bacon.

Herndon, James. (1971). *How to Survive in your Native Land*. New York: Simon and Schuster.

Hiemstra, Roger. (1988). Translating Personal Values and Philosophy into Practical Action. In Roger G. Brockett (Ed.). *Ethical Issues in Adult Education*. New York: Teachers College Press.

Hiemstra, Roger. (2000). *The Educative Community*. Lincoln, NE: Professional Educators Publications.

Highet, Gilbert. (1950). *The Art of Teaching*. New York: Knopf.

Hill, Dave, McLaren, Peter, Cole, Mike, & Rikowski, Glenn. (2002). *Marxism against Postmodernism in Educational Theory*. New York: Lexington Books.

Hirsch, E. D. (1987). *Cultural Literacy*. New York: Random House.

Hirschberg, Cornelius. (1960). *The Priceless Gift*. New York: Simon and Schuster.

Hogan, David J. (1985). *Class and Reform: School and Society in Chicago, 1880-1930*. Philadelphia: University of Pennsylvania Press.

Holford, John & Jarvis, Peter. (2000). The Learning Society. In Arthur L. Wilson & Elisabeth R. Hayes (Eds.), *Handbook of Adult and Continuing Education*, (643-659). San Francisco: Jossey-Bass.

Hollinger, Robert. (1994). *Postmodernism and the Social Sciences: A Thematic Approach*. Thousand Islands. CA: Sage.

(STOP 17)

R p. 261

Holst, John D. (2002). *Social Movements, Civil Society, and Radical Adult Education*. Westport, CT: Bergin & Garvey.

Holt, John. (1967). *How Children Learn*. New York: Pitman.

hooks, bell. (1994). *Teaching to Transgress: Education as the Practice of Freedom*. New York: Routledge.

Houle, Cyril. (January 1955). How Useful is a Liberal Education. *Adult Leadership*.

Houle, Cyril. (1972). *The Design of Education*. San Francisco: Jossey-Bass.

Houle, Cyril & Nelson, Charles A. (1956). *The University, the Citizen and World Affairs*. Washington, DC: American Council on Education.

Howie, George. (1969), *Educational Theory and Practice in St. Augustine*. New York: Teachers College Press.

Humanist Manifesto I and II (1973). Washington, DC: American Humanist Association.

Hutchins, Robert. (1936). *The Higher Learning in America*. New Haven, CT: Yale University Press.

Hutchins, Robert. (1953). *The Conflict in Education in a Democratic Society*. New York: Harper & Row.

Hutchins, Robert. (1968). *The Learning Society*. New York: Britannica Books.

Ianinska, Silvana, Wright, Ursula, & Rocco, Tonette S. (2003). Critical Race Theory and Adult Education: Critique of the Literature in Adult Education Quarterly. *AERC 2003 Proceedings of the 44th Annual Adult Education Research Conference*, (175-180). San Francisco: San Francisco State University.

Ihde, Don (1977). *Experimental Phenomenology*. New York: G. P. Putnam.

Illich, Ivan. (1970). *Deschooling Society*. New York: Harper & Row.

Illich, Ivan. (1973). *Tools for Conviviality*. New York: Harper & Row.

Inbody, Tyron. (1995). Postmodernism: Intellectual Velcro Dragged Across Culture? *Theology Today*, 51, 4, 523-538.

Inkster, Ian. (Ed.). (1985). *The Steam Intellect Societies: Essays on Culture, Education and Industry Circa 1820-1914*. Derby, Eng.: Saxon Printing.

Institute for Cultural Action. (1974). *Liberation of Woman: To Change the World and Re-Invent Life*. Geneva, Switzerland: Institute for Cultural Action.

Institute for Cultural Action. (1975). *Toward a Woman's World. Geneva*, Switzerland: Institute for Cultural Action.

Jacobs, Ronald L. (1987). *Human Performance Technology: A Systems-Based Field for the Training and Development Profession*. Columbus, OH: ERIC Cleaning House on Adult, Career, and Vocational Education, Information Series No. 326.

James, William. (1902/1972). *The Varieties of Religious Experience*. New York: Longmann.

James, William. (1909). *The Meaning of Truth: A Sequel to Pragmatism*. New York: Appleton.

Jansen, Theo, & Wildemeersch, Danny. (1998). Beyond the Myth of Self-actualization: Reinventing the Community Perspective of Adult Education. *Adult Education Quarterly*, 48, 4, 216-226.

Jarvis, Peter. (1992). *Paradoxes of Learning: On Becoming an Individual in Society*. San Francisco: Jossey-Bass.

Jarvis, Peter. (1997). *Ethics and Education for Adults*. Leicester, England: National Institute of Adult Continuing Education.

Kallen, Horace. (1962). *Philosophical Issues in Adult Education*. Springfield, IL: Charles C. Thomas.

Kaplan, Abraham. (1964). *The Conduct of Inquiry: Methodology for Behavioral Sciences*. New York: Chandler.

Karan, Robert. (1974). *An Introduction to Behavior Theory and its Application*. New York: Harper & Row.

Karrier, Clarence, Violas, Paul, & Spring, Joel. (1973). *Roots of Crisis: American Education in the Twentieth Century*. Chicago: Rand McNally.

Katz, Michael B. (1968). *The Irony of Early School Reform*. Boston: Beacon Press.

Keddie, Nel. (1980). Adult Education: An Ideology of Individualism. In Jane Thompson (Ed.), *Adult Education for a Change*. London: Hutchinson.

Keller, Fred. (1977). Behaviorism. *Collier's Encyclopedia*. Vol. 4. New York: Macmillan Educational Corporation.

Kett, Joseph F. (1994). *The Pursuit of Knowledge under Difficulties: From Self-Improvement to Adult Education in America*, 1750-1990. Stanford, CA: Southern California Press.

Kidd, J. Roby. (1973). *How Adults Learn*. (rev. ed.). New York: Association Press.

Kinkade, Kathleen. (1972). *A Walden Two Experiment: The First Five Years of Twin Oaks Community*. New York: William Morrow.

Kirk, Russell. (1965). A Conservative View of Education. In Phillip Phenix (Ed.), *Philosophies of Education*. New York: Wiley.

Kneller, George. (1958). *Existentialism and Education*. New York: Wiley.

Knowles, Malcolm S. (1970; 1980). *The Modern Practice of Adult Education*. New York: Association

Knowles, Malcolm S. (1975). *Self Directed Learning*. Chicago: Association Press.

Knowles, Malcolm S. (1977). *A History of the Adult Education Movement in the United States*. New York: Krieger.

Knowles, Malcolm. (1989). *Making of an Adult Educator: An Autobiographical Journey*. San Francisco: Jossey Bass.

Knowles, Malcolm S. & Associates. (1984). *Andragogy in Action: Applying Modern Principles of Adult Learning*. San Francisco: Jossey-Bass.

Koerner, James. (1965). *The Miseducation of American Teachers*. Baltimore, MD: Penguin.

Kolesnik, W. B. (1975). *Humanism and/or Behaviorism in Education*. Boston: Allyn and Bacon.

Komisar, B. Paul & McClellan, James E. (1961). The Logic of Slogans. In B. Othaniel Smith & Robert H. Ennis (Eds.), *Language and Concepts in Education: Analytic Study of Educational Ideas*, (195-214). Chicago: Rand McNally.

Kozol, Jonathan. (1972). *Free Schools*. Boston: Houghton Mifflin.

Kozol, Jonathan. (1975). *The Night Is Dark and I Am Far From Home*. New York: Bantam Books.

Kristeva, Julia. (1984). *Revolution in Poetic Language*. New York: Columbia University Press.

Kuchinke, K. Peter. (2003). Comparing National Systems of Human Resource Development: Role and Function of Post-baccalaureate HRD Courses of Study in the UK and US. *Human Resource Development International*, 6, 3, 285-301.

Lagemann, Ellen Condliffe. (1989). The Politics of Knowledge: The Carnegie Corporation, Philanthropy, and Public Policy. *History of Education Quarterly*, 27, 2, 205-220.

Laird, Susan. (1988). The Concept of Teaching: Betsey Brown vs. Philosophy of Education. In James Giarelli (Ed.), *Philosophy of Education*: 1988. Normal, IL: Philosophy of Education Society.

A Latino National Conversation. (2001). Great Books Foundation. www.greatbooks.org.

Lawson, Kenneth H. (1975). *Philosophical Concepts and Values in Adult Education*. Nottingham, Eng.: Barnes and Humby.

Lawson, Kenneth H. (1982). *Analysis and Ideology: Conceptual Essays on the Education of Adults*. Nottingham, Eng.: University of Nottingham.

Lawson, Kenneth H. (1998). *Philosophical Issues in the Education of Adults*. Nottingham, Eng.: Continuing Education Press.

Lazerson, Marvin. (1971). *The Origins of the Urban School: Public Education in Massachusetts, 1970-1915*. Cambridge, MA: Harvard University Press.

LeClerq, Jean. (1961). *The Love of God and the Love of Learning*. New York: Fordham University Press.

Lee, Ming-Yeh. (2001/2002). Learning within the Community, Learning from the Community. *Adult Learning*, 12, 4/13,1, 6-9.

Levering, Robert and Moskowitz, Milton (2000). The 100 Best Companies to Work For. *Fortune*, 141, 1, 82-106.

Lindeman, Eduard C. (1961; 1926). *The Meaning of Adult Education*. Montreal: Harvest House.

Lindeman, Eduard C. (1956). *The Democratic Man: Selected Writings of Eduard Lindeman*. Edited by Robert Glessner. Boston: Beacon Press.

Londoner, Carroll A. (August 1972). The Systems Approach as an Administrative and Program Planning Tool for Continuing Education. *Educational Technology*, 22-30.

Lyotard, Jean Francois. (1979; 1984). *The Postmodern Condition: A Report on Knowledge*. Minneapolis: University of Minnesota Press.

Maher, Frances A. (1987). Toward a Richer Theory of Feminist Pedagogy: A Comparison of "Liberation" and "Gender" Models of Teaching and Learning. *Journal of Education*, 169, 3, 91-100.

Malcolm X. (1964). *The Autobiography of Malcolm X*. New York: Grove Press.

Maritain, Jacques. (1943). *Education at the Crossroads*. New Haven: Yale University Press.

Maritain, Jacques. (1962). *The Education of Man*. Donald & Idella Gallagher (Eds.). New York: Doubleday.

Marrou, Henri I. (1956). *A History of Education in Antiquity*. New York: Sheed and Ward.

Martin, Everett Dean. (1926). *The Meaning of a Liberal Education*. New York: Norton.

Maslow, Abraham. (1954). *Motivation and Personality*. New York: Harper & Row.

Maslow, Abraham. (1976). *Education and Peak Experience*. In Courtney D. Schlosser (Ed.), *The Person in Education: A Humanistic Approach*. New York: Macmillan.

Matuszowicz, Peter, F. (2001). Philosophy in Program Management. *Adult Learning*, 11, 2, 17-19.

Mayo, Peter. (1999). *Gramsci, Freire & Adult Education: Possibilities for Transformative Action*. London: Zed.

McFague, Sallie. (1987). *Models of God*. Philadelphia: Fortress.

McGucken, William. (1942). The Philosophy of Catholic Education. In *Philosophies of Education*. National Society for the Study of Education, Forty First Yearbook, Part I. Chicago: University of Chicago Press.

McKenzie, Leon. (1977). The Issue of Andragogy. *Adult Education*, 27, 4, 225-229.

McKenzie, Leon. (1978). *Adult Education and the Burden of the Future*. Washington, DC: University Press of America.

McKenzie, Leon. (1982). *The Religious Education of Adults*. Birmingham, AL: Religious Education Press.

McKenzie, Leon. (1991). *Adult Education and Worldview Construction*. Malabar, FL: Krieger.

McLagan, Patricia. A. (1983). *Models for Excellence*. Arlington, VA: ASTD Press.

McLagan, Patrick. (1989). *Models of HRD Practice*. Alexandria, VA: ASTD Press.

McLaren, Peter. (1993). *Paulo Freire: A Critical Encounter*. New York: Routledge.

McLaren, Peter. (1994). *Politics of Liberation: Paths from Freire*. New York: Routledge.

Merriam, Sharan B. (1979). Benjamin Franklin's Junto Revisited. *Lifelong Learning: The Adult Years*. 2, 18-19.

Merriam, Sharan B. (Ed.), (1982). *Linking Philosophy and Practice*. San Francisco: Jossey-Bass.

Merriam, Sharan B. & Caffarella, Rosemary S. (1999). *Learning in Adulthood* (2nd ed.). San Francisco: Jossey-Bass.

Mezirow, Jack. (1989). Transformation Theory and Social Action: A Response to Collard and Law. *Adult Education Quarterly*, 39, 3, 169-175.

Mezirow, Jack. (1991). *Transformative Dimensions of Adult Learning*. San Francisco: Jossey-Bass.

Mezirow, Jack. & Associates. (1990). *Fostering Critical Reflection in Adulthood: A Guide to Transformative and Emancipatory Learning*. San Francisco: Jossey-Bass.

Mezirow, Jack & Associates. (2000). *Learning as Transformation: Critical Perspectives on a Theory in Process*. San Francisco: Jossey-Bass.

Miller, H. &. McGuire, C. (1961). *Liberal Education*: An Evaluative Study. Chicago: Center for the Study of Liberal Education of Adults.

Minzey, Jack. (1977). Community Education—Another Perception. *Community Education Journal*, 2, 3, 58-61.

Misiak, Henry & Sexton, Virginia Standt. (1973). *Phenomenological, Existential, and Humanistic Psychologies: A Historical Survey*: Grune and Stratton.

Monette, Maurice L. (1977). The Concept of Need: An Analysis of Selected Literature. *Adult Education*, 27, 116-127.

Monette, Maurice L. (1979). Need Assessment: A Critique of Philosophical Assumptions. *Adult Education*. 29, 83-95.

Moody, Harry. R. (1976). Philosophical Presuppositions of Education for Old Age. *Educational Gerontology*, 6, 1, 1-16.

Moore, George E. (1903). *Principia Ethica*. Cambridge, Eng.: Cambridge University Press.

Morris, Van Cleve. (1966). *Existentialism in Education*. New York: Harper & Row.

Murchland, Bernard. (1979). Reviving the Connected View: Reforming the Liberal Arts. *Commonweal*, 106.

Nadler, Leonard & Nadler, Zeace (1989). *Developing Human Resources*. (3rd ed.). San Francisco: Jossey-Bass.

Nadler, Leonard & Nadler, Zeace (1994). *Designing Training Programs: The Critical Events Model* (2nd ed.). Houston: Gulf Publishing.

Neill, Alexander S. (1960). *Summerhill*. New York: Hart Publishing.

Noddings, Nel. (1995). *Philosophy of Education*. Boulder, CO: Westview Press.

Noll, James W. & Kelly, Sam P. (Eds.). (1970). *Foundations of Education in America: An Anthology of Major Thoughts and Significant Actions*. New York: Harper & Row.

Norris, Christopher. (1993). *The Truth about Postmodernism*. Oxford: Blackwell.

Nussbaum, Martha C. (1997). *Cultivating Humanity: A Classical Defense of Reform in Liberal Education*. Cambridge, MA: Harvard University Press.

Nye, Robert D. (1975). *Three Views of Man*. Monterey, CA: Brooks/Cole Publishing.

Ohliger, John (1974). Is Lifelong Adult Education a Guarantee of Permanent Inadequacy? *Convergence*, 7, 2, 47-58.

O'Malley, John. (1993). *The First Jesuits*. Cambridge, MA: Harvard University Press.

Parson, Steve. (1978). Cooperative Extension Guide to Community Education Development. In *Yearbook of Adult and Continuing Education*, (1978-1979). Chicago: Marquis Academic Media.

Paterson, R. W. K. (1979). *Values, Education and the Adult*. Boston: Routledge and Kegan Paul.

Patterson, Cecil Holden. (1973). *Humanistic Education*. Englewood Cliffs, NJ: Prentice Hall.

Pearson, Elaine M. & Podeschi, Ronald L. (1999). Humanism and Individualism: Maslow and His Critics. *Adult Education Quarterly*, 50, 1, 41-55.

Perkinson, Henry. (1977). *The Imperfect Panacea: American Faith in Education 1865-1976* (2nd ed.). New York: Random House.

Perry, Ralph Barton. (1956). *The Humanity of Man*. New York: George Braziller.

Perspectives (Spring 2003). Wisconsin Humanities Council, 30, 1. www.wisconsinhumanisties.org/assets/perspectivesPDFs/spring03.

Peters, R. S. (1967a). *Ethics and Education*. Boston: Routledge and Kegan Paul.

Peters, R. S. (1967b). What Is an Educational Process. In R. S. Peters. (Ed.), *The Concept of Education*. Boston: Routledge and Kegan Paul.

Phillips, D. C. (1995). Counting Down to the Millennium. In Wendy Kohli (Ed.), *Critical Conversations in Philosophy of Education*. New York: Routledge.

Phillips, D. C. & Soltis, John. (1991). *Perspectives on Learning* (2nd ed.). New York: Teachers College Press

Plumb, Donovan. (1995). Declining Opportunities: Adult Education, Culture, and Postmodernity. In Michael R. Welton (Ed.), *In Defense of the Lifeworld: Critical Perspectives on Adult Learning*. Albany: State University of New York Press.

Podeschi, Ronald L. (1987). Andragogy: Proofs or Premises? *Lifelong Learning: An Omnibus of Practice*, 11, 3, 14-16.

Popham, W. James. (1971). Probing the Validity of Arguments against Behavioral Goals. In Miriam B. Kapter (Ed.), *Behavioral Objectives in Curriculum Development*. Englewood Cliffs, NJ: Educational Technology Publications.

Popham, W. James. (1973). The New World of Accountability in the Classroom. In Julia DeCarlo & Constant Mason (Eds.), *Innovations in Education for the Seventies: Selected Readings*. New York: Behavioral Publications.

Powers, Edward. (1982). *Philosophies of Education*. Englewood Cliffs, NJ: Prentice Hall.

Pratt, Daniel D. (1988). Andragogy after Twenty-Five Years. In Sharan B. Merriam (Ed.), *An Update of Adult Learning Theory*. New Directions for Adult and Continuing Education, No. 57. San Francisco: Jossey-Bass.

Pratt, Mary Louise. (1992). Humanities for the Future: Reflections on Western Culture. In Darryl J. Gless & Barbara H. Smith (Eds.), The *Politics of Liberal Education*. Durham, NC: Duke University Press.

Pratte, Richard. (1971). *Contemporary Theories of Education*. Scranton, PA: Intext Educational Publishers.

Rachal, John R. (1993). Computer-Assisted Instruction in Adult Basic and Secondary Education: A Review of the Experimental Literature, 1984-1992. *Adult Education Quarterly*, 43, 3, 165-172.

Rachal, John R. (2002). Andragogy's Detectives: A Critique of the Present and a Proposal for the Future. *Adult Education Quarterly*, 52, 3, 210-227.

Randall, John Herman Jr. (1948). The Spirit of Philosophy. In F. Ernest Johnson (Ed.), *Wellsprings of the American Spirit*. New York: Harper & Row.

Ravitch, Diane. (1982). *The Troubled Crusade: American Education 1945-1980*. New York: Basic Books.

Ravitch, Diane. (2000). *Left Back: A Century of Failed School Reforms*. New York: Simon and Schuster.

Rikowski, Glenn & McLaren, Peter (2002). Postmodernism in Educational Theory. In David Hill, Peter McLaren, Mike Cole, and Glenn Rikowski. *Marxism Against Postmodernism in Educational Theory*. (3-14), New York: Lexington Books.

Robinson, James. (1924). *The Humanizing of Knowledge*. New York: George H. Doran.

Rogers, Carl R. (1965). The Place of the Person in the New World of the Behavioral Sciences. In Frank T. Severin (Ed.), *Humanistic Viewpoints in Psychology*. New York: McGraw-Hill.

Rogers. Carl R. (1967). The Process of the Basic Encounter Group. In James F. T. Bugental (Ed.), *Challenges of Humanistic Psychology*. New York: McGraw-Hill.

Rogers, Carl R. (1969). *Freedom to Learn*. Columbus, OH: Charles E. Merrill.

Rorty, Amelia (Ed.). (1966). *Pragmatic Philosophy: An Anthology*. New York: Doubleday.

Rorty, Richard. (1992). Two Cheers for the Cultural Left. In Darryl J. Gless & Barbara H. Smith (Eds.), *The Politics of Liberal Education*. Durham, NC: Duke University Press.

Rosenau, Pauline. (1992). *Post-Modernism and the Social Sciences*. Princeton, NJ: Princeton University Press.

Ross-Gordon, J. Winter. (1990). Serving cultural diverse populations: A Social Imperative for Adult Education. *New Directions for Adult and Continuing Education*, No. 48. 5-15. San Francisco: Jossey-Bass.

Rothwell, William J. & Cookson, Peter S. (1997). *Beyond Instruction: Comprehensive Program Planning for Business and Education*. San Francisco: Jossey-Bass.

(STOP 18)

Rothwell, William J. & Sredl, Henry J. (1992). *The ASTD Reference Guide to Professional Human Resource Development Roles and Competencies.* Vol. 1 (Second Edition). Amherst, MA: HRD Press.

Rousseau, Jean Jacques. (1762/1979) *Emile or On Education.* Translated by Allan Bloom. New York: Basic Books.

Rush, Benjamin. (1786/1969). Thoughts Upon the Mode of Education Proper in a Republic. In S. Alexander Rippa (Ed.), *Educational Ideas in America: A Documentary History.* New York: McKay.

Russell, Bertrand. (1912). *The Problem of Philosophy.* London: Home University Press.

Ryle, Gilbert. (1949/2000). *The Concept of Mind.* Chicago: University of Chicago Press.

Ryle, Gilbert. (1967). Teaching and Training. In Richard S. Peters (Ed.). *The Concept of Education.* (105-119). London: Routledge and Kegan Paul.

Sadovnik, Alan R. (1995). Postmodernism in the Sociology of Education: Closing the Rift Among Theory, Practice, and Research. In William T. Pink & George W. Noblit (Eds.), *Continuity and Contradiction: The Futures of the Sociology of Education.* Cresskill, New Jersey: Hampton Press.

Sartre, Jean Paul. (1949). *Nausea.* Lloyd Alexander (Trans.) London: Purnell and Sons.

Sarup, Madan. (1989). *An Introductory Guide to Post-Structuralism and Postmodernism.* Athens, GA: University Press.

Scheffler, Israel. (1960). *The Language of Education.* Springfield, IL: Charles Thomas.

Schlesinger, Arthur Jr. (1992). *The Disuniting of America.* New York: Knopf.

Schuster, Diane Tickton. (2004). *Jewish Lives, Jewish Learning.* New York: UAHC Press.

Seller, Maxine S. (1978). Success and Failure in Adult Education: The Immigrant Experience, 1914-1924. *Adult Education,* 28, 83-89.

Shaull, Richard. (1970). A Forward to Paulo Freire's *Pedagogy of the Oppressed.* New York: Seabury.

Sheats, Paul. (1938). *Education and the Quest for a Middle Way.* New York: Wiley.

Shor, Ira & Freire, Paulo. (1987). *A Pedagogy for Liberation: Dialogues on Transforming Education.* South Hadley, MA: Bergin and Garvey.

Silberman, Charles. (1970). *Crisis in the Classroom.* New York: Random House.

Simpson, Elizabeth Leonie & Gray, Mary Ann. (1976). *Humanistic Education: An Interpretation.* Cambridge, MA: Ballinger.

Skinner, Burrhus F. (1938/1999). *The Behavior of Organisms.* Cambridge, MA. B. F. Skinner Foundation.

Skinner, Burrhus F. (1948/1960). *Walden Two.* New York: Macmillan.

Skinner, Burrhus F. (1968). *The Technology of Teaching.* New York: Appleton-Century-Crofts.

Skinner, Burrhus F. (1971). *Beyond Freedom and Dignity.* New York: Alfred A. Knopf.

Skinner, Burrhus F. (1974). *About Behaviorism*. New York: Alfred A. Knopf.

Sleezer, Catherine M., Conti, Gary J., & Nolan, Robert E. (2003). Comparing CPE and HRD Programs: Definitions, Theoretical Foundations, Outcomes, and Measures of Quality. *Advances in Developing Human Resources*, 6, 1, 20-34.

Smith, Barbara H. (1992). Cult Lit: Hirsch, Literacy, and National Culture. In Darryl J. Gless & Barbara H. Smith (Eds.), *The Politics of Liberal Education*. Durham, NC: Duke University Press.

Soltis, Jonas F. (1968). *An Introduction to the Analysis of Educational Concepts*. Reading, MA: Addison-Wesley.

Sork, Thomas J. (2000). Planning Educational Programs. In Arthur L. Wilson & Elisabeth R. Hayes (Eds.), *Handbook of Adult and Continuing Education* (171-190). San Francisco: Jossey-Bass.

Sparks, Barbara & Peterson, Elizabeth A. (2000). Adult Basic Education and the Crisis of Accountability. In Arthur L. Wilson & Elisabeth R. Hayes (Eds.), *Handbook of Adult and Continuing Education* (263-277). San Francisco: Jossey Bass.

Spencer, Herbert. (1860). *Education: Intellectual Moral and Physical*. New York: Appleton.

Spielberg, Herbert. (1975). *Doing Phenomenology*. The Hague, Netherlands: Martinus Nijhoff.

Spikes, Frank A. (1978). A Multidimensional Program Planning Model for Continuing Nursing Education. *Lifelong Learning: The Adult Years*, 1, 4-8.

Spring, Joel. (1973). Anarchism and Education: A Dissenting Tradition. In Clarence Karrier, Paul Violas & Joel Spring. *Roots of Crisis: American Education in the Twentieth Century*. Chicago: Rand McNally.

Spring, Joel. (1975). *A Primer of Libertarian Education*. New York: Free Life Editions, Inc.

Stanage, Sherman. (1987). *Adult Education and Phenomenological Research: New Directions for Theory, Practice, and Research*. Malabar, FL: Krieger.

Stewart, David & Mickunas, Algis. (1974). *Exploring Phenomenology*. Chicago: American Library Association.

Stirner, Max. (1967). *The False Principles of Education*. Translated by Robert Beebe. Colorado Springs, CO: Ralph Myles.

Stone, Lynda. (1992). Philosophy, Meaning Constructs, and Teacher Theorizing. In Wayne Ross et al. (Eds.), *Teacher Personal Theorizing*. Albany: State University of New York Press.

Stubblefield, Harold. (April 1979). *The Aim of the American Adult Education Movement in the Nineteen Twenties: A Historical Analysis*. Paper presented at the Adult Education Research Conference, Ann Arbor, MI.

Stubblefield, Harold W. & Keane, Patrick. (1994). *Adult Education in the American Experience: From the Colonial Period to the Present*. San Francisco: Jossey-Bass.

Thompson, Jane (Ed.). (1980). *Adult Education for a Change*. London: Hutchinson.

Thompson, Norma. (1984). Adult Religious Education: Life and Nurture. In Marvin J. Taylor (Ed.), *Changing Patterns of Religious Education*. Nashville, TN: Abingdon.

Thorndike, Edward L. (1932). *The Fundamentals of Learning*. New York: Teachers College, Columbia University.

Thorndike, Edward L., Bregman, Elsie O., Tilton, J. Warren, & Woodyard, Ella. (1928). *Adult Learning*. New York: Macmillan.

Tisdell, Elizabeth J. (1993a). Feminism and Adult Learning. In Sharan B. Merriam (Ed.), *An Update of Adult Learning Theory*. New Directions for Adult and Continuing Education, No. 57. San Francisco: Jossey-Bass.

Tisdell, Elizabeth J. (1993b). Interlocking Systems of Power, Privilege, and Oppression in Adult Higher Education Classes. *Adult Education Quarterly*, 43, 4, 203-226.

Tisdell, Elizabeth J. (1998). Poststructural Feminist Pedagogies: The Possibilities and Limitations of a Feminist Emancipatory Adult Learning Theory and Practice. *Adult Education Quarterly*, 48, 3, 139-156.

Tisdell, Elizabeth J. & Taylor, Edward W. (2001). Adult Education Philosophy Informs Practice, *Adult Learning*, 11, 2, 6-10.

Tolbert, Michelle. (2001). *English Literacy and Civics Education for Adult Learners: Special Policy Update*. Washington, DC: National Institute for Literacy.

Tolstoy, Leo. (1967). *Tolstoy on Education*. Translated by Leo Wierner. Chicago: University of Chicago Press.

Torraco, Richard J. (1999). Advancing Our Understanding of Performance Improvement. In Richard J. Torraco (Ed.), *Performance Improvement Theory and Practice*, (95-112). Academy of Human Resource Development and Berrett-Koehler Communications.

Tough, Allen. (1971). *The Adult's Learning Projects*. Toronto: Ontario Institute for Studies in Education.

Toynbee, Arnold. (1963; 1960). Education in the Perspective of History. In Ronald Gross (Ed.), *The Teacher and the Taught*. New York: Dell.

Tuition-Aid Concepts at Kinberly-Clark Show Dramatic Results. (December 1977). Training and Development Journal. 8-10.

Tyack, David & Cuban, Larry. (1995). *Tinkering toward Utopia: A Century of Public School Reform*. Cambridge, MA: Harvard University Press.

Tyler, Gus. (1979). The University and the Labor Union: Educating the Proletariat. 2, 32-37, 64.

Tyler, Ralph. (1949). *Basic Principles of Curriculum and Instruction*. Chicago: University of Chicago Press.

Usher, Robin, Bryant, Ian, & Johnston, Rennie. (1997). *Adult Education and the Postmodern Challenge: Learning beyond the Limits*. New York: Routledge.

Van Doren, Mark. (1943). *Liberal Education*. Boston: Beacon.

van Manen, M. (1990). *Researching Lived Experience: Human Science for and Action Sensitive Pedagogy*. New York: State University of New York Press.

Verdun, John Jr., Miller, G., & Greer, C. (1977). *Adults Teaching Adults.* Austin, TX: Learning Concepts.

Verner, Coolie. (1959). *Methods and Techniques: An Overview of Adult Learning Research.* Chicago: American Education Association.

Vincent, John. (1959; 1886). The Rationale of the Chautauqua Movement. In C. Hartley Grattan (Ed.), *American Ideas about Adult Education,* 1710-1951. New York: Teachers College Press.

Vogel, Linda. (1991). *Teaching and Learning in Communities of Faith.* San Francisco: Jossey-Bass.

Wandersman, Abraham, Poppen, Paul J., & Ricks (Eds.), (1976). *Humanism and Behaviorism; Dialogue and Growth.* Oxford: Pergamon Press.

Watson, John B. (1913/1948). Psychology as the Behaviorist Views It. In Wayne Dennis (Ed.), *Readings in the History of Psychology.* New York: Appleton-Century-Crofts.

Watson, John B. (1914/1930). *Behavior: An Introduction to Comparative Psychology.* New York: Norton.

Watson, John B. (1919). *Psychology from the Standpoint of a Behaviorist.* Philadelphia: Lippincott.

Weinberg, Carl. (Ed.), (1972). *Humanistic Foundations of Education.* Englewood Cliffs, NJ: Prentice Hall.

Weitz, Morris. (1966). General Introduction. In Morris Weitz (Ed.), *Twentieth Century Philosophy: The Analytic Tradition,* (1-12). New York: Macmillan.

Welser, Carl F. (1978). The Flow of Community Education in Historical Perspective. *Yearbook of Adult and Community Education,* (1978-1979). Chicago: Marquis Academic Media.

Welton, Michael R. (1993a). The Contribution of Critical Theory to our Understanding of Adult Learning. In Sharan B. Merriam (Ed.), *An Update on Adult Learning Theory.* New Directions for Adult and Continuing Education, No. 57. San Francisco: Jossey-Bass.

Welton, Michael R. (1993b). Social Revolutionary Learning: The New Social Movements as Learning Sites. *Adult Education Quarterly.* 43, 3, 152-164.

Welton, Michael R. (1995). The Critical Turn in Adult Education Theory. In Michael R. Welton. (Ed.), *In Defense of the Lifeworld: Critical Perspectives on Adult Learning,* (11-38). Albany, NYL State University of New York Press,

Westbrook, Robert. (1991). *John Dewey and American Democracy.* Ithaca, NY: Cornell University Press.

Westwood, Sallie. (1980). Adult Education and the Sociology of Education: An Exploration. In Jane Thompson (Ed.), *Adult Education for a Change.* London: Hutchinson.

Whipple, James. (1960). *A Critical Balance.* Chicago: Center for the Study of Liberal Education for Adults.

Wilson, Arthur L. (1993). The Common Concern: Controlling the Professionalization of Adult Education. *Adult Education Quarterly,* 44, 1, 1-16.

Wilson, Arthur, L. & Hayes, Elisabeth, R. (2000a). A Selective History of the Adult Education Handbooks. In Wilson, Arthur, L. & Hayes, Elisabeth R. (Eds.), *Handbook of Adult and Continuing Education*, (3-14), San Francisco: Jossey-Bass.

Wilson, Arthur, L. & Hayes, Elisabeth, R. (2000b). On Thought and Action in Adult and Continuing Education, In Wilson, Arthur, L. & Elisabeth R. Hayes, (Eds.), *Handbook of Adult and Continuing Education*, (15-32), San Francisco: Jossey-Bass.

Wilson, James Q. (1978). Harvard's Core Curriculum: A View from the Inside. *Change*, 10, 40-43.

Wisdom, John. (1952). *Other Minds*. Oxford: Blackwell.

Wisdom, John. (1966). Philosophical Perplexity. In Morris Weitz (Ed.), *Twentieth Century Philosophy: The Analytic Tradition*, (282-296). New York: Macmillan.

Wittgenstein, Ludwig. (1921). *Tractatus Logico-Philosophicus*: London: Routledge and Kegan Paul.

Wittgenstein, Ludwig. (1953). *Philosophical Investigations*. Oxford: Blackwell.

Youngman, Frank. (1986). *Adult Education and Socialist Pedagogy*. London: Croom Helm.

Youngman, Frank. (2000). *The Political Economy of Adult Education and Development*. London: NIACE & Zed Books.

// AUTHORS

JOHN L. ELIAS is Professor of Religion and Education at Fordham University, New York. He is also the author of *Philosophy of Education: Classical and Contemporary; Foundations and Practice of Adult Religious Education, Studies in Theology and Education Psychology and Religious Education; Moral Education: Secular and Religious;* and *Paulo Freire: Pedagogue of Liberation;* and *A History of Christian Education.*

SHARAN B. MERRIAM is Professor of Adult Education at the University of Georgia, Athens, Georgia. She is the author, coauthor, or editor of *Qualitative Research in Practice, A Guide to Research for Educators and Trainers of Adults; The Profession and Practice of Adult Education; Qualitative Research and Case Study Applications in Education; Linking Philosophy and Education, Research Learning in Adulthood; The New Update on Adult Learning Theory; Adult Development and Learning: Multicultural Stories; Adult Education: Foundations of Practice;* and *Selected Writings on Philosophy and Adult Education.*

273

NAME INDEX

Adams, Frank, 74
Addams, Jane, 59
Adler, Mortimer, 12, 25, 26, 39, 43
Adorno, Theodor, 151, 175
Allport, Gordon, 13
Aristotle, 2, 5, 12, 18, 19, 20, 28, 35, 111, 114, 115, 195, 196
Askov, Eunice N., 104
Atkinson, Elizabeth, 229
Augustine of Hippo, 19, 34
Ayer, A. J., 191

Bacon, Francis, 20, 52, 84
Bagnall, Richard G., 230, 232-234, 237, **239-242**, 244
Baudrillard, Jean, 219, 222
Baumgartner, Lisa A., 141
Beck, George, 20, 25
Belenky, Mary, 14, 180
Bellah, Robert, 57, 144
Benne, Kenneth, 12, 67, 71
Berger, Brigitte, 45
Bergevin, Paul, 7, 12, 51, 66, 71, 73, 131, 204
Bernstein, Basil, 170
Blakely, Robert, 12, 73, 74
Bloom, Allan, 12, 42-45

Blundell, Sue, 179, 180
Boone, Edward J., 108
Bourdieu, Pierre, 170, 175
Bowers, C. A., 56, 150
Bowles, Samuel, 79, 150
Brameld, Theodore, 14, 149, 150, 249
Bridenbaugh, Carl, 21
Brockett, Ralph, 7
Brookfield, Stephen, 13, 136, **141-142**, 177, 178, 183, 209
Broudy, Harry, 8, 18, 68
Brown, Ted, 100
Buber, Martin, 13, 113, 119
Bugental, James F. T., 116

Caffarella, Rosemary, S., 135
Caire, Kaleem M., 96
Camus, Albert, 13, 113
Candy, Phillip C., 135
Carlson, Robert, 80
Carnavale, Anthony P., 102
Cervero, Ronald, 103
Chomsky, Noam, 91
Clark, M. Carolyn, 141
Collard, Sue, 141
Collins, Michael, 109, 168, 170, **174-176**, 238

SUBJECT INDEX